Tonight, I'm surrounded by candles, all cuddled in on the outdoor patio, reading diligently. And, so far, my words and thoughts are just taken aback at the authenticity, rawness and openness of the daughters' heartbreaking stories.

Daughters Betrayed By Their Mothers is a life-changer for anyone who has suffered betrayal by her mother and is in search of answers. Having experienced betrayal in my own mother-daughter relationship, I discovered portraits of women's experiences that mirrored my own, and in this way, I found solace and answers. There are tears of both sorrow and joy in the beautiful, brave stories of harm and hope. It is a must-read. *Daughters Betrayed By Their Mothers* changed my life.

—Charlotte Carson, Editorial Director,
ClearLifeMagazine.com

Holli Kenley tackles a difficult subject in her book, *Daughters Betrayed By Their Mothers: Moving From Brokenness To Wholeness*. As a champion for childhood abuse survivors, I was very deeply moved by Holli's book. My biggest take-away is that, as the daughters profiled in the book confronted and addressed their mother-wounds, many were also, at times, healing co-occurring disorders and/or other forms of childhood trauma or relational challenges. In my work as an advocate for abuse survivors and as a survivor myself, I've found the co-occurring healing process related to mothers to be a key component for identifying repetitive subconscious patterns that many of us were not aware of prior to diving into that particular relationship.

I absolutely recommend *Daughter's Betrayed by Their Mothers*, especially to women dealing with childhood trauma, even if this is a topic they haven't thought of exploring. **So much of what Holli illustrates through her research is that one of the most important relationships —the mother/daughter bond—can be the key to understanding relationship patterns throughout life.**

—Kiersten Hathcock, founder Little Light Project, Inc.,
a non-profit organization

Powerful, reflective and reassuring to all who read it. Holli Kenley's *Daughters Betrayed By Their Mothers* reminds us that no matter what hurt we have experienced, the opportunity to heal and be whole is always possible.

—Cyrus Webb, *Conversations LIVE* radio show host
and Amazon *Top 500 Reviewer*

Messages of hope and resolve were the paramount themes that permeated throughout *Daughters Betrayed By Their Mothers: Moving From Brokenness to Wholeness*. The daughters profiled were able to become strong and successful women, despite the deep pain that they endured. The book showed that, as long as the healing work is put in from the many healing modalities available, one can overcome the most painful of circumstances.

I appreciated how each daughter was able to share her unique experience and how she sought out various means to help in the healing process. By sharing the various approaches, these women showed that there are many roads to healing. This understanding provides hope and empowers those in similar situations to continue to search for the path that is right for them.

The book's expansion of the word betrayal beyond its typical connotation allows readers to connect to the book on a variety of levels. As many other books limit the scope of the meaning of betrayal, *Daughters Betrayed By Their Mothers* sets out to demonstrate that betrayal happens in many forms, often going unnoticed, yet has tremendous consequence in all aspects of life. While the mother-daughter bond is often considered to be one of the most nurturing, safe and loving bonds known, the book explores what happens when this distinguished expectation is not met.

As a health and wellness coach, I quickly came to discover that health and wellness is way more than just diet and exercise. I look forward to recommending *Daughters Betrayed By Their Mothers: Moving From Brokenness to Wholeness* to clients who have had similar experiences and may be unaware of how these experiences not only affect them emotionally, but also in all aspects of their journey towards their most complete and healthy lifestyle.

—Omar Cumberbatch, founder The Health Coach Academy

Daughters Betrayed By Their Mothers brings a new slant to our understanding of the love, pain and diversity in the mother/daughter relationship. Each narration fills the heart with compassion for the daughters, as they delve further into the potent topic of a mother's betrayal. Kenley, once again, has written about a heart-worthy topic. Brava!

—Barbara Sinor, PhD,
author *Finding Destiny* and *Tales of Addiction*

Motherhood is universally regarded as a source of loving understanding. Kenley reveals the dark underside of this belief. She vividly portrays incidents of betrayal by her interviewees' mothers as well as by her own mother. With courage and openness, Kenley explores the deep wounds inflicted on women by their mothers.

One of the consequences of the betrayal is that it involves not only the mother and the daughter, but the whole family. Some of the questions that Kenley asks are about the family – father and siblings— and the role the betrayed daughter holds within the family unit. The abuse by the betraying mother can take various forms, such as emotional, verbal, physical, or sexual mistreatment and exploitation. There is also abandonment and a lack of protection. The results, even worse and long-lasting than those kinds of abuse are, in Kenley's words, "a deeply personal scouring of my inner being."

Future healthy relationships are challenging due to the ancient lack of trust, the distorted mirroring by the mother and the lack of healthy modeling. The primal betraying moves on to betrayal by others. The journey of recovery is lengthy and arduous.

However, healing brings its own gifts. *Moving From Brokenness To Wholeness* is Kenley's apt subtitle for this book. She stresses the importance of acceptance, which produces a sense of calm. Forgiveness, the ability to practice self-care, inner strength, empowerment and the growth of self-esteem create new meaning in life. Compassion and understanding are a part of this, as well as the capability of giving to others. **Informative and insightful, this book is a wonderful guide to reclaiming the self.**

—Shoshana Kobrin, LMFT, author of self-help books,
sculptor, and consultant

Daughters Betrayed By Their Mothers:
Moving From Brokenness to Wholeness

Holli Kenley

Loving Healing Press

Ann Arbor

Daughters Betrayed By Their Mothers: Moving From Brokenness to Wholeness
Copyright © 2018 by Holli Kenley All rights reserved.

2nd Printing – July 2018

Author Photo: Aris Affairs Photograph

Library of Congress Cataloging-in-Publication Data

Names: Kenley, Holli, 1951- author.
Title: Daughters betrayed by their mothers : moving from brokenness to
  wholeness / Holli Kenley.
Description: Ann Arbor : Loving Healing Press, [2017] | Includes
  bibliographical references and index.
Identifiers: LCCN 2017050077| ISBN 9781615993475 (pbk. : alk. paper) | ISBN
  9781615993482 (hardcover : alk. paper)
Subjects: LCSH: Mothers and daughters. | Parent and adult child. | Adult
  child abuse victims. | Betrayal.
Classification: LCC HQ755.86 .K46 2017 | DDC 306.874/3--dc23
LC record available at https://lccn.loc.gov/2017050077

Published by
Loving Healing Press
5145 Pontiac Trail
Ann Arbor, MI 48105

Tollfree USA/CAN: 888-761-6268
FAX 734-663-6861

www.LHPress.com
info@LHPress.com

Distributed by: Ingram Book Group (USA/CAN/AU), Bertram's Books (UK/EU)

Contents

A pearl is a beautiful thing...
produced by an injured life.

Stephan Hoeller

Acknowledgements

Acknowledging Other Gems In My Life

Lani Stoner – You are like an amethyst stone. Your remarkable editorial talents brought clarity of thought to my words. Your wisdom and command of the English language calmed my spirit knowing the Daughters' voices were treated with the highest regard for coherency and continuity.

Bekah Kleinman – You are like a blue topaz which is a traditional stone for writers, scholars, artists and intellectuals. Your prowess in the field of journalism as a writer and an editor elevated the integrity of the lengthy transcriptions. Moreover, the gentle fidelity with which you approached the process comforted my spirit.

Victor R. Volkman (CEO, Loving Healing Press, Inc.) – You are like an opal which is strongly associated with emotions. In the past ten years since our paths have intersected, your unwavering promotion of spontaneity, imagination, dreams, and healing has been evidenced in the publication of my books. Because of your belief, I am living out my passion – bringing healing to others.

Dan Kenley – You are like a diamond, able to absorb my thoughts along with their strengths and weaknesses and transform them into meaningful messages. Your remarkable insights into my writing are amplified by your intuitive gifts of listening, reflecting, and revising. My work is truly a reflection of the brilliance and beauty you cast onto others.

Preface – Opening The Shell

Their stories touch upon the deepest and darkest of pains,
knowing you have a mother but you don't.

Betrayal. It is an uncomfortable word. It is complex. It is often hard to talk about.

Mothers. It is a subject which conjures up many emotions. It is complicated. It can be very difficult to talk about.

Discussing them in relationship to one another? A rare conversation.

A little over three years ago, I began entertaining the idea of exploring betrayal, mothers, and their daughters. Because of my personal wounds incurred from betrayal by my own mother and because of my ongoing professional commitment to advancing recovery from any kind of betrayal injury, I was curious about the wounding of other daughters betrayed by their mothers. More importantly, I wondered about their healing journeys and what paths they traveled to claim their wellness. Thus, I dedicated a year of thinking through and organizing the structure of what would come to be "The Daughters Project."

First, I designed a "Letter of Invitation" (Appendix A) which explained the purposes of "The Daughters Project" and the criteria for participation. The "Letter of Invitation" also clearly defined key terminology such as *betrayal, brokenness,* and *wholeness.* Secondly, I drafted a "Consent To Participate In An Independent Project" (Appendix B), outlining in detail the application procedures for the daughters' study as well as clarifying ethical and legal issues. The "Informed Consent" also delineated the structure of the interviewing process which consisted of a thirty minute pre-interview conference, a four to five hour intensive interview, and a half hour post-interview conference. Thirdly, I developed "Interview Questions" (Appendix C) to be utilized for the study. Lastly, I began compiling a list of names from daughters who had expressed interest in participating in "The Daughters Project." At the same time, I remained open to where the study would lead me and to other daughters who might come my way.

In designing "The Daughters Project," I had the flexibility of my own timeline as well as the opportunity to present my findings in a manner which I felt would benefit a broad audience. Although I closely adhered to the protocol of a formal qualitative study, the final product resembles a non-fiction novel rather than an academic publication. Based on interviews conducted with daughters who met the criteria for the study and who chose to participate, "Daughters Betrayed By Their Mothers: Moving From Brokenness To Wholeness" is a collection of factual accounts (with name substitutions made upon request) describing their painful mother-wounding and their powerful recovering journeys. Each daughter's story is embedded within a larger narrative chronicling my journey as a researcher.

Part One: Our Stories "Daughters Betrayed By Their Mothers" begins with my narrative – *Flying Solo*. I responded to the same questions which were asked of all daughters and in the same order. Not only was it important to me to share my truths with readers, but I also wanted to experience what I would be expecting of other daughters. Each narrative begins with a *Reflection* in which I described my thoughts and feelings regarding the process of "The Daughters Project." Readers are also introduced to each daughter and learn how she became part of the study. Each *Reflection* is followed by the *Setting*. Readers become further acquainted with each daughter from information submitted in her application biographical sketch and from our pre-interview conference. In addition, when and how the interview was conducted (phone, Skype, in person) is described. From there, daughters disclosed their betrayal narratives and their journeys to wholeness in the order of the questions provided covering the following areas: *Beginning, Background, Betrayal Narrative, Brokenness From Betrayal, From Brokenness To Wholeness, and Wholeness To*. Based on the post-interview conference, in the concluding *Follow-up Reflection*, readers discover how each daughter felt about her participation in the study and bask in the glow of her final thoughts and feelings. In this section, I described my emotions as each daughter and I brought closure to our time together.

After completing the daughters' interviews, I spent several weeks analyzing the themes which guided the study: examining the life experiences and life messages of daughters betrayed by their mothers; exploring similarities and differences in their recovering journeys "Moving From Brokenness To Wholeness"; and extrapolating new meanings for myself and readers from the voices of daughters healing from betrayal injury. **Part Two: An Analysis,** *A Strand of Pearls,* is intended to guide health care professionals in their work with betrayal injury and to offer comforting insights for those of shared suffering.

"Daughters Betrayed By Their Mothers: Moving From Brokenness To Wholeness" is an intimate exploration into the lives of daughters who were wounded by their own mothers and who chose wellness over victimhood. Their stories touch upon the deepest and darkest of pains, *knowing you have a mother but you don't.* The daughters' journeys of healing their fractured selves and of honoring their voices are a testament to the power of choice, perseverance, and resiliency.

Searching for truth in unchartered waters is a delicate process. It cannot be rushed. It requires timely precision. It is much like *opening the shell* of a real pearl oyster.

> The procedure begins by placing the oyster shell on a solid protected surface and then gently inserting a dull knife into the indentation on the shell's top right side. While carefully sliding it across to its left side and slowly pressing the knife downward, the shell will open just slightly. With consistent light pressure, the shell will open more fully revealing a hidden gem.

I invite you to take a journey as we tenderly open up a conversation around stories of betrayal, mothers, and daughters, and we witness the rare beauty of real pearls produced by an injured life.

Part One: Our Stories

1   "Flying Solo" – Holli

Reflection

I started on "The Daughters Project" in September 2014. After spending the weekend with my daughter, tapping into her knowledge of conducting a qualitative study and going over the required forms, I returned home. I reviewed the notes I took and put them down for a while. I was working on another project, a novel, and decided I needed to finish my commitment to that process. I think, deep down inside, I knew I wasn't ready to write about my mom. My daughter suggested I take time to write down my feelings as I journeyed through this difficult territory. I knew she was right. Throughout the ensuing year, I moved forward with my novel – *Another Way*. However, in my quiet time when I chose to reflect upon my mom, I began sorting and sifting through my thoughts about her as well as my plans for "The Daughters Project."

Another year passed and much transpired. More betrayals. More pain. More healing. I trusted what my inner voice was telling me—it was time to move ahead.

* * *

It is a warm summer day, August 2015. It is my intention to interview daughters, who like me have been betrayed by their mothers, and who have worked hard on their wellness. I want to find out how they were betrayed and how it affected them, but more importantly, I want to learn about their recovering journeys. I wonder if their paths will be similar to mine. I wonder what we will have in common, if anything. I want to know the differences too and how those aspects of our lives affected each of us. I wonder if there will be comfort in knowing each of us is not alone, not having a real mother to guide our way. I want to know what each of us has done with our lives and why. I want to know how we are as mothers, if we chose to be one. There is much to explore. There is much to say, even though it is hard to do so.

I know I need to talk about myself first. If I expect other daughters to disclose their narratives, I too must be willing to do so. I want to. I've worked on my betrayals regarding my mom for a long while. I have written about them indirectly in some of my writings; however, I have not fully disclosed my entire journey. I am ready now. I need to start at the beginning.

Setting

Unlike the daughters I will be interviewing, I am not recording myself. However, I am going to respond to the same questions which I have provided to them. And unlike most of my clinical writings, my narrative will be an informal piece. I want it to be reflective of my voice and of the emotions I carry with it.

While writing at my computer, I am in one of my favorite rooms in my house—my office. It is decorated in warm colors with framed covers of my published books and my degrees. Photos of my family are all around me, neatly displayed on walls and positioned strategically on book shelves. Through the large window to my left is a beautiful display of nature. The dark soil is home to numerous varieties of sturdy pines and scrubby-looking oaks. Massive layers of lava rock provide much-needed protection from water erosion while framing our backyard in a natural and subtle way. Often during the day as I am writing, I will look up and see a family of deer saunter by. Or on occasion, a grotesque-looking javelina will snort its way across the grassy trail.

My office is a place of peace. I spend hours here, mostly by myself. It is where I can think, reflect, and create. It is where I will respond to the questions about my own mom which I will be posing to other daughters. It is where I will write my story.

Beginning

1. **How do you refer to your *mom*? Do you use that noun, or do you use a different one? Other? Can you talk about that?**

A person's name is important. It holds value. When I am speaking to someone, I almost always use the individual's name in the conversation. Even when I am speaking about someone, I am conscious of how I am using her name. It is no different with my mom. As I think about how I have referred to her over my life, I have used "my mom" or "mom." On occasion, I've used the words "my mother."

Sadly, there have been times, even in the past year where I have used the words "my betrayer" or even more indifferently "the betrayer." I use the word "betrayer" when I have felt rejected by her. I am not able to get out the word "mom" when I experience the pain of her disregard or dismissal of me. Using the word "betrayer" is like using a form of protection for me. The word seems to safeguard me from feeling close to her. I can define her, distance myself from her, and shield myself from ongoing injuries. I am very aware of when I am doing this—and I know why. Because of my interest in betrayal, I know when there is ongoing betrayal or chronic occurrences how important it is to put protective measures into place. It is easy to fall into the trap of feeling worthless or powerless to change anything. When I use the word "betrayer," I feel like I am placing the injustice where it belongs—on her. I am able to free myself from feeling like the betrayal is holding me hostage.

2.   How does it feel to talk about your mom?

Today, and as is true for most days, when I talk about my mom I feel *acceptance* for what has been and what is. Acceptance is a peaceful place, no conflict and no confusion. No wishing it was different. Acceptance comes with years of awareness into and understanding of our family's unhealthy dynamics and of tireless but rewarding work on myself.

When I think of my mom or talk about my mom, there is loss. I also know *acceptance* is the last stage of grief—of loss. Having to give up a healthy mom at an early age, I have revisited the stages of grief many times—denial, anger, bargaining, depression, and acceptance. Presently, I cycle through them quite fluidly and always embrace the anticipated calm which accompanies acceptance.

Along with the peaceful feelings which come with acceptance of my mom's betrayals, I also do not feel any guilt or shame when talking about my mom or them. I hold no ill-will toward her and have no hidden agendas or motivations in disclosing my truths about her and my relationship with her. At the same time, I am careful about how and when I talk about my mom, and about how much I want to disclose. I am always keeping a pulse on my being, doing what is best for me. What is most important to me is honoring my truths. If talking about my mom is going to contribute to my healing journey, I carefully evaluate it and decide. Sharing my own journey in this project, "Daughters Betrayed By Their Mothers," is an ongoing and integral part of my journey. This is about honoring myself, my voice, and my truths. It is not about her.

3. **Has that changed over time? Is it different today than a year ago? 5 years ago? Other?**

The strength I feel today in talking or writing about my mom was not always present. Because my betrayals from my mom started at such an early age and were ongoing, I detached from her emotionally early on in my life. When I recall my thoughts of her and of talking about her, I protected myself by being very guarded in the degree of my disclosures. Although I did not disrespect her or disregard her openly in any way, I just did not talk about her very much. I did not share my true feelings about my mom until I was much older and when I was ready to confront them myself.

Over the years, as I chose to address my mom's betrayals of me, I did, of course, have many different feelings talking about her. I remember feeling incredibly angry, disappointed, and resentful. At times I was so hurt, even thinking about her left me feeling sickened. Before I embraced my journey of healing, I held many of my feelings inside, not able to talk about them or her. I remember thinking that by "talking about her...I was betraying myself even more." At the time, I didn't really understand that thinking, but years later I would come to know I was doing what I needed to do to prevent further damage to myself.

4. **We've talked about the connotations of the word "betrayal." How does this word feel for you? How does it feel to use it in relating to your mom?**

As I am writing this, I am thinking about how confusing betrayal felt as a little girl. Although I didn't use the word "betrayal," I felt like I was holding a secret. I felt like something was wrong with my family. I wanted to tell someone but was afraid if I did, I would be in trouble, or even worse, I would be blamed. I remember I desperately wanted someone to make my family better. I carried these thoughts with me throughout my childhood and into my teen years.

Strangely, for most of my adult life, I have felt very comfortable around the word "betrayal." It is something that I have been forced to know, intimately and early on. It has been a part of my life for as long as I can remember. In my career as a therapist, I worked largely in the areas of abuse, trauma, grief and loss; and thus, I was well-acquainted with betrayal on many levels. I don't want to imply my experiences with betrayal made it easier to navigate; it was and still is difficult work. Being familiar with it makes me less fearful of it.

However, even with my personal and professional background navigating betrayal injury, I was blown off course by the last squall of betrayals. In May of 2015, my mom betrayed several other family members and me on multiple levels. My mom lied about me to others, and she lied to me about my sisters. We were blamed for things we did not do. The climax of the betrayals crushed my sisters and me when my mom disowned us. For the first four months, I could barely speak of her. When I did, I referred to her as "The Betrayer." Although there was horrific brokenness around this series of unconscionable betrayals, at the same time I was also grieving my father and uncle whose passing immediately preceded my mom's betrayals.

I am aware of how grief and betrayal can be easily intertwined; and yet each one carries with it distinct characteristics. After working through the stages of grief due to triple loss—the physical deaths of my dad and uncle and the relational death of my mom—I am now in a place of acceptance. After recovering and restoring the broken pieces from my mom's most recent series of betrayals, I am once again in a place of wholeness.

When I started thinking about "The Daughters Project," I wondered if other females might struggle with the word "betrayal," not only in expanding upon the different kinds of betrayal as well as integrating betrayal's broad connotations into their lives, but also in subscribing these applications to their mothers. Talking about betrayal and engaging in an exploration of it, especially when it concerns our mothers, is like wading into dark waters, uncertain as to the depth of stigmatization it often carries with it or to the degree of shame we experience. Today, I no longer carry any secrecy, stigma, or shame over the betrayals from my mom. Today, I am ready to speak my truths.

Background

5. How would you describe your family as you were growing up?

I believe betrayal is like a cancerous growth. When its inception is deeply lodged within an unhealthy family system, vulnerable conditions become further weakened. Without early intervention and treatment, the source struggles. Ongoing, ensuing dysfunction provides fertile ground for betrayal to take hold and spread. Tragically, my family fell into this diseased dynamic.

When I think about my environment growing up, it was chaotic. My parents were very young when they married. I believe they were ill-equipped, both physically and emotionally, to handle marriage let alone a fast-growing family. Four daughters came into their lives within seven years. Being the second oldest, I remember there was always much to be done and not enough time to get it done right. There was always a sense of tension in the air, like something or someone could snap at any time. Money was very tight and I remember my mom complaining to us about not having enough to pay bills or buy milk. I worried about not having enough food, never eating more than my share. What was so confusing to me was there was always money to buy alcohol. Both my parents drank every night before dinner. When the drinking started, anger entered our home. My dad would get mad at the slightest things, especially with my mom. Almost every night at dinner, there was some kind of blow-up followed by the slamming of doors or cupboards. Holidays seemed to be the worst. There were major explosions with blame-filled remarks targeting any one of us. My mom didn't say anything to help us understand what was going on. She always made excuses for my dad and for herself.

Our household was also filled with criticism. No one ever measured up or was enough. Neither my older or younger sisters nor I could reach the standard which was set, although we all performed at high levels in almost everything we did. My youngest sister, who struggled physically, emotionally, and psychologically and who was unhealthily enmeshed with my mother, was not held to the same standards. I remember being belittled and berated for insignificant or minor things. It tore away at my self-worth and contributed greatly to my insecurities and shyness.

My mom and dad were very authoritarian in their parenting. While it seemed they didn't really care about how my sisters and I felt about things or how their behaviors were affecting us, their rules were strict, unreasonable, and without justification. It was "because they said it was." When one of us did mess up, my mom and dad overreacted, imposing restrictions which were illogical and emotionally detrimental. I know I was compliant most of the time, fearful of the consequences I might face. I believe this to be true for two of my sisters as well.

6. How many siblings, parents in the home, other family?

When I think of my family growing up, it felt repressive. It was not an environment in which children could flourish. Happy moments revolved around my parents "highball hour" (at least for a short time) and time we spent with my grandparents, either summers in Nevada or when they would come and visit us. My Pappy and Grandma spoiled us. There was plenty of money for food and other treats. Life was easier and more gentle during their stay. My parents seemed less stressed and on better behavior. I remember feeling more safe when my grandparents were with us.

As I would later come to understand in my Al-Anon work, I was the classic lost child and rescuer. Even as a little girl, I was a pleaser—the peacemaker—and wanted to try to make everything better. I was also very shy, very introverted. I envied my older sister (just one year older) who was outgoing and gushing with personality. When we were little, my mom dressed us like twins because we were so close in age and in size. I liked that others thought we were twins. I always felt closer to my older sister than to my mom.

When I think back to when my sister and I were five and four, memories of my mom are vague but good. She worked hard to clean the house, cook, and take care of us. When I was four, my first younger sister was born. We moved into a new, nicer and bigger house. I remember I loved my younger sister. She was a good baby and she was very cute. Even though my mom was busier, she still made time for us—keeping us clean, washing our hair, making doll clothes, and teaching us how to do our chores. However, my mom did not show her love outwardly or express it verbally. She always seemed preoccupied, and I felt a detachment from her at an early age...a sort of distance or coldness. It was hard to understand. I felt sad and alone.

When I turned six, my mom gave birth to one more daughter, my youngest sister. From that point, everything in my life and my two other sisters' lives changed. The new baby was fussy, cried constantly, and even as an infant she seemed angry. My mom became even more detached. She seemed anxious, on edge, and demanding. Although my mom was a stay-at-home mom, with four children there was always much to be done. My dad, who was a school band teacher, also worked other jobs such as teaching private lessons and playing gigs in a jazz band in order to keep up with mounting expenses. He was not at home much. It was during this time where my older sister and I became our mom's "worker-bees."

My older sister and I did whatever we were taught and told to do. And, we did it extremely well. In fact, we did it perfectly. Along with regular chores of making our beds and clearing and cleaning dishes, at an early age we took on more and more responsibility. As we continued on into elementary school, we vacuumed and dusted the house. We cleaned the bathrooms. We changed the beds. We learned to iron, and to do so with perfection. My mom purchased an Ironite (a mangle) like the kind which is used in professional cleaners. As a small, petite girl, I learned how to work it, often fearful of burning myself. I ironed sheets, pillow cases, and other large pieces of clothing. I didn't understand why everything had to be ironed. It was hard work; it was hot and uncomfortable. I also learned to iron using a regular-sized iron. I ironed shirts, pants, dresses, and blouses. I ironed handkerchiefs, underwear, and silky slips and other under garments. I ironed for hours on the weekends. Six people. Lots of clothes.

There were numerous other chores related to our family's endless laundry. I remember when our washing machine broke, and then our dryer. There was no money to fix it. For several years, every weekend my older sister and I would load up a week's worth of laundry into baskets, put them in our little red wagon, and walk down the street to the local laundromat. We spent the most of the morning there—washing, drying, and folding clothes. When we returned home, we put everyone's clothes in their proper places and sorted those items which needed ironing. I don't remember my mom ever thanking my sister and me for anything we did. It was just expected. It was our job. We did what we were told.

Although there was always a lot of work to do, I didn't know anything different. It was the way our home was. I didn't feel important. I didn't feel valuable. Mostly I felt invisible, except when told there was work to do. My mom seemed self-absorbed and distant, detaching more from my older sister, my younger sister and from me. She was consumed with taking care of my youngest sister, whose various diagnoses, disorders, and demands required more and more of her time. I began to feel unsafe as our household was becoming more and more angry. Although my mom and dad always drank—always had cocktails before dinner—as the drinking increased so did the tension and the blow-ups. Before my dad came home from work, my mom ordered us to be quiet, not to speak at the dinner table, and to get our work done. She didn't talk to us about what was going on, she didn't explain, she didn't "mother" us. She did not guide us through the turmoil. I felt I was on my own.

7. How would you describe your role?

Almost entirely, my role remained the same throughout my middle and high school years. When I was in middle school, added responsibilities and pressures were placed on my older sister and me when my mom returned to college to obtain her nursing degree. At a young age, my older sister and I took over the cooking and cleaning. When my mother wasn't at school or studying, she was sleeping. She was simply not available—physically, emotionally, or psychologically. My father remained absent a lot, working his various jobs. The tension and fighting between my youngest sibling and my two other sisters reached volatile and explosive levels. I felt like the parent, like the mom in the home. It wasn't until years later when I would understand how normal that was in an alcoholic family dynamic.

Growing up I had a few girlfriends whose households and roles within them were very different from mine. Two of my friends had moms who were incredibly loving and giving. Their homes felt warm and safe. Although my girlfriends had responsibilities and chores, their mothers "mothered" them in ways which were so foreign to me. After spending time with their families, I would often return home feeling more confused by my mom's absence and aloofness toward me. I couldn't make sense out of her lack of involvement in my life or interest in my well-being. Those feelings of confusion contributed greatly to my growing sense of worthlessness.

Betrayal Narrative

8. **When did you first start thinking about your betrayal narrative with your mom? What was that like for you?**

Although I was only six when my youngest sister was born, the shift in my mom's "mothering" of my other sisters and me was deeply felt. Being a very sensitive child, I felt alone. Even though my mom was present physically, I felt abandoned emotionally. I was too little to understand what was going on; however, I knew things were not right in our household. Over the years as my mom continued to detach and distance herself, the injustices seemed to pile up, one on top of the other.

9. **How would you like to share your betrayal narrative now?**

    • Is there a chronology to your betrayal/s with your mom?

    • Was there a pattern of betrayal? Episodes? Re-occurring?

10. **When you feel ready, please share your narrative.**

As I begin to share my narrative more fully, I choose to do so by describing the layers of betrayal. Although there are many different experiences which contribute to the different layers, the memories I have chosen to write about are the ones which have stayed with me the most, signifying their importance to me and their impact on me.

The first layer is best described as meanness toward me. With the birth of my youngest sister, I took on more responsibility. I worked very hard to please my mom, doing whatever I was asked to do in order to help out. I wanted to be a good daughter and a responsible older sister. Although I felt I was not a perfect child, I did the best I could for being six years old. Even though my persona was quite shy and very compliant, if my mom felt I disrespected her or talked back, I was given a choice—to have my mouth washed out with soap or peppered. I hated both options, but would typically choose soap. Its after-effects were not as long-lasting. Even today, I can picture myself standing on a little stool, leaning over the sink gagging and choking as my mom demanded, "Open your mouth" and proceeded with the ritual.

Although there are many worse and more horrific forms of child abuse, the soap-washing of my mouth felt like a deeply personal scouring of my core being. Because I was already not one to speak up easily this brutal washing further diminished my feelings of worth, resulting in a more quiet restrained voice and an even more responsible compliant child. As the meanness continued, I developed a fear of my mom, uncertain as to when she would get mad and impose the ritual again.

The next layer of betrayal is a difficult one to write about. It is one which moved my feelings about my mom from being a mean mom to a new level—being a punisher. Although I had learned to anticipate and to control my environment to whatever degree I could, as a little girl of eight I did not foresee the consequences of my choices.

For most of my life growing up, my family spent our summers in Nevada visiting our grandparents and other relatives. It was a time of freedom and fun. It was an escape. My sisters and I had many cousins from my mom's side who were loving, caring, and easy to be around, as were my aunts and uncles. One warm afternoon, my grandparents and parents took us to the local horse races. This was something we did every summer. Although to this day I can't remember why, but during the middle of the races I asked my mom and dad if I could go back to my grandmother's house. Because the races were not finished, they of course declined my request. I was persistent.

I said, "I want to go home."

My mom sternly replied, "If you want to go home, then go. But you'll have to walk back."

Because we were several miles away from my grandparents' house, she didn't think I would go. But, I did. I left our seats and the stadium, and headed at least a mile down a long dirt road toward the highway.

Hearing my named being screamed from behind me, I stopped before reaching the highway. When my mom caught up with me, she spanked me. It was not an ordinary spanking. With each step I took, my mom struck me with every force of her being. It felt like hatred being spread across my body mixed in with layers of anger, resentment, and madness. I was crying uncontrollably. I was afraid. I was in pain. Wearing a little dress, there was not much protection on my legs or rear end from her blows. By the time we reached our car, I was beaten, blistered, and bleeding. My body shook as I whimpered, pleading for her to stop.

The incident was never spoken of or mentioned again, until just a few years ago when it was minimized, joked about, and dismissed by my mom. What I knew then and every time I've thought about it after was, with every blow which accompanied every step I took, another layer of distrust and damage was painted onto my soul. Every mark on my body and every memory of it reminded me of how I was responsible for making my mom angry, and how I was punished for it.

As a little girl, my family's unhealthy structure continued to fracture and become more fragmented. The word "betrayal" was not part of my vocabulary. However, within its cancerous camouflage, betrayal shows up in many different forms. It is often hard to recognize, until it presents without any masks to disguise it. The mask came off of my mom when I was eleven years old. She was no longer a protector, like a mother should be. She became a violator of my trust and a silencer of my voice. Although this incident is still hard to talk about, it is important to my betrayal narrative.

I was visiting a teen female neighbor who lived across the street from my parents. She was a little older but much bigger than I was. With no adults at home, she turned a game of tag into an opportunity to attack and assault me. I fought her with all my might, struggling to break her grip and get out from underneath her. After several minutes of clawing and kicking, I was able to slide out from under her grotesque weight and run back home. With my clothes torn and tattered and my body shaking with fear, I screamed to my mom who was washing something in the kitchen sink. Crying and trembling, I grabbed hold of her arm.

"Mommy, Carla hurt me." Barely able to speak, I continued. "She chased me around the house and then threw me to the ground…" I choked on my words. "She started touching me…"

Before I could finish, my mom glared at me. With her hands still in the sink, she responded. "We don't talk about those kinds of things. Nothing happened to you. Quit your crying."

I pleaded. "But mommy, she did…she is so big and I couldn't get away…she held me down, hurting me. But I slid out from under her arms…"

My mom became angry. "I won't talk about this. Go change your clothes right now." And then she added, "And Holli, don't talk about this to anyone. Ever."

At that very moment, any trust I had in my mom vanished. I no longer felt safe in her presence. I knew I was on my own, and I knew I would need to take care of myself. I also learned my words held no value. I could not and should not speak up—ever. From that point forward, my mom—the silencer—took away the voicing of my truths. I repressed the event, burying it deeply within my core. Although I would not address it until many years later, my mom's mask was off. I would not see her the same way.

As I grew into my tween and teen years, the layers of distrust and detachment continued to form. I accepted more responsibility at home, working to please my mom with whatever I was asked to do and taking on more parenting roles with my younger siblings. I also worked very hard in school and in my musical interests.

From middle school and into high school, when my mom wasn't working or sleeping, she was focused on my youngest sister whose problems, both physical and psychological, were escalating. By the time I was in my last years of high school, the layers of abandonment I felt from her had solidified. She simply wasn't available or interested in being present for anyone else but my youngest sister. By the time I left for college, I was comfortable being on my own.

Over the years, my sisters and I married and had children. My older sister and I both moved away and remained away, except for short intervals. Although my two younger sisters remained in close proximity to my parents, my mom and youngest troubled sister never differentiated or individuated from one another. With my disturbed sister under her wing, my mom became the justifier of her injustices to my two other sisters and me.

Thus, the layers of betrayal have thickened exponentially. From my early twenties until present day, the toxic coatings range from unfounded accusations of not being there for my younger sister; unhealthy alliances between my mom and youngest sister damaging and destroying family gatherings, special events or individual celebrations; to a plethora of my troubled sister's real as well as fabricated illnesses, court dealings, dangerous relationships, and life-threatening diseases or dramas which served to erode further the fabric of our fractured family. During all these years, there has been little to no recognition of me as a daughter. There was no room for me. I became accustomed to it.

With a great deal of recovering work under my belt and embracing wellness in my own life, many years ago I came to accept the reality of my relationship with my mom. I have chosen to be kind, respectful, and loving. For example, I've never missed sending a card or calling on her birthday and Mother's Day. During visits, I've helped out with any needs of hers and done so with a caring spirit. Because I developed a very close and loving relationship in my adult years with my dad, I called often to speak with him, welcoming the opportunity to talk with her as well. However, my mom never had much to say to me. I held no expectations of her. I was in a place of peace, until recently.

Fueled and fed by years of weakened toxic environs, betrayal's cancerous growth spread throughout our family system. The malignancy reached a critical stage, subsequently poisoning its paternal carriers and paralyzing their dutiful descendants. On April 8, 2015, both my mother and my father methodically planned, carried out, but did not complete a dual suicide. An overdose of medications did not grant them their last wish, but instead cast the final layers of brokenness onto an already fractured family. Both parents were found and hospitalized; my dad in critical condition and my mom serious but stable. My dad was moved home and passed on April 16th, 2015, under hospice care. Although my mom recovered, she was transferred to a nursing home for further rehabilitation. As our family hung in the balance by a thread, I both anticipated and expected for there to be additional betrayals with ensuing fallout. However, I was not quite prepared for the enormity or finality of being disowned by my mom.

Because I live a great distance from my mom, I called the nursing home frequently to check on her. My three sisters were nearby helping out; and thus, there was no need for my presence. Within a few days, bitter accusations and disputes started to arise between my mom and youngest sister against my two other sisters. It continued to escalate with disastrous consequences. My youngest sister moved into my mom's house with her family, changed the locks, and took control of everything and of my mom.

During the chaos, I continued to call my mom, desperately defending my sisters and myself against a pile of lies and pleading with her to reconsider the baseless foundations for them. There were moments during our calls when I felt as though she heard me, but she would not change her mind. After a week of upheaval and with threats being waged against my other sisters and me by my youngest sister, I made one last call to my mom.

When I called, I asked her for one request. "Will you please listen to what I have to say? Allow me time to finish? And then, I will listen to you?"

My mom agreed. For the next two hours, I talked to her about our family. I spoke softly and gently but with conviction. I described the brokenness—a family built on lies and secrets and enveloped in denial and shame. And with a heavy heart, I spoke of the betrayals, not just mine but those my sisters had shared with me. She listened.

When I was done, I asked her if she wanted to respond. My mom acknowledged what I said. She did not deny or dismiss it. There was a sadness in her voice and an owning of sorts about various pieces. However, there were no apologies. Toward the end of our conversation, I needed to know what she wanted—from me and my two sisters—if anything.

I took in a deep breath. "Mom, with Stephanie (youngest sister) moving into your house, how will I have any relationship with you? She won't allow it."

My mom knew well what I meant. She cautiously replied, "Well, I will try and call you when I can."

I went on to describe my concerns about Stephanie's unhealthiness and her inability to take care of my mom. I told her how I was worried about her safety and long-term quality of care. My mom continued to listen, even agreeing at times but not wavering in her position.

Before we ended our conversation, I made one last request guessing this might be the last opportunity I ever had to speak with her again. And although I knew, without question, what her response would be I wanted my mom to know where my heart was—in a place of love and forgiveness.

My voice was strong and filled with compassion. "Mom, choose us (my other two sisters and me). We love you. We can help you. Even though I live far away, I will be there for you. We can help you get settled—stay in your home or move to a smaller place. Whatever you want or need. We will be there for you."

My mom's reply was short. "I can't. I need to be with Stephanie."

I spoke once more. "Mom, she is not well. She cannot take care of you. Please, this once…this time. Choose me…choose us."

Her voice was firm, but soft. "I can't."

I understood. I accepted what had been true for most of my life. I paused, waiting for the anchor lodged in my throat to come lose and allow my words to flow. "I love you, Mom. Goodbye."

She whispered, "I love you, too."

Over the next several weeks, a few more layers of betrayal followed—a certified letter from my mom and Stephanie warning my sisters and me to stay away from my mom's house and cruel voicemails telling us of the awful individuals we were.

I don't know if there are more layers to come. I don't know what is more final than being disowned.

Brokenness From Betrayal

11. How did your mom's betrayal /s affect you? What do you remember thinking, feeling, and doing?

Although I have described many of my feelings underneath my layers of betrayal, my brokenness manifested itself in all kinds of emotions, thoughts, and behaviors. Until I embraced a path a wellness, my broken foundation, for the most part, contributed to a fractured sense of self.

When I was very young, my dominant thought was I could not trust anyone or anything. There was no one else to rely on except myself (and my older sister). I was not close to my father, so there was not another adult to turn to. With the chaos and confusion in our home, I was constantly feeling anxious and hyper-sensitive. I could not turn to my mom for comfort. She was not available. This belief remained with me throughout my adult life, even while I began my recovering work.

Along with the lack of trust, I did not feel safe around other people or in my environment. After the assault at age eleven and my mom's dismissal of it, these feelings, of course, intensified. Whenever I was frightened or nervous about anything, I typically kept my feelings to myself believing no one would believe me if I shared what was going on, or even if someone did, that nothing would be done. I did not feel I had a "voice;" and thus, I kept quiet. I kept to myself. I spent a lot of time thinking about my family, my life, and my environment, especially in comparison to my friends and their families. However, I was very vigilant, always wondering if someone might hurt me; therefore, I continually assessed my circumstances in order to implement protective measures. I rarely took risks, afraid of what might happen.

It was also during this same time, although I was only eleven, I remember promising myself two things. "First, I will do whatever it takes to get out of this environment. I will study, practice, work and save money, maybe get a scholarship, it didn't matter. I will do what I have to do to go away to college and get out of this house."

And then, without really knowing the depth of what I meant, I made another promise to myself. "Secondly, what is going on in my house, I will never repeat. And, if and when I am a mom someday, I will never, ever be like my mom. I will do it differently."

Not feeling as though I could trust anyone or anything, not feeling safe, and not believing what I felt or said mattered, all contributed to my feelings of being alone and being on my own. My mom was there, and yet she wasn't. Whatever I was going to accomplish or do with my life, I would need to do it by myself. As I would write years later about my younger years, I knew I was *flying solo*.

12. What life messages came to you from your mom and/or in your relationship with her?

In my recovering work and in my work as a therapist, I have come to know and understand how powerful life messages are. They are an individual's internal dialogue (or messaging) which is composed from each person's unique life experiences and perceptions of them. Life messages come from any external source and they form our personal truths about ourselves and our inner-personal value.

At an early age, my life experiences and the messages I perceived from them taught me I was invisible. My youngest sister was the only one who mattered. With the ongoing harshness from my mom, I learned I was not enough. I didn't matter. I was not important. With the ensuing violations of trust, my messages became more damaging. I was not lovable. I was not worth protecting. I did not have a voice.

Another life message which was instilled in me as a young girl was my mom was like a Queen Bee and I was there to serve her. I worked very hard, always doing what I was told and to the best of my abilities. As compliant as I was in doing all my chores and carrying through with all my responsibilities, as well as with my school work and practicing, my mom never acknowledged me or what I did. She, in fact, took the credit. As I grew older and took on more responsibility, especially after my mom returned to school and then work, my life message was, "My role is to serve my mom."

Another message which was very confusing to me as a little girl was "my needs are not important." From my friends' households, I didn't see their moms behaving the same way. A memory which remains unpleasant to this day is when my mom would take long baths. I, along with two of my sisters, were busy bees getting our chores done. Soaking in the tub, she would sing a verse from a song… "When my ship comes in…" and she would go on to describe all the things she would get and do. I remember feeling sad and angry. It felt like all she could focus on was herself and her wants. When I saw her in the tub with bubbles all around her, I resented how the Queen had time for daydreaming, but not for me.

One of the most painful life-messages which I perceived from my mom and I have struggled with encapsulates most of the other messages. It is a tape I've played in my mind many times growing up and continued to do so into my adult life.

"If I don't matter, if I am only here to serve my mom, and if she is not available for me in any way, I must not have been wanted…I must not have been wanted…I was not wanted."

Even as a little girl, I took really good care of all my belongings and possessions—clothes, dolls, books, and so on. I could not understand that if something was important or if it was valuable, how someone would not want to take care of it, unless it was not wanted in the first place. My tape continued.

"If someone or something is not wanted, then it doesn't matter how it is treated. And in fact, if there is resentment or anger over this person or thing for making life more busy and complicated, then use it to make things easier."

As hurtful as this message was, playing it over in my mind helped me to make some sense out of my reality and to accept it. I believe it was during my middle school years when I learned neither I (nor any of my sisters) was "planned." In fact, my mom explained to us the inadequacies of the contraceptive devices she and my dad used. For me, it solidified the belief or the message that I was not wanted.

Although all of my sisters had nicknames which were not flattering, mine put a label on the layers of messages I carried with me, *Horrible Holli*.

One final and powerful message which emerged as a tween and strengthened into my adolescent years, was, "If I want my mom's attention, all I need to do is be sick." As I observed the deterioration of my youngest sister's emotional and physical health (both real and feigned), I also witnessed how my mom became more obsessed and absorbed with her wellbeing. I saw the degree of attention my sister received and, at times, I was very envious. Whenever I did get sick, my mom was the "nurse" I needed, taking really good care of me. When I was better, the attention was over. However, as I grew older detaching more from my mom, I knew I would rather have no relationship with her than use illness to get her attention. Even as a young teen, wellness became a subconscious goal.

13. What were their short-term and long-term implications or impact on you?

As with the betrayals themselves, the impact of their life messages on me also came in layers, each one adding another coat of predominately unhealthy patterns of thinking, behaving, and feeling.

Inner-personally as a young girl and adult, my life messages fueled my lack of self-worth. I was extremely insecure and had very low self-confidence. I did not feel pretty. I did not feel anyone could or would love me. However, I desperately wanted to love and be loved in return.

In spite of my shyness, I did develop some wonderful female friendships during my school years and in college. I dated quite a bit in high school, never wanting to get too serious with any guy. I didn't want to derail my plans for college. When I started having stronger feelings for a boy, I would usually do something to sabotage it, causing the guy to break it off with me. I had one serious relationship in my senior year in high school with a freshman from a local university. He was kind. He was safe. He did not pressure me about anything—sex, drugs, alcohol. I felt very much in love with him but shortly after I left for college, our relationship ended.

After entering college, a pattern of unhealthy relationships with men started to emerge. I dated a lot, falling quickly and deeply for a guy. Then, as I did in high school, I would sabotage it by becoming over-possessive or needy. The relationship would end, usually quite badly. I remember how the feelings of pain, shame, and rejection felt normal to me, almost safe in a way. Although I didn't understand it at the time, I didn't feel like I deserved to be loved.

My pattern of unhealthy short-lived relationships continued until prior to my junior year when I began dating an older man, a university teacher's assistant who was working on his PhD. He was smart. He was an alcoholic. He was emotionally and psychologically abusive. He was selfish and manipulative. He used me and abused me. I did not sabotage the relationship. I kept going back for more. I didn't feel like I deserved anything more. I had no self-worth. I held no value. Toward the end of my junior year, I married him. The relationship was sick. It got worse over time. He had multiple DUI's, arrests, and we were deeply in debt. He became more angry and abusive. After two years, I made a plan in my mind to get out of the marriage and away from him. Just like I did with my mom.

Although I worked hard to change my life around and get it on track, my wounds ran deep and I was unaware of their impact on me and my relationships with men. I dated a bit, ending relationships as soon as I felt uneasy or unsafe. In my later twenties, I met and married a wonderful man. We had a beautiful daughter together; however, I know now that because of my unattended wounds from childhood, my voids and needs could not be met by him or anyone, and we divorced after six years of marriage.

In my early thirties, I met and married my husband Dan. With his encouragement, I began my recovering journey, healing and unhooking myself from my patterns of self-destructive feelings, thoughts, and behaviors.

14. Are there other pieces to your brokenness which are important to share?

Most of my brokenness impacted me in very destructive ways. However, there is one aspect to my brokenness which is really important to me and one which I share often today as I speak to audiences. It is actually a positive piece.

Because I learned early on I was not able to depend on anyone or anything else, I became very self-reliant. As I invested into my academics and into my musical pursuits, something incredible started to happen. I began receiving accolades, awards, and recognition for my accomplishments. Whether it was being mentioned for Honor Roll or winning a musical competition, I made the connection in my mind that when I invested into things which gave back to me, I felt my sense of worth and value increase. And, relishing those foreign feelings of worth as they grew, I was even more motivated to continue making strong investments and healthy choices into those same areas. I learned to be focused, driven, and to perform at my highest level possible.

The life message I carried within me was there were areas outside of my personal circumstances in which I could feel safe to invest. Learning to *fly solo* taught me how I could soar. No one could stop me. This message, which emerged out of layers of brokenness, has served me well all throughout my life.

From Brokenness To Wholeness

15. When did you first start thinking about your brokenness in relationship to your mom?

Becoming aware of one's brokenness, for most individuals, is a process. It is a painful process. It is one which is shrouded in shame and secrecy. It was no different for me. By the time I was in my late-twenties, there was an internal tug of war going on inside me. On one end of the worth-rope I was proud of my accomplishments—becoming a teacher, enjoying a loving relationship with my husband, and establishing a stable life. Pulling at the other end, I was filled with feelings of worthlessness, embarrassment, and self-condemnation over the poor choices I had made in my past along with their ensuing consequences. When I allowed myself time to reflect upon my feelings, especially those of worthlessness, I recommitted myself to continue working hard at living my life in a healthier and different way than I was raised.

However, it was during the period of time when my husband and I started planning for a child that I first thought about my brokenness in direct relationship to my mom. I was twenty-seven when I became pregnant. I was incredibly happy and excited. I loved working on the nursery and planning for the baby's arrival. When my daughter was born, I remembered my promise I made to myself at age eleven, "I would not be the mom I had. I would do it differently. I would be everything she wasn't." Over the years, as I was raising my daughter, many painful memories would surface. Although I did not seek out any help, I really started making my first connections into my layers of brokenness with the onset of my daughter's birth.

16. When did you first consider addressing your injuries, wounds, or brokenness? What was that like for you?

Sometimes, recovering comes in through the back door. Time and time again, I remember clients who came in to seek help for "what they thought was the issue" when it was something much different. As a therapist, I addressed what was in front of me, giving the underlying issues time to surface while providing the space for clients to feel safe with me and establishing a trusting rapport with one another.

It wasn't until I was in my early thirties when recovering came to me in an unexpected way, through a different door. Strangely enough, mine started with my dad, not my mom. When I think about it now, he was actually more present in my life and he was more safe. Although I was extremely angry with him and resentful for the authoritarian way in which we were raised, in addition to the chaos and commotion around the alcoholism, I didn't feel betrayed by him like I did my mom.

With encouragement from my husband Dan, I began reaching out to my dad by telling him I loved him. It was extremely difficult, especially when I heard nothing back from him. However, I welcomed in foreign feelings of forgiveness and renewal. After about eight months of continually expressing my love, either in person or over the phone, my dad reciprocated. Although it was a new beginning in our relationship, what I took notice of was how I was changing. I no longer felt powerless over my pain.

17. **How would you like to share your journey *From Brokenness To Wholeness*?**

    - Are there different stages?
    - Has there been ongoing work?

18. **When you are ready, please share your journey *From Brokenness To Wholeness*.**

During the same period of time I reached out to my dad, I also began seeing a counselor. After being diagnosed with what was called then "premenstrual syndrome" (PMS), I realized I had adopted really unhealthy coping mechanisms in order to manage my bouts of anger and depression. With a young daughter at home, I desperately wanted to get to the root of my moods, address them, and not repeat unhealthy behaviors of my mom or dad. I worked really hard in counseling, changing my thinking, feeling, and behaving. It was a significant first layer in my recovering. However, I don't remember addressing under-lying issues or the betrayals I felt as a child. Regardless, my life took on more stability—emotionally, physically, and psychologically. With a move away from my hometown a year later, I felt even stronger and healthier.

Another unanticipated door opened in my recovering journey when my husband and I decided to move to Southern California, five hundred miles away from my family. After spending a couple of years adjusting to our new jobs and getting acquainted with our desert environs, we chose to live in the mountains a short distance from our work positions and at an elevation away from the intense heat. Establishing a home and a life in a wide open grassy valley surrounded by large pines was freeing and renewing. The high desert topography reminded me of my summers in Nevada, and the comfort it brought to my mind, body, and spirit was like a creamy salve gently spread across layers of torn tissue. Each day, each month, and each year, as I walked among Nature, I drew from Her beauty and Her goodness and integrated healing lessons into my life. Mother Nature became my teacher, my mentor, my nurturer—replacing the one I did not have.

The longer I was away from my childhood environment and the stronger I began to feel, the more aware I became of my brokenness in relationship to my mom and my family. I no longer was afraid of it or the power it held over me for so many years. Several doors of recovering had opened, and I was eager to keep knocking on others.

Although I taught English and history for eleven years at middle school, my bachelor's degree was in French and music. When I changed school districts, I was required to obtain an additional credential in order to teach English at the secondary level. In my composition class at our local state university, the professor's first assignment was to write a descriptive personal narrative. Without hesitation, I chose to write on "My Unhealthy Family." It was the first time I had put down my thoughts in writing. It felt strange. It felt validating. My voice and my truths spilled out. They no longer could be silenced.

Also during this period of time, I began teaching at a new middle school. One of the older more seasoned teachers took me under her wing. She was loving and kind. She became a confidant. After sharing with her privately about the paper on "my unhealthy family," she asked me if I would like to attend Al-Anon with her. Although I didn't know what Al-Anon was, she explained it to me. And she shared how both she and her husband were recovering alcoholics and from alcoholic families. I agreed to go with her, feeling quite anxious. I was just beginning to give a voice to my past. I wondered if this recovering door was the right one for me to open.

The minute I stepped into the first meeting, I felt at home. The stories of others were mine. No judgment. Complete acceptance. I didn't speak for months. I just listened. There was healing in doing so. I heard the word "codependency" for the first time. I was fascinated by it and I set out to read and learn everything I could about it. *Codependent No More* (Beattie, 1986) became my first recovery book. I read it from cover to cover, working all the activities and writing down my thoughts and feelings. I also read *Perfect Daughters* (Ackerman, 2002). Feeling as though the author had written my autobiography and having my experience explained with empathy and intelligence, I began opening numerous recovering doors and exploring them. I started to make sense out of my family—the alcoholism, the chaos, the absence of parents, and my mom's role—not only as an alcoholic but as a codependent herself. As I continued attending meetings and educating myself on alcoholic family systems, and especially the roles of children, layers and layers of awareness moved me into a place of understanding, and of wanting to know more.

As I continued to attend Al-Anon meetings, once again I felt a surge of wellness within me take hold. Working the 12 Steps, I discovered the power of reclaiming myself, my worth, and my voice. Feeling empow-ered, I began writing my first recovery book—*The PMS Puzzle*. Although I did not write about my brokenness with my mom, I disclosed my personal journey with PMS along with a comprehensive holistic approach to treatment. In addition, I reached out to help women suffering from PMS (later termed Premenstrual Dysphoric Disorder) by facilitating psycho-educational support groups. After leading the groups for several years and wanting to know more about human behavior, I returned to graduate school to obtain a master's in Psychology and become a licensed marriage and family therapist.

During the three year span it took me to finish my degree, I continued my healing on several levels. I continued my work in Al-Anon and I constantly turned to Nature, observing—listening—and reflecting on the lessons She offered. As time passed, wellness integrated itself into my being and became my compass. As I prepared myself to enter the next recovering door—graduate school—I would awaken layers of awareness, unravel their meaning, and incorporate their healing applications into my life.

The first layer of awareness unveiled itself during a class on "family systems." One of the final assignments was to construct a family geno-gram, a pictorial diagram which maps out the patterns and relationships within the emotional unit—using all the information we had learned in the class to deconstruct and analyze our families. The professor cautioned us to take our time, explaining how it could be a very painful exercise.

During the next several weeks, I thought about and prepared myself for the assignment. I knew it would be tough, but I felt ready. I laid out a large poster board on our dining room table and began painting my family's portrait: births, members, family history, medical and psycho-logical issues, relationships, marriages, children, roles, alliances, birth orders, disorders, and so on.

With every symbol I drew—circles, squares, jagged lines, straight lines, etc.—along with writing down their representations and additional descriptors, I cried and I grieved. As I carefully penciled in the multiple lines between my mom and my youngest sister signifying their enmeshed relationship while adding in the symbols for abandonment, detachment, and neglect between my mom and me, I gave myself permission to release the betrayals of my past. Although I still had much more to learn about the "pathology" behind the unhealthiness of my mom, her behaviors, and her relationship with my sister, I felt a growing calm of acceptance replace the gnawing pain of past rejection. I continued to work hard on my genogram until it was complete, crafting a portrait of brokenness—A Fractured Family.

By the time I was done and ready to present the portrait of brokenness to my professor and fellow students, I could feel layers of awareness, insight, and understanding take hold within me. Although I was nervous the night of class in which I was scheduled to share my genogram, I felt safe in the empathic group structure which the professor had cultivated and nurtured. As I talked about my family and my mom, my voice was strong. As I spoke of my relationship with my mom, heads nodded and eyes watered. No judgment. No dismissal. Only unconditional regard and acceptance. What I was continuing to discover about myself is that for me, knowledge is empowering and shared suffering is healing.

The second layer of awareness revealed itself to me during the same period of time. As a requirement for graduation, students needed to secure a counseling internship at a place of their choosing. After applying, being accepted, and attending mandatory training to intern at a well-respected women's shelter, I took on several responsibilities: working at the shelter once a week; working the crises lines one night a week; counseling individual clients several times a week; and co-leading a psycho-educational group for women in a two-year transitional housing program. As I worked in the various positions along with attending mandatory supervision, I found I connected easily with the women.

Although many women came from highly dangerous relationships and environments, I found comfort in knowing other females had mothers who betrayed them (as well as other family members) and who also felt a great deal of shame around their experiences. They, too, carried around self-deprecating life messages of self-blame and self-hatred. Their feelings of worthlessness and powerlessness haunted them and defined them. While working with my clients and reflecting on their recovering journeys, I began to peel away and release many of my outer layers of shame: not having a mom to protect me, care for me, and want me. I was not alone. Other women experienced it too. Other women were healing from it too.

The last layer of awareness which presented itself to me while I was getting my degree took hold during therapy. Each student was required to be in individual counseling during our masters' program. Although I remember addressing mostly issues which were coming up in reference to my clients, the shelter, and my classes, I remember feeling very safe with my female counselor. She was kind and gentle. She was honest and truthful. I trusted her, a feeling which was foreign to me, especially with older women. Because my husband and I had relocated to the Bay Area of California two years previously for his job and we were moving back to the mountains after my graduation, she suggested I continue my counseling upon returning to our home.

With compassion and unconditional positive regard, she spoke softly as we said our goodbyes, "Holli, I think there may be more there for you to work on. Take your time. Take care of yourself." Although it would be over ten years before I would unearth the deepest of my betrayals from my mom, my experience in therapy with an older woman who validated and affirmed me contributed significantly to my feelings of worth, both personally and professionally.

With each additional layer of awareness, insight, and understanding into my brokenness and with the ensuing recovering levels each brought, I felt a new "Holli" taking hold. I felt like I had stepped outside of the dysfunctional dance of my family and into a place where I could do my own dance, on healthy terms. I no longer felt "a part of them" but "apart from them." Then, rather unexpectedly, a few months before my husband and I returned to our mountain home, a door opened to re-engage with my family. After cautiously considering the ramifications, I walked through the door.

As was a common occurrence in our family, my youngest sister became enraged with my two sisters and me over an incident within her personal life. However, this time the turmoil reached a breaking point causing my mom to turn completely against us as well. Against the advice of most professionals in the field of psychology, I felt I had just enough training under my belt to facilitate a family intervention. With my two sisters and their husbands on board and with my parents in agreement to talk through the situation, we scheduled a time for a family meeting. Without my youngest sister present, each member was instructed to address three questions: What am I feeling? Why am I feeling this way? And what are three things I need to move forward?

When I reflect upon that day over twenty years ago, I am actually amazed at how well it went! Each of my sisters spoke their truths, as did I. Although my father was completely aware of the unhealthy dynamic between my mom and my youngest sister, he walked a fine line between acknowledging my mom's feelings as well as being there for the three of us.

In the end, nothing changed for the better. And in fact, my mom became livid afterwards feeling she had been singled out and blamed for all our family's problems. She and my youngest sister became more aligned than before, and my mom distanced herself from my two sisters and me even further. However, with the degree of knowledge I had acquired at that time about human behavior and family systems, I knew I was on the right track. I would continue healing myself, tending to my wounds, and setting healthier stronger boundaries moving forward. Neither I, nor anyone, could change my mom (or our family structure) unless she chose to change and do the work as well. I had no reason to believe it was ever going to happen. There was freeing of my spirit within that acceptance. With every level of additional insight, I was breaking through my betrayals from my mom and releasing their hold on me.

After returning to our mountain home and acclimating ourselves, my husband and I began reestablishing our professional careers paths. However, within the business of my schedule, both as a teacher and a therapist, I would often recall the words of my prior therapist, "Holli I think there may be more there for you to work on. Take your time. Take care of yourself." It was time. I was ready to open another door.

Because of my positive experience with an older female therapist, I made a few inquiries in the area I was working locating a well-respected psychologist who maintained a small private practice in her home. We quickly established a very safe and trusting relationship. My therapist gently guided me through the healing of my inner child, using hypnosis to access areas of trauma. I did a tremendous amount of journaling, utilizing it as an integral form of processing and releasing. And although I uncovered many of the repressed events relating to the betrayals from my mom, I was not able to root out the core trauma from age eleven. However, by the end of our sessions spanning about ten months, I felt an integrated and purposely-formed healing take hold, replacing the fractured pieces which had lain dormant for so long. As we concluded our time together, I thanked my therapist for the role she played in my work, allowing my transference toward her as a mother to serve as a tool for rebuilding worth in myself and trust with others. At our last session, my therapist recommended a book she thought might shed some light on my mom's relationship with my youngest sister. Just the title— "The Normal One: Life with a Difficult or Damaged Sibling"—left me running to open that door!

I love reading a book which feels like it was written *just for me and to me*. Dr. Jeanne Safer's *The Normal One* was one of those. Not only was her book informative, but it was extremely restorative. Understanding how my feelings of being invisible and growing up too fast because of the demands of an unhealthy sibling were very "normal" in a family like mine, brought new levels of release and renewal. When I was younger I recalled saying to myself many times, "The one child who requires the most, receives the most. The rest of us get little or nothing." *The Normal One* validated that truth, pulling me away from resentment and propelling me toward further recovery.

Over the next five years, I continued my wellness program—reading, journaling, working 12 Steps, walking in the mountains—and integrating familiar as well as newly discovered practices into my routine. My relationship with my mom was distant both physically and emotionally; however, I was always kind and loving toward her. I learned to expect nothing from her; and thus, I was able to avoid re-injury and maintain my peaceful place of being.

My next recovery door presented itself to me in a very natural form, writing. Although I had always loved to write and I had one book published in the early 90's, during the summer of 2006 I began entertaining the idea of authoring a book about betrayal. Because I heard the words "I feel so betrayed" come up so much in my work as a therapist and because I had experienced betrayal in my life, I was both fascinated by it and frustrated by what I felt was a lack of thorough understanding of its etiology, symptomology, as well as effective interventions for addressing it.

After many months of reviewing my clinical notes and analyzing case studies, both past and present, in the fall of 2007 I began drafting my first findings about betrayal. As soon as I started typing words into my computer, I believed writing *Breaking Through Betrayal* would not only help others, but I knew it would augment my healing. From the definitions of betrayal in Chapter One which poured out of me—*an investment into someone or something met with rejection or abandonment; a profound trust which is profoundly violated; a belief which is shattered or truth which is becomes a lie*—to the five- part recovering in Section III—*Revive and Restore: Mind, Body, and Spirit*—I put into practice what I wrote. From chapter to chapter, from exercise to exercise, I did the hard work. During the writing about chronic or ongoing betrayals, I grieved over the multitude of losses. I gave myself time and permission to release residual or fresh grief, and I renewed myself in the process. I carefully crafted exercises throughout the book which protected me from additional harm from my mom and which strengthened me on my recovering journey. With added layers of understanding of betrayal accompanied by healthy changes in my thinking, feeling, and behaving, my betrayals no longer *defined* me—they *refined* me. Almost a decade after the intervention with my mom, I was reminded of what I thought about betrayal then and what I knew about it now—*it was and is my responsibility to right myself.* However, my most difficult door still awaited my opening.

After selling our home in the mountains, in the fall of 2008 my husband and I relocated to a small town in central California, twenty miles from my parents. Although I felt I had enough healing under my belt and our motivations for returning to the area were heartfelt, after living there just a few weeks my emotional wellness suffered greatly. Triggers were everywhere. I began having nightmares and flashbacks. I became unusually angry, especially around my mom. I felt I was *losing myself.*

Although I put into place all the exercises and wellness practices I knew, I could not get a handle on what was going on with me. Finally, in the winter of 2010, I located a therapist in a nearby town who specialized in abuse and trauma. Once again, I opened the recovery door and walked through it. I put my trust in the hands of a gifted, gentle, older woman. Slowly and compassionately, she guided me through peeling away the deeply buried layers of pain and shame, and unearthing the assault from age eleven. As we moved through its delicate removal, releasing residual layers of guilt, self-blame, self-hatred, and more shame, I faced my most painful truth—at the moment in time when I needed my mom more than anyone else in the world—when I cried out for her to see me, protect me, and care for me, she betrayed me.

My body trembled and shook like a fragile structure during an earthquake. Plastered cracks within my being opened up and tiny fissures exploded. Tears flowed; then gushed. As the release continued, my therapist wrapped my soul in her arms and cradled my spirit. Her blanket of warmth felt like a mother's love, safe and unconditional. I soaked it in, allowing its integration within my being. Although there was still more releasing to do over the next few months, layers of forgiveness—of myself and of my mom—began to form and fill in the spaces where shame and pain resided for so many years.

In the summer of 2011, I once again moved away from my betrayal environment. I returned to the familiar desert terrain of Southern California where I began writing about my recovering. Over the next six months, my husband retired and was able to join me. In the winter of 2011, we relocated to the beautiful mountains of Arizona. Once in Nature's womb, I continued my healing and my writing. Although I never intended my journals to be published, I knew that if writing *Mountain Air: Relapsing and Finding the Way Back…One Breath at a Time* added layers of healing to my personal journey as well as provided me with critical insights into relapse of all kinds, I believed offering these experiences of shared suffering to readers might do the same.

As I write my narrative today, I am strong. I am well. I still work on my recovering, keeping myself open to new doors. It is ongoing. It is a part of who I am.

Wholeness To ...

19. Where are you today in your relationship with your mom (whether living or not)?

When I was creating the interview questions for *Wholeness To ...*, I thought long and hard about them. I don't see wholeness or wellness as a destination or a perfect place, but as another door which opens to additional rooms for living in accordance with our healing truths and purposely cultivating healthy ways of being. I am also well aware that relapse is a part of recovery and there may be times where we are required to step back into prior recovery rooms and rework our processes or programs.

My work on myself with regard to my mom has brought me to the door of wholeness. Each day I choose to walk through it, embracing what practices I need in order to honor myself and my truths and to do so with a loving spirit.

As I am writing my narrative, I do not have a relationship with my mom. This was her choosing. When I think about her, I feel sad for a few moments. I allow that feeling to be there. I honor it. And then, I let it pass. If it starts to linger, I say a prayer for her, sending positive thoughts her way.

Once in a while when I am doing a household chore—cooking a fancy dinner, decorating the dining room table, or planning for a special holiday or gathering—I will think of my mom and say to myself, "I know how to do this because I was trained so well at such a young age." It is not a positive thought. It is not a negative thought. It is just a thought.

Over the years as I have learned more about our family with buried secrets being exposed and background histories being explored along with my work in psychology, I've come to understand my mom more. It does not excuse her behavior. It explains it.

I am at peace with her. I am in a place of acceptance.

20. Today, where are you with yourself?

Although my journey of wellness with my mom has been a long one, I feel good about myself today. With a great deal of humility, I feel proud of myself. And, I've worked hard to get here!

21. How do you feel about yourself today? Why?

When I think back to the destructive life messages of my youth and compare them to the life messages which fill my rooms of Wholeness today, I am so grateful for the journey I'm on.

22. What life messages do you say to yourself now?

As I keep stock of my emotional current reality and wellbeing, I often find myself replaying the following life messages:

I was a good daughter.
I am a good daughter.
I am a good person.
I am a good friend to others.

As I think about my role as a wife, I feel incredible fulfillment and satisfaction. With each year of my marriage, my life messages have become more solidly integrated into my being.

I am a giving wife.
I am a grateful wife.
I am a loving wife.
I am a loved wife.

As I think back to the two promises I made to myself over fifty years ago, I first reflect upon what I have accomplished in my roles as a teacher, therapist, author, and presenter. I am both humbled and honored by these life messages and in their presence in my life.

I am a strong woman.
My voice is important.
My work is important.
I am important.
I matter.

And lastly, I think about my role as a mother and my promise to my daughter. Although I was not a perfect mom, I purposely mothered her in all the ways I was not. Her wellbeing was always paramount. Loving her, affirming her, nurturing her, and guiding her through life's struggles, as well as successes, has been my greatest joy. As I reflect upon the loving letters, cards, messages, and poems my daughter has written or spoken to me over the years and as she continues to do so today, her words confirm that I kept my promise and that there is a living legacy of its proof.

My most precious life messages are in her words.

Happy Birthday
My mother's touch is worth the highest price.
Ever so gently, soft, graceful fingers glide over my skin.
Love seems to spread over me ever so perfectly.
Yes, my mother's touch is worth the highest price.

My mother's love is worth the highest price.
Through wrong and right her love never seems to change.
Her love and direction has supported me since day one.
Yes, my mother's love is worth the highest price.

Which I shall never sell for as long as I live.
Alexis—Age 15

In thinking over my journey and all my current life messages, I am convinced that *flying solo* produced strong wings which have carried me far.

23. As you continue to work on your wholeness, what areas are important to you?

As I continue to move through my wellness rooms and cultivate healthy ways of being, one of the toughest areas for me with any kind of challenge, but especially a betrayal, is remaining *still* for a period of time before responding in whatever way may seem appropriate and healthy. When something unpleasant or hurtful takes place, I've learned the way I feel about it on a specific day will most likely not be the same in a day or two. And even if it is, by allowing my heightened emotions to settle down, I am more likely to respond in a healing way rather than a harmful way, if I am *still*. Because of my control issues as a codependent and wanting people and situations to be "fixed right away," I often do not give myself enough time to sift and sort through my feelings and/or give others enough time to do the same.

I write about being *still*. I talk about it. I continue to work on it!

On a professional note, I will continue doing what I have been doing for over ten years now—working in the field of psychology as a writer, speaker, and workshop presenter. I will keep knocking on doors and continue wondering how I can bring wellness into the recovery rooms of others. I am still fascinated by human behavior. I am passionate about exploring *why* we do what we do, examining causation. And I am driven to discovering healing interventions or offering recovering paths in order for others to embrace a more well and whole place of being.

Embarking on this project, "Daughters Betrayed By Their Mothers: Moving from Brokenness To Wholeness," is by no means an easy task! But then, anything worthwhile rarely is. If *one* more daughter is helped by my narrative and by the other daughters'…if *one* more is made to feel understood… if *one* more is encouraged or motivated to take that first critical step in recovering… if *one* precious daughter sees herself in one or more of the narratives and experiences the inexplicable healing which comes from shared suffering—my core will glow in rays of wholeness.

I will keep doing what I am doing, until I no longer can.

24. From your betrayal experience with your mom, what life lessons have served you well and which ones continue to do so?

As I continue to move through *Wholeness,* each day I make a conscious effort to be mindful of living in accordance with my healing truths. I tap into the life lessons learned from both my childhood betrayal experiences with my mom and my ensuing recovering.

At a very young age, my only source of recognition came from excelling in music and academics. I learned the more I invested into people or things which gave back to me, the better I felt about myself. And, in return, I made healthier choices. The life lesson I learned was even though I could not choose my environment or control my personal circumstances, I did have a choice about how I felt about myself. No one could take that from me. Not my mom, not anyone. However, it was my responsibility to choose it and act upon it.

Another important piece to this lesson which I have carried with me is if I stumble and fall, or if I fail, or if, by no fault of my own, someone or something derails me, I can always begin again. With every betrayal I experienced, from my mom and from others, I kept going. I picked myself back up, found help, and continued my hard work. I continued to invest and reinvest into myself and my wellbeing. I continued to give back to myself by doing the hard work. I didn't get bitter. I got better.

From my years of recovering from betrayals from my mom; from learning about and understanding the unhealthiness in my family system; and from getting off the drama rollercoaster which my family road all of my life, another life lesson I carried with me is I have choices in how I want to live my life. One very important decision I made at an early age was not repeating the same behaviors or patterns of my family. I took stock of what was happening. Even though it didn't make sense to me at the time, I knew I wanted a different life. And yes, I made mistakes along the way. I chose unhealthy behaviors and relationships. And then, I remembered what I wanted and what I promised myself and I made a choice. I chose wellness.

One of my most important life lessons came to me a little later in life. Because my sense of trust was violated at such an early age by my mom, I learned not to trust. Not only was this harmful to me but it was damaging to my relationships as well. As I worked on my recovering, I learned not only how to trust but also how to be mindful about my levels of trust. For example, I learned I could be selective about where, when, and in whom and to what degree I chose to invest of myself and my resources. This new life lesson was a difficult one to embrace and implement, especially being a codependent person. However, it has served me well. If individuals come into my life who are not healthy or current relationships bring drama into my life, I trust what I need to do. I reset boundaries and shore up others. At times, I have let go of friendships.

The umbrella life lesson I carry with me daily is *I am only as good for others as I am to myself.* My wellness remains my priority.

25. Where do you wish to go from here? Is there something beyond wholeness?

As my journey with *wholeness and beyond* continues, I am open to where it will lead me. I will write this book. And then, the next. I will remain receptive to the messages coming my way while keeping a pulse on my passions and what is purposeful. As I continue down my path, if it is to be, I will write another. As long as I have something to say which I believe might help others live more whole lives, I will obey the calling.

Giving back is my platform for ongoing recovering.

Giving back is my greatest reward.

And I trust without question that because of my journey *flying solo*, it will serve to strengthen the wings of others required to do the same.

2   "A Hero Lies in You" – Ann

Reflection

In a few hours, I will be interviewing my first participant—Ann—for "The Daughters Project." Preparing for this interview, I've spent several months organizing my ideas and formulating what I believe to be a sensitive yet thorough script with which to guide our conversation. I have also neared the completion of writing my own narrative regarding the betrayals with my mom, enabling me to connect more intimately and intuitively with what I am asking of Ann.

During the past few weeks, I've thought about Ann and her willingness to be my first interviewee. Meeting in graduate school twenty-one years ago, we were drawn to one another with respect to our mutual passion for becoming marriage and family therapists. As we grew our friendship over the years, it became clear that we shared many other experiences and we both navigated from a deep desire to live our lives from a more whole and well place of being. Although our paths have taken on their own unique challenges and recovering journeys, we have shared in our common pain and bonded over our experience of shared suffering—betrayal by our mothers.

A little over a year ago, I first approached Ann about "The Daughters Project." Without any hesitation, she expressed a strong interest in participating. As the months and weeks have drawn closer to our interview date, I've checked in with Ann regarding her willingness, readiness, and preparedness. She has not once waivered. As I check in with myself, I know that I am ready as well. However, I feel a heavy responsibility to Ann, and to the other women I interview. Regardless of our levels of recovering, speaking about our mothers, especially mothers who have betrayed their daughters, is a formidable task. While I want to remain present and open to Ann's experiences, I also want to cover specific themes and lessons within our conversation. Thus, I need to keep an internal pulse on the direction and flow of our interview. Most importantly, within the designated time allotted for our interview, I want to honor Ann's voice and her truths by allowing her the ample space she needs to express herself freely and fully.

While my thoughts are filled with mindful intention, my spirit is illuminated with purposeful anticipation.

Setting

Because I live several hours away in a neighboring state and I had previously scheduled a vacation in Ann's hometown, we decided to meet at her house for our interview. As I walked up to her front door and knocked softly, I felt the butterflies in my stomach settling down just slightly. Within moments, Ann answered. Her warm smile and gentle hugs assuaged any remaining fluttering. She ushered me into her lovely home, comfortably decorated in tones of winter white with Christmas red accents strategically placed on elegant tables and sprawling inviting couches. Ann's talent for detail and striking décor was evident through-out her home. It is a reflection of her personality and character.

"Where would you like to sit?" Ann quickly asked, wanting to make sure I was comfortable.

"I think the dining room table would be great," I responded. "That way, I can lay out my tape recorders, forms, and questions." I hesitated, "If that is OK?"

"Of course. What would you like to drink?"

As Ann moved into the kitchen to prepare her iced coffee and my water, I began arranging my materials on the large glass pedestal table. I looked over at Ann, thinking about her busy schedule and how appreciative I am that she has made time for our interview. Ann is in her mid-sixties, a single woman divorced for many years. She is a licensed marriage and family therapist and works very long hours for a large recovery center specializing in the field of addiction. She also maintains a small private practice. In her limited free time, she enjoys spending time with family and friends and she has always loved to travel. I know how precious her weekends are to her, thus, I am even more sensitive to sticking to our four-hour interview time frame.

"Are you sure you just want ice water?" Ann chuckled as she mixed together a delicious looking coffee concoction.

"Yes, thank you. That's perfect." I finished testing and checking my recorders—one old fashioned tape recorder and one fancier digital one. My questions were neatly arranged on the table with a small alarm clock facing me. My mind was focused on the task at hand. My thoughts were centered on Ann.

"I'm just going to grab some paper so I can take a few notes as we go along," Ann added. "That way I can keep my mind on track!" She giggled as she gathered up a notepad from her office. As she settled herself into her chair at the end of the table, I am reminded of how much Ann has to juggle. Although I work almost fulltime as an author and speaker, my schedule does not demand of me the same rigorous hours as it does for Ann. Her work is difficult and it is draining. And, as she does with anything or anyone she cares about, Ann gives one hundred percent of herself.

"Are you ready?" I faced Ann and waited for her.

We looked at each other, our eyes connecting knowing that what we were about to embark upon was unchartered territory for us both. Yes, we have shared our betrayal narratives over the years. We have worked through them with our therapists and recovering practices. We have cried with one another. We have been there for one another. And now, we are in a place where we are both ready to share those narratives, not only with one another but with others. And although there can be an un-spoken power differential between interviewer and interviewee, I have worked tirelessly on creating a format and cultivating a setting around "The Daughters Project" which is conducive to an environment of equality.

"Yes," Ann sighed. "I wish I had had more time to prepare…but then I always think that." We both smiled as I turned on the tape recorders.

Beginning

I glanced down at my questions under the first section, *Beginning*. The first question is one I have thought about for many years and one which I think is critical for our discussion.

"Ann, how do you refer to your *mom*? Do you use that noun, or would you prefer to use a different one? Can you talk about that?"

Thoughtfully, Ann responded, "It was basically mom or mother. Most of the time I called her mom. If I was agitated or was talking to other people about her, I called her mother." She paused, "There were no other names."

Picking up on the word "agitated," I asked Ann if there was any other thinking or feeling behind the word.

"That is a good question. The word mother has more emphasis; it would get her attention. She was always busy. If I was agitated and upset, that word would get her attention more." Ann added, "That word is less intimate. If I was frustrated or angry or not happy about something, the word mother did not have that happy nice mom [sound]."

"So, for our interview today, are you comfortable using the word 'mom'?" I wanted to make sure Ann felt safe in our references to her mom."

"Yes. Although it will be interesting as we go throughout the interview, to see what word I use and what emotions I have around it. Mom is fine."

As we moved into the second question, I felt a mutual ease settle in. It was like a light fog had lifted allowing the space between us to clear our path ahead. The next question was tough and I knew we both would need the welcomed warmth which had filled the room.

"Ann, how does it feel to talk about your mom?"

"Actually, I am a little scared. I have an expectation and a belief that I have done so much work around this that it is not going to be a big deal. But I guess I still have feelings after crying in the garage a few days ago finding those Christmas ornaments." Ann explained how her mom did so much around Christmas, cooking and decorating. She continued, "I felt as though I had come to the other side, loving her for who she was and appreciating the good things she had done." Ann paused, thinking. "I guess she died about ten years ago. So how do I feel about talking about it? I don't know… I don't want to start crying. Because I feel like I cried for years, once I discovered that I did not have a happy relationship with my mom. She wasn't the kind of mom I saw that my friends had, at least that I could see." Ann took in a breath, letting it out slowly. "I am open…totally open. There is a part of me that doesn't want to get so emotional because I am so tired. But I am OK with it." With a stronger voice, she added, "A good test for me."

Because I felt this was such an important area in our journeys with our moms, I moved into the second part of this question. "Has talking about your mom changed over time? Is it different today than it was a year ago? Five years ago? Other?"

"Oh yes. Until I started doing this work forty years ago, I was in total denial how it affected my life. I had resentments growing up…well, for years until I started working on it. Growing up, she was just 'mom.' It wasn't until I went to marriage counseling and to Al-Anon, because my ex was an alcoholic, that the pain started coming up about my childhood—and how I didn't really have an emotionally available mom. Then, because of the therapy and all the work I was doing, it was really hard [to talk about her]."

Ann continued, "My therapist asked me to write a letter about her. It took me months to write it, and it took me almost a year to get through it and read it. I would totally lose it...and cry, and cry, and cry. So, at that time, it was very difficult."

I listened closely, looking at Ann. Her words came more firmly, more confidently.

"Then I started doing 12 Step work, step work around her, and started to tell her I loved her." Her voice intensified slightly. "And then I was punished by my older sister when I would talk about mom, the negatives about mom. I was ostracized by her [sister], so I wouldn't talk about it with her. There was that phase. Just a very turbulent time around what our relationship was about."

Ann took in a deep breath, calming herself, recentering her thoughts. "Then I moved into more healing after therapy. I did more resentment work toward her with 12 steps and my sponsor. After more pain of discovering stuff and being more aware of how she was treating me (because she was still alive then), I was more on a vendetta against her internally. Then, I came to a place in my own healing of accepting her for who she was."

As Ann continued to describe her transitioning of careers by moving into the recovery business where she honed her skills in the addiction field, she explained how she uncovered an important insight—her mother had all the symptoms of a dry drunk [a person who does not drink or use drugs but still behaves in dysfunctional ways]. It was in her position at the recovery center where she began to talk about her mom in an entirely different and somewhat unexpected way.

Ann's voice took on a tone of authority and accomplishment. "I started to talk about her in my teaching and working with my clients. I talked about denial and about what our childhoods were really like. And how I was the way I was—afraid to speak or to speak in public, to stand up for myself...all the behaviors that I learned in childhood trying to adapt to her that made me who I am today—which are not healthy behaviors. So, I talked about her as a teaching tool..."

I noticed how Ann's words continued to take on strength as she moved into her present reality with her mom.

"So, I feel right now that I have done so much work around her that I am in a really good place because I don't have that negative energy. I know she did the best she could and with what she had. So, I feel comfortable talking about her."

I almost wanted to shy away from the next question. We had reached a vista in our climb up an emotionally challenging mountain, basking for a moment in the clarity of path taken. And yet, I needed to bring in the reason for our being together. Betrayal. The word hung in the air, waiting to be pulled in.

"Ann, we've talked about the connotations of the word betrayal in previous conversations. How does that word feel for you? How does it feel to use it in relating to your mom?"

Ann paused for a minute. She went on to describe how she didn't really know the word until she began her study into psychology. In her mind, betrayal was always associated with affairs in marriage rather than mother-daughter relationships. However, as our friendship grew, we continued our conversations around betrayal, and we read and discussed additional articles on the subject. Over time, Ann considered other connotations and connections of betrayal with all kinds of relationships.

Ann thought carefully before speaking. "Betrayal to me sounds like, or means to purposely hurt someone else. When I think of my mother, I got it that she didn't do any of this on purpose. It was just who she was. She learned it from her mother. The more I learned about my mother's role with her mother, it was not great. I remember grandma—I was scared of her."

I sensed there was much more there to disclose. However, I waited for Ann. I was following her lead in this tender territory.

She spoke with firmness and finality. "I'm learning more about betrayal and opening up my mind. When I think of it as emotional abuse, it is easy for me [to connect it with betrayal]."

Again, I waited. A heaviness descended upon us again like a blanket of grief. I know these moments well. It is just best to let them be…and to let them pass. As the blanket slid away, I sensed the space was clear for our next area of investigation—background.

Background

In order to understand the context of Ann's experiences with her mom, I asked her to describe her family as she was growing up.

In a methodical manner, Ann explained that her family was the typical "50's" family living in an all-white middle class neighborhood of Southern California. Her dad was a patent attorney who worked long hours while her mom was the perfect wife, serving dinner at 6:15 pm every night, raising four kids, and cleaning and taking care of household needs. Ann described her dad as being a perfectionist with a kind, sweet and passive personality. Her mom, on the other hand, was aggressive and hyper, with nicotine and caffeine addictions. Ann was raised with three siblings: a sister four years older, a brother two years older, and another sister who was two years younger. Ann recalled that education, music, and attending church were important factors of her growing up years. And although Ann was confident that her family must have been financially secure, a strong work ethic was modeled by the adults, and expected from Ann and her siblings.

Wanting to dig a bit deeper into the dynamics of Ann's family, I reworded my question about history and background, inquiring about the tone or atmosphere of her home life and about her role within the family.

Without hesitation, Ann jumped in. "I was the lost child. That's me. Lost. Away from the family dynamic which could be so chaotic. My brother fought a lot with my mom and I just stepped back. My older sister was busy, busy, busy. My younger sister came in and she was the baby." Ann took in a deep breath, and then added, "My younger and older sister, in my opinion, got more positive feedback. My whole message growing up was *mom loves my sisters more than she loves me.*"

Ann continued to describe how she was closer to her dad. She recalled how her mom was mean to her and how she, "just tried to stay out of the way." Although her mom never physically abused her or her siblings, her mother's unpredictability was unsettling. As the weightiness of the conversation intensified, Ann shared, "When one of us did something wrong, we all got punished...it was a little scary."

Feeling that this part of our conversation was difficult, I didn't want to push too hard. Suddenly, Ann perked up.

"My role? I helped. I did chores. I did not feel as smart as my older siblings so I spent time in my room studying." Ann took in another deep breath and exhaled slowly, "I was so tired of my mother saying negative things to me, I didn't talk to her for months during high school." Ann paused, "I wanted to see if anyone noticed.... Yes, I just wondered if anyone would notice. And another thing, it was kinda like punishment for my mom." Ann added, "Where did I learn that? I learned that from my mom. If she got angry with her friends, she would just cut them out." Ann went on to describe how her silence continued for many months. Eventually, her dad questioned her about it and scolded her for it.

I wasn't sure if Ann was finished. We sat in silence for a few moments. Observing her affect as she embraced the quiet, the calm space gave her time to release past pain. As I reflected on Ann's family dynamics and her role, I recalled how the betrayal of a parent to a child not only harms the child, but its destructive grasp is far-reaching. The betrayal toxins spread their fumes throughout the family, infecting and affecting all members to some degree and with differing manifestations. Betrayers call in for reinforcements, demanding loyalties from family members. Spouses and siblings take sides and form alliances, adding layers of betrayal onto prior betrayals. Recalling these familial injuries and injustices is like sifting through ashes. The fine soot runs through our fingers, leaving a film of remembrance. It takes time to sort through it, taking from it that which we want to hold on to. It takes even more time to wash away the particles which do not serve us well.

I waited for Ann as she sifted through her thoughts and released those memories which did not contribute to her narrative. Moving into her betrayal narrative would require both her courage and clarity of mind.

Betrayal Narrative

After taking a short break, Ann and I refreshed our drinks and resituated ourselves comfortably in the soft dining room chairs. Although we had covered some aspects of Ann's betrayal narrative in an earlier part of our conversation, we were now headed into tender territory.

Again, I asked, "Are you ready?"

She smiled and answered, "Yes."

"When did you *first* start thinking about your betrayal narrative with your mom? And what was that like for you?"

Ann paused. "Could you ask that again? I want to make sure I am clear on the question."

I remember I struggled with this question when I was writing it. So, I was prepared to reword it. "How old were you when you felt there was something missing or wrong in your relationship with your mom? When did you first feel that you were not getting from your mom what you needed—or that you felt betrayed by her?"

"When I was a little girl, my mom was our Brownie leader. Other girls would say how wrinkled she was and that she was so mean. Yes, that she was so mean. I was embarrassed. I also remember feeling lonely. I couldn't talk to my mom. There was no intimate conversation because she was angry all the time. Although I felt love from my dad, I never felt love from my mom." Ann continued, "During Christmas, mother would always count our presents. She wanted us all to have the same amount but I was always short one. I would ask about it but it was discounted. This really stood out for me." And then Ann added, "Birthday parties were the same thing. My two sisters always got more; it seemed to me everything I got was about half. I always looked for discrepancies." With a tone of sadness, Ann confirmed, "The message I got was that I just was not as good as my two sisters." And adding, "It started very young. I just adapted. I was the lost child so I would go to friends' houses. I spent time away from my family."

Picking up on Ann's early experiences and feelings, I moved into the next question regarding her betrayal narrative. "In preparing to share your betrayal narrative in more detail, how would you like to explain it so that readers can have an understanding as to its presence in your life?"

Ann did not hesitate to ask for clarification. "I'm not sure exactly what you mean?"

"Was your betrayal an ongoing experience? What there a pattern? Was it reoccurring or episodic? Was it a one-time event? Does this make more sense?"

Within a second, Ann responded. "It was always the same. She never changed. Until she died at 87, she was the same." Ann took in a breath, "During holidays and family gatherings, she picked on someone, she had terrible moods, and she ruined the holiday or event."

I waited as Ann explained.

"As I entered into recovery, I realized she was going to be this way. My siblings continued during her life to get upset. My last years with her, I wasn't disappointed because I expected it."

Ann briefly described how a conversation later in life with a beloved aunt confirmed her perceptions about her mom. With a quiet resolve, Ann accepted that her mom was never going to change.

While I was changing the tape in one of my recorders, Ann looked over a few notes she had scribbled on a piece of paper. She expressed concern about repeating some of the same information she had shared previously as we readied ourselves to move into her full betrayal narrative. I attempted to assuage her concerns by encouraging her to allow her process to be fluid and natural. If there were parts of her narrative which were repetitive, that too was important to her story.

Ann took a sip of her iced coffee.

Placing the tape recorder between us again, I looked up and faced Ann, "When you are ready, please share your narrative."

Ann hesitated. I waited. There seemed to be something holding her back. I wasn't sure what it was and I didn't want to rush her. Ann spoke up, "I'm not sure what to say that I have not already said... is there something more you are looking for?"

I understood Ann's confusion. Over the years in the telling of my betrayal experience, I shared it mostly in bits and pieces. My betrayal narrative was like a jigsaw puzzle from which I would take out a piece, examine it, think about it, and put it back into place. It was usually when I was in therapy when I would explore the entire spectrum of my betrayals with my mom, and even then, it was examined in sections or several pieces which made up one part of the picture. I drew upon that reference as I reworded the question for Ann.

"If you were to think about your relationship with your mom as a picture, what would be in it? And what would it say to you?"

Ann promptly responded, "I guess I could describe that as the messages I believed growing up. Because of her behavior and not being able to have intimate conversations with her, or share emotions with her, or have her present when I needed support...or observing behaviors where she did treat other family members terribly and me feeling so hurt for them—the message that I got which is what I describe at work as walking on eggshells like you do with an alcoholic. I didn't know when she was going to be calm or get angry about nothing. It was so confusing...unsettling...hard to relax. I missed the closeness that I saw other kids have."

Ann's words flowed, spilling out the messages from her betrayal canvass. "Another message was... *go outside the home and find people that love you and care about you and that you can be comfortable with, and share who you are and what you want.*"

Ann took in a deep breath. "Part of my story is that I got used to that behavior. I couldn't figure it out but I knew that other mothers were not like that. I didn't know if it was bad or good then..."

I listened intently as the pictorial messages continued to pour out.

"The message I got was *something is wrong with me...you are not good enough...you are not as smart as your siblings...you are always late...*" Ann paused, regaining her strength. "I felt ashamed...I felt shame all the time, and then I felt guilt. I felt like a bad person. Something must be wrong with me because I did not feel love from her...just more frustration. I felt she was saying...'Just get away from me. I don't like who you are'." Ann paused. "Those messages led to my fear of abandonment. I thought... *people are going to leave me because I am not good enough.*"

Ann took in another deep breath, making room for another message to surface. "I learned from my mom...'silence is golden'. I tried to compete with my three siblings, but the message was *keep your mouth shut.* If I opened my mouth, there was usually an argument with my brother or my mom. Also, I never felt heard. There were two reasons. First, I just shut down after trying to talk. And...I would get in trouble for saying the wrong thing at the wrong time or not saying it the right way. I learned I did not have a right to express myself, and if I did, it would be wrong. I would be wrong."

Ann continued sharing her picture, one that also contained messages which were confusing to her and that didn't seem to fit into the betrayal puzzle. While her mom was emotionally abusive, she provided for her basic needs and for those of her siblings. In fact, she provided for them physically quite well.

I followed Ann's lead, sensing there were more messages to uncover. Ann's demeanor softened as she shared her next message.

"Another message I got was *motherhood was not a fun thing. It is too hard.*" She took in a breath. "Therefore, I never wanted to be a mother...never wanted to have kids. I had no desire. I'm not sad that I didn't have kids. I've questioned myself. Even my ex-husband questioned me. But I saw her role. I saw what she was like and thought, 'I'm not going to do this. She is not happy'."

Ann and I sat quietly for a few moments, once again allowing the heaviness in the room to lift. The pieces of Ann's puzzle seemed to be floating all around us, as if waiting for more to join them. I waited for a few more minutes before I spoke.

"Thank you, Ann, for sharing your messages." I paused again. "As you entered into young adulthood and beyond, did your messages change? Were they the same? Can you speak to that?"

"Well, at seventeen I left and went to college. I lived overseas. I didn't really go back home again, unless to visit. I always wanted to get away from home, in one way or another. I wanted to see the world. I had no desire to go back home or even live near them."

Ann described more about her life away from her parents during her college years and into adulthood. As Ann's mom aged and after her dad died, Ann began having nightmares about who was going to take care of her. Because she was divorced at the time, Ann felt her siblings might expect her to take on the responsibility of their mother. Although Ann's mom was settled comfortably into a condominium, Ann began to experience familiar betrayals.

"I would drive to see her after working long hours. After getting there and visiting for just a few minutes, she would turn on the TV." Ann paused. "At times, she did seem happy to see me. But by then, I had done quite a bit of work on myself. I was more accepting of her."

I sensed Ann was struggling a bit. I gave her room to sort through the pieces, examining any final messages.

Ann quietly added, "I just felt sad about my life, especially when I started doing the work on it. I realized how much I missed having a mom, even though she was there physically."

The images of the orphaned piece joined the others, floating about carrying messages of loneliness and of loss. As we both honored the messages with our silence, Ann prepared herself to share more specifically her *Brokenness From Betrayal*. The picture puzzle would take on deeper meaning.

Brokenness From Betrayal

In covering Ann's beginning, background, and betrayal narrative, she had made clear references to her brokenness. However, it was at this time in our interview process where we would move into even more tender ground. I know well how each betrayal piece carries with it varying levels of impact and injury. And although Ann had done tremendous work around her betrayals with her mom, it was important to me that I remain sensitive to the potentially painful process and their disclosures.

"Ann, you have referenced several times, especially in sharing your life messages, how *not having a mom* affected you. Can you expand upon or elaborate on the impact of her emotional and psychological betrayals... and on your brokenness from them?"

As Ann listened to the question, I found myself rewording it in several different ways, filling in the quiet space between us. I stopped myself, giving Ann the room she needed to uncover her truths.

Ann spoke with calmness and firmness. "In general, it impacted my ability to have healthy relationships, particularly with men." She paused and then elaborated, revisiting a piece from her prior messages, "It impacted me with not wanting to be a mom, not wanting to have children. Never feeling comfortable around children. Especially young children...babies. I am scared to be around them." Ann's words seemed to catch her a bit off guard.

Pushing just a bit further, I asked, "What do you think is behind that?"

She paused, thinking. "I don't really know except not having been around babies... They scare me...They are so vulnerable, so dependent on you." More forcefully she added, "For some reason, I did not want anyone dependent on me. I'm not sure where that comes from. I don't feel good enough... Even to this day if someone asks me to hold a baby, it is scary for me."

The air felt heavier again. Lots of broken fragments floating about. I sat quietly.

"I think it goes back to the motherhood thing...seeing my mom so unhappy. I think not knowing how to give love...especially to little ones." More silence. "Gosh...that is yucky...just realizing how that is probably the problem I have in my relationships."

Ann was sorting through all the pieces, openly sharing their impact upon her.

"It has also affected me in that I learned years ago that I married my mother. He [my ex] was angry, judgmental, and I walked on eggshells, couldn't please him...couldn't make him happy. That was exactly what my relationship was with my mother. I always tried to make her happy... and I always failed. Always. I did everything I could that a good daughter would do and I always failed."

Ann took in a deep breath, as her thoughts and feelings came spilling out.

"Even before my marriage, I ended up with abusive men...in one form or another. I didn't have many relationships in high school. I had a crush on my brother's friend, who was not available. I guess it got me out of any type of intimate relationship. I would always pick the men who were unavailable. And some were emotionally abusive and somewhat physically abusive. Also... I never felt pretty enough. I was running with some really nice gals, but they were all very pretty...they all had men after them. I always felt less than as far as beauty...I never felt pretty."

Ann paused and added, "My low self-esteem is coming up which has affected me." Ann chuckled somewhat nervously. "Accepting unacceptable behavior from men. I remember when I was younger, getting involved with a wonderful man [from a foreign country] who I was engaged to, and I was going to relocate to his country. He turned out to be married with a family." Ann paused for a moment, "I guess that is sort of emotional abuse...he was not available." Ann sorted through the brokenness, picking out another shard.

"From that, I went overseas and met another man. I don't know...he had so many passports. I went to Africa with him. He carried a knife with him that he kept by the bedside table. This became acceptable to me. He said we needed it because we were in Africa. I normalized that."

She explained in more detail. "He showed me attention. When I think about it as far as my mom, I was craving attention from men so much especially if I had chemistry—and I seemed to have chemistry with unavailable or abusive men or men who were questionable. It got dangerous in Africa...so I left and came back home. He followed me home and kept the knife on the bedside table, which seemed to be okay with me. Then, one night he put the knife to my neck and that was it. I got so scared. I needed to get him out of my apartment. He'd gone through all my savings I had and he damaged my car. I got him out of my house."

Ann took in a deep breath, but kept pulling out the brokenness. "After that relationship, I went on to marry my husband who had a loaded gun beside his bed our whole life. He was often suicidal and homicidal...I lived with that for almost twenty years. I seemed to accept unacceptable behavior with danger and emotional abuse. It seemed to be okay because he provided for me...and he loved me. "

Ann did not hold back. After her divorce, she described a series of relationships with men who were alcoholic, or addicted, and/or emotionally and verbally abusive.

Pacing herself and slowing her breathing, Ann described her most recent relationship. "He was an alcoholic who quit drinking...my ex-fiancé who turned out to be a sex addict, which totally destroyed our relationship. When I go back and look at my mom and the behavior I accepted from her, it has just followed me throughout my life. It has impacted my ability to have healthy relationships. I have made a lot of progress in getting out of relationships faster, rather than getting more involved. I've had to learn what is really unacceptable behavior in a relationship...sometimes I don't know what unconditional love is. I don't even know... I don't know how to give, and I don't like it when people are too dependent on me. It's like not wanting to have kids...I don't know if I can handle it. If I do [let people become more dependent on me], I tend to get hurt...there is probably a lot more in there."

The relational pieces to the betrayal puzzle hovered around us. So many shattered memories. Their jagged edges reminders of past pain. As Ann gathered her thoughts, I gave the pieces time to settle. I waited for a sense of stillness to return. Her eyes met mine, signaling their readiness to continue.

Gently, I spoke, "Ann, we've been talking about relational, emotional, and psychological brokenness. Are there other areas of your life which were impacted by your betrayals from your mom? If so, would you mind speaking to that?"

Ann jumped in, "Food...my mother was a good cook and made sure we had our meals every day. It was wonderful on holidays. And she always had snacks: a cookie drawer and jar. And the only time she would stop moving at night is when she would have popcorn and

snacks...oh my gosh...that's exactly what I still do in front of the TV."
Ann laughed. She waited a moment. Then, she became more serious.
"That was like comfort...the only time to feel her love. She was
providing food for us on a regular basis. She was there to provide food
and for our physical needs."

Ann went on to describe how she became conscious of her weight
when her mom put her on a diet at age thirteen. Although Ann was on a
swim team and in good shape, she was not built like Twiggy. Ann
disclosed how every day after school when she would come home and
her mom was not talking to her (which was about ninety-nine percent of
the time), she would grab cookies, ice-cream, and junk food and go up
and binge in her room.

Ann's voice became very solemn, "This went on for years, and years,
and years. When I went away to college, I learned what bulimia was. I
would just gorge myself with food. It went on and off through my
twenties." Ann named the brokenness. "Food provides my support...it
numbs me. I've learned working in the addiction field, what I've been
doing to myself." Ann's voice softened, "Yes...that is my addiction...my
physical need for food."

Ann's authenticity and openness continued to fill the room as her
container of brokenness released the pieces—all different shapes and
sizes. All integral parts to her narrative. All testaments of how betrayal
enters our lives and invades our bodies, minds, and spirits. Her full
picture was taking shape, and although I wanted to dig a bit deeper, I
was keeping a pulse on her levels of strength.

"We've covered relational, emotional, and physical aspects of your
brokenness. And earlier, you shared about your life messages you
received from your mom and about yourself. Is there anything more you
would like to add as we begin to conclude this section?"

Without a moment's hesitation, Ann responded, "I am not good
enough. I cannot do it good enough. I call it *the not enough syndrome*. I
am not enough. Nothing I do is right. I can't speak good enough. I can't
dress good enough. I am not pretty enough. My house is not clean
enough—perfectionism. I am always striving to do better and nothing is
ever good enough. It is exhausting." Ann chuckled. "It is still happening
today...but not as much." Ann sighed. I waited. Her quiet posture
punctuated the end of our conversation.

Suddenly, the air seemed to shift. All the scattered pieces of brokenness slid into place within the frame of Ann's canvass—*I am not enough*.
Each, with its sharp edges and cracked surfaces solidified its position

within her life message, creating a mosaic of a daughter shattered by betrayals. And yet, Ann's picture was far from finished.

As I reached over to change my tape, I sensed Ann's uneasiness. Uncertain as to whether Ann was satisfied with her closing remarks within our last segment, I lingered a bit longer checking and re-checking my tape recorders. She fiddled with her pen and paper, making a few notations.

"Is there something else?" I asked.

"There may be," she responded. "I don't know. I need to think about it some more."

"We have plenty of time," I added.

"For now, I'm ready to move on...to share the next part of my journey."

From Brokenness To Wholeness

As I was getting ready to ask the first question in this section of our interview, I recalled the difficulty in the wording of it. Although I believe that many individuals are open to disclosing their struggles throughout their lives, I think it is often more difficult to pinpoint their inception, especially when it is in relationship to a person with whom your care was entrusted. Therefore, I moved into the first question gently.

"Ann, as you continue to reflect on your betrayal narrative, when did you *first* start thinking about your brokenness in relationship to your mom?"

Ann spoke with authority, "It was a very specific time when I went to couple's therapy to try and save my marriage, which was in 1991. In one visit, my therapist told my ex to go to AA and I was to go to Al-Anon. My ex disagreed [with me going to Al-Anon] and we got in a fight...so I started going to Co-Dependence Anonymous (CODA). My ex did go to couple's counseling weekly for a few months before he quit. After he quit, I went back to my therapist and he asked me if I would like to continue. He asked me, 'Have you noticed every time you bring up your childhood, you start crying?' I told him, 'No'. When I thought about crying, which I did, it seemed vague to me. I thought I was focusing on my ex and my marriage." Ann paused for a moment, "I agreed to come because I was curious about this pain from childhood. Looking back, I was in total denial... I knew and felt that my mom did not love me...but I had no idea about the pain around it!"

Ann recalled the events as if they had just happened.

"When I went back, I didn't want to cry in front of him... and I remember a comment he made to me. 'If you are not going to be honest with me, you are wasting your money. So, try to take a risk and be as honest as you can with me.' I remember that stuck out because I always wanted to look good. So, I kept going."

Ann described how one of her assignments her therapist gave her was to write a letter to her mom. "I thought it was weird...but whatever. Well, I went back home to write the letter and I couldn't write it. All these feelings started coming up...these painful feelings... I couldn't write the letter. I'd go back and tell the therapist I couldn't write it. When he asked me why I said I had a perfect childhood.... I now know I was in total denial of the pain. That went on for weeks. Then, I finally started writing it...that was very hard. I'd cry and put it away...I'd cry and put it away."

Identifying her recovering pieces, Ann seemed energized by the healing they carried with them.

"Finally, I got it written...probably a couple of pages. I took it in and tried to read it. The pain and the feelings were so bad I could never finish it. I would start over and over again." Ann started to chuckle. "I'm laughing about it now cause when I think back...that is what denial is. I was in such denial of that pain that I had carried about not having a mom available to me emotionally, or feeling support, or feeling unconditional love, that I just couldn't go there." A tone of tenderness surfaced in Ann's voice. "Now, I can relate to people who can't go to these painful places...because I was forty-something by then."

I listened intently, amazed at the composure with which Ann collected the shattered pieces, filed their sharp edges, and fit each one into the wholeness puzzle making it more complete, more comprehensible.

"That is when it became apparent that I had an issue with my mother...a deep-seated painful hurt. I had not at that time connected with how it had affected my life except that I didn't have a mom like other people. Eventually, I got through the letter. It took almost a year, going weekly, to sit and read the entire letter without stopping and crying. My therapy was no longer about me and my ex... but about my childhood, me, and my mom."

I understood how healing segments can easily overlap and I wanted to give Ann the time she needed to separate out what was important to her. The different sections singled themselves out.

"From my therapy, I uncovered two important insights. What I learned from my childhood and from my mom is that I was responsible for her happiness which means I am responsible for everybody's happiness, which is what I tried to do with my ex-husband also. Because my mom was always angry and upset, I was responsible for making her a happy person. What I learned is, I am powerless over that. I can't make anyone happy. They have to make themselves happy. In recovery, I learned as long as I am focused on making everyone else happy, there was no room for me. Understanding that was a big deal for me...it helped me a lot."

Ann paused, looking over a few notes. I waited for her thoughts to form.

She added, "The other insight which went along with the messages *I am not good enough or smart enough,* was facing the loss of my sense of self." Ann spoke firmly, reciting the questions she began asking herself during recovery, and also what she had written in her journals. "Who am I? What am I feeling?" Ann referred back to her recovery journals from years previously and added, "As I was reading them, I saw the desperation of not knowing who I was and thinking I was worthless. However, in therapy and the 12 Steps, I began to see a way out of my self-condemnation. I realized I 'learned' I was not good enough and if I 'learned' it, it is worth a try to 'relearn' who I am." Sometimes healing pieces are brilliant and big. Sometimes they are subtle and small. Either way, they all make up integral parts of the recovery puzzle.

Ann further described how during the same time as she continued her therapy, she still attended CODA meetings to deal with her ex and some about her mom and her childhood. Eventually, she discovered how it all came together. As Ann continued her work in therapy for two to three years exploring her relationship with her mother, she also uncovered how she had married her mother. "I learned that all these behaviors which were unacceptable to other people, because other people were telling me my ex was abusing me but I couldn't hear it. Well, it was what I was used to. I had married the personality of my mother. What I learned from that is God keeps putting the same people in our lives until we change, and that I had no idea about all this behavior I had accepted. I put myself in dangerous and unacceptable relationships because someone would show me what appeared to be love. My need for love and attention contributed to all these unhealthy relationships. It has been a pattern."

Knowing how retelling of our betrayal recovering can unearth particles of shame in that we often continue to repeat unhealthy patterns both during and after our therapy, I appreciated the level of Ann's openness in her narrative and ownership of her choices. And knowing firsthand how recovering doesn't mean we are perfect, I recalled Ann's words from earlier in our conversation, "I've made a lot of progress getting out of relationships faster rather than getting more involved."

Wanting to explore a little deeper, I probed, "Breaking through the denial and digging out the roots of the betrayal injuries is such hard work, Ann, as you described. If I heard you correctly, you were willing to commit to the hard work for two to three years. Are there other areas of your recovery work you would like to share which you moved you *From Brokenness To Wholeness?*"

"One of the things which was so important is that I didn't really want to end therapy. First of all, my therapist set boundaries with me... After being in 12 Step meetings where you hug everybody, I would try and hug him and he would say, 'No, no, no...we don't do that. This is a boundary. We don't touch.' I remember how that hit me. It was like a boundary I had never heard of before," Ann laughed softly.

"Another thing I took when we finished, was thinking about how just talking gave me so many insights and healing. I wondered if I could do this? I thought...maybe I'll go look at that master's program... I was interested in psychology and healing behaviors." Ann's excitement grew. "After all these years, I asked myself how could I learn all this? How could I be in such denial, and by someone listening to me and asking me questions...it was like WOW! I think maybe I want to try this. If I can make a living this way—helping people?!" Ann's joy was over-flowing.

Ann described how she was scared to death. She remembered she didn't feel like she was any good in school. However, from her therapy Ann took with her a newly discovered purpose and driving motivation to enter graduate school and change her career path.

The room seemed to be filling with light and the recovering pieces appeared to be dancing in our midst. I eagerly moved through the related recovering questions.

"Are there other parts to your journey which are important to share?"

"A couple of main things. Basically, it is about 12 Steps. It was a very interesting experience tying that in. Number one, I was told to go by what the therapist recommended. But I ended up going to CODA because my husband wouldn't allow me to go to Al-Anon. He said it was bad. So, I started those meetings regularly, and all I could do was cry in them because it was me. I didn't want to share...I was too afraid to talk. I would go to therapy so I could learn to talk in a 12 Step meeting. I had no confidence in my speaking. But I liked going to the meetings. It was helping me as far as my marriage and learning what a healthy relationship is because I had no idea. I would read this list and say, 'Oh my gosh! I'm everything on this!' I had no idea what boundaries were or appropriate behavior was or healthy relationships and how I mistreated myself. The whole list was right there in front of me. I cried a lot and I wouldn't speak, but I kept going."

Ann described how over time, she began to speak a little at a time—just her name and then the word "pass." It was recommended to Ann that she obtain a sponsor through Al-Anon because the CODA groups were very new at the time and didn't have them. Eventually, she started Al-Anon, attending for two years and going to as many meetings as possible.

"I was in so much pain between my divorce and new stuff coming up from childhood, but I didn't want to get a sponsor." Ann's voice was strong, "I don't trust women. One of my messages was *don't trust women—they are not there for you.*" She took in a deep breath. "It was very hard to ask for a sponsor…it took me two years to do that. I wasn't comfortable with women even though I had some good girl friends."

Softening her voice again, Ann added, "But eventually, I did choose a sponsor. That was a whole new experience. She became the mother I never had. She was tough. She guided me through the steps. She set boundaries with me. She helped me through my divorce and warned me that I shouldn't be in any relationships until I was more healed and knew what healthy relationships were. She was absolutely right. Every time she told me not to do something and I did, it was wrong." Looking directly at me with a depth in her eyes I rarely saw, Ann spoke, "It was probably my first trusting intimate relationship. She was like a mom." Silence. And then more. "She got me on a spiritual path. She just became a guiding force as a parent and loved me unconditionally. No matter what I did wrong, she was still there for me."

Ann described the impact and importance of work and relationship with her sponsor. She credits her sponsor for modeling the kinds of behaviors necessary in working in the addiction field and with Ann's successes in her own professional path. Ann shared poignantly, "I owe so much gratitude to her. She's been the mom I never had."

Allowing the beauty of that wellness piece to shine and sparkle, we both basked in its glow for a few moments. Somewhat reluctantly, I moved on.

"Other people…other places which contributed to your wholeness?"

"The recovery center where I work…with addicts and alcoholics," Ann's voice took on a vibrancy. "Continuing to use the steps, continuing to see with all of them…what their relationships are with their parents, how it has affected their lives. And the abandonment by their parents—physical, or parents who work all the time—the hole or void that is there which they are filling with other stuff. I am reminded every day and I am learning every day the impact of missing unconditional love from parents or the presence of a loving person in a child's life. The impact of it not being there... I am still on a learning curve, and it reminds me of the work I still need to do, especially in relationships." Ann took in a deep breath. She spoke firmly, "My work is huge as far as being another force in my life. It teaches me how to be a better person and a better woman."

The recovering pieces of Ann's puzzle filled the air and fell into place and I wanted to stop right there, allowing them to shimmer without interruption. However, the canvass of wholeness awaited its creator's unique touches.

"Is there anything more to add as far as how you would describe your journey *From Brokenness To Wholeness*? Has it been in stages? Has it been continual? Other?"

Ann laughed aloud, "LONG!" And I joined in.

"Ongoing!" We both laughed harder. Ann caught her breath, "It has not stopped since 1991. From being in recovery, to my spiritual work, to 12 Steps, to learning more tools and therapies in our field of psychology, it is just an ongoing process. And another thing, in the work I do, it teaches about letting go and forgiving and setting healthy boundaries that I need to keep doing. I am reminded every day what I need to work on. The lessons are with us every day."

Ann stopped the flow of words abruptly. Her tone was serious, her mood serene. She strategically placed a few purposeful pieces of wholeness onto her canvas.

"I am grateful that I have the awareness." With a calm intensity, Ann continued. " I am grateful that I have been able to heal and love my mother for who she was. I am grateful that this has happened to me because I know it has made me a better human being."

I sat mesmerized by the shower of wholeness around us when suddenly Ann's voice regained in strength, sprinkled with a bit of sarcasm.

"But it is ongoing and I would like a vacation from it!! I really would! I just want to have fun!!"

As our laughter bounced around the room, we decided to take a short recess. Both of us knowing our recovering is never over and that one path leads to another, I was excited to learn where Ann's journey with wholeness was leading her next.

Wholeness To ...

With our drinks once again refilled and our minds refreshed, we returned to the dining room table. I adjusted the recorders, making sure they both were picking up our voices and recording properly. I moved right into the first question.

"Ann, where are you today in relationship with your mom and in your journey with wholeness? And where are you with yourself?"

"I can say that it seems like every year my relationship, or my beliefs about the relationship, are more positive. She died at 87...and the last couple of years were really hard. Her mind was right on until the day she died. She didn't suffer cognitively at all. She was as smart as a whip, although she didn't believe so. I learned she had low self-esteem and all this other stuff was a cover-up. I learned that...but maybe I'm getting off center here..."

I waited, following Ann's lead. The sections to Ann's wholeness were conceived and nurtured from different areas of her experience. I understood this well, and gave her ample space to cultivate and harvest them.

"Thinking back to when I was working with my therapist, I told him my mother never told me she loved me. And he asked me, 'Well, have you ever told her you loved her?' I said, 'No, we don't talk about love in the family'." Ann explained, "One time when my parents were out visiting me, but before leaving to go back, they came by my place of work. As they were pulling away out of the parking lot, they rolled down the window. I remember it was a hot afternoon and I was scared to death. I put my head inside the car and said, 'I love you guys...' and they rolled up the window!" Ann's throat choked out a burst of laughter. "I'm laughing now and I was laughing then because I had shocked them. Instead of feeling hurt, it just showed me how uncomfortable they were with that word."

Ann's voice returned to a more serious tone, "So that shows the progress I had made over the years." She paused. "There were a couple of times where my mom eked out in a phone message 'I love you' and hung up really fast. It wasn't to me, but it was on my machine."

Ann described her gratitude for her work in the 12 Step program and with her sponsor. She disclosed how when her father died, she was not able to get in to see him. As she shared her guilt over not being able to get there fast enough to say goodbye to her dad, she was adamant how she did not want to go through that with her mom.

"I wanted to go in and spend time with her with in a loving spirit, even if she turned on the TV or did things I didn't like or if people came up to me and said 'she is mean.' I wanted to be able to love her and for who she was and for the things she did do for me." With strength in her voice, Ann added, "The big event I often share with patients is that I had totally given up my expectation that I would make her happy. Years before she died—thank you to recovery and my own work—I learned I am not responsible for her happiness or for my ex's happiness...but I could still love them."

As the spaces between the broken pieces filled with healing lessons of love and understanding, Ann continued to weave together where her journey to wholeness had taken her.

"Two days before she died, I went in to be with her. We didn't know she was going to die but she had been moved to the highest level of care. I remember I looked at her, she was still in the bed and she was still clear...and I put my hand on her. I said, 'Hey mom...you know I love you.' She looked at me with that stern German face and said, 'I know and there is nothing I can do about that now!'" Ann burst out laughing, "Those were about her last words to me! I can laugh now instead of cry because that was my mom—tough German lady. I don't know what she said to the rest of my siblings but it is okay..." Ann glowed as she spoke. "I was so grateful that I did this work around her because I could tell her that and mean it. So that shows to me the progress which I have made, accepting her for who she was." Ann's mom died a few days later.

The beauty in moving from *Wholeness To* is just that. It doesn't stop. Once we open ourselves to truth and growth, the harvest continues. I quietly sat and Ann shared hers.

"A year or two passed when I started seeing more of the positives. A few years ago, I wrote a list of all the positives that she had done and what I gained from her. It is a pretty good list." For the first time during our interview, Ann could not speak. Sometimes, wholeness shows up that way- like a wave splashing over us, engulfing us and saving us at the same time.

"In fact, that is what makes me emotional right now..." Ann came up for air. "She was a good mom in her own way..." Another deep breath. "I am grateful that I can see the good, and how she worked her butt off for us." With wholeness spilling out, Ann added, "This is where I can help my patients. It doesn't do away with the pain I had all my life. It doesn't do away with it, but I have to learn from it. I have to heal myself and grow from it."

Ann sat quietly for several minutes, and then shared more of her insights about her mom which she had come to discover over the years. She described how she learned that her mom was very interested in the injustices suffered by Native Americans and the injustices around the Civil War. Her mom cared about oppressed people and how life was not fair for them. Ann spoke of how her mom was president of the City

Council of Girl Scouts and of other positives in her mom's life. Ann also learned how her mother suffered from very low self-esteem, never having the education she wanted and thus, she was always reading and trying to better herself. These pieces too, each in their own way, added to Ann's journey, altering painful perceptions and moving her into peaceful acceptance.

With a tenderness in her voice, Ann revisited her most recent loving memory of her mom—going through a box of Christmas decorations her mom had given her. Ann's voice broke, and her tears flowed, "I pulled out these little things that we put on the tree....and so..." Ann was once again engulfed in emotion, "I'm only crying for joy... that I can see she wasn't all bad. I can see the good in her. Her meanness I know now, because I teach it, is that underneath anger is fear and sadness. So, she was angry most of the time...afraid of not being good enough for my dad. I've learned more things about her which help me understand why she was the way she was."

With the wholeness pieces integrating smoothly into Ann's puzzle, I moved into a related question which Ann and I had touched upon during our pre-interview conference.

"Ann, you mentioned the word 'gifts' in reference to your mom when we talked a couple of weeks ago. Is that the same as the positives you are talking about now?"

Ann affirmed my perception, describing the work she does at the recovery center, "Working for over fifteen years with alcoholic and addicted men, I credit my ability to set boundaries, to be really tough, and to not get hooked in or manipulated by their anger to my mom's qualities of being assertive or aggressive...and of being strong." In a completely different area of life, Ann also described how her mom made the holidays special by decorating, buying, etc. Ann spoke compassionately, "I see my love for doing the same kinds of things around the holidays as a gift from my mom."

As I was focusing on Ann's words, she interjected an important qualification.

"I wanted to add something. My mom died in '95, and I didn't become aware of these gifts until years after. I had a really hard time seeing it until after she died. Even though I had done a lot of work and had come to a place of acceptance for who she was, I did not see the gifts then. I had come to a peace...to acceptance, but did not see the gifts."

"How and when did you begin to see these positives as gifts?" I asked curious of their transformation.

"My ongoing work with my therapist around my work and my relationships but also working the 12 Steps and my spiritual work....and a lot more work on my passions and not judging others. I've continued to do my spiritual and self-awareness work, both by choice and by the work that I do every day with addicts and alcoholics, including my work around powerlessness and taking self-inventories...all of it. As I have continued to work on myself, the gifts started emerging. Who am I to be judging other people? I mean, look at my life. It has not been perfect, and I have not had to raise kids. It has been an ongoing process."

Once again, the openness and honesty with which Ann claimed her successes in wholeness along with acknowledgment of her struggles illuminated the integrity of her process. I was eager to hear more.

"We talked earlier about your life messages growing up and how they impacted you, especially in relationship to your mom. How do you feel about yourself today and what are some of the dominant life messages you say to yourself now?"

Ann paused. Then spoke resolutely, "That I still need more work. That I am a good person even though I continue to doubt my abilities. I think too much. I am self-critical, although I have made huge progress in the area of perfectionism. Although I am still hard on myself, my message is...becoming a better human being is a life project." She took in a deep breath.

"Sometimes, I do get tired of the life messages and having new lessons, but I also know it is part of the process and I know I've made huge progress. My message to myself is being grateful and having faith that good is coming out of the challenge, if I use it that way. Being grateful for all the stuff I have been through has given me special abilities that other people don't have. All this past stuff is helping me to help other people."

Understanding that wholeness is never complete, that there are always pieces which need more attention or which surface indiscriminately depending on life's circumstances, Ann reflected on more interpersonal messages.

"Right now, I struggle with messages—*why aren't I married, why don't I have a relationship*? On the other side of that, I won't accept unacceptable behavior anymore. So, I am getting to a point if God wants me to be single, I will be single and happy for all the good things." Ann continued, "I also still have a lot of negative messages around the work I do, which continue to pop up. Not so much in private practice, but at the recovery center."

With conviction in her voice, Ann added, "Another message is I need to put myself around people who are on the same path as me—people who are aware, who care about other people, who care about self-exploration, and who are not always judging everybody else. They are looking at themselves. I have had to let go of some friends or put boundaries up around other friendships. I want to surround myself with people who will care about me for who I am."

I know well what Ann means and of its importance. After years of working on a canvass of wholeness, both its development as well and its protection become a priority. Support of like-minded individuals contributes to its sustainability. And yet, there remains room for new pieces as the canvass takes on deeper legitimacy and longevity.

As I approached the end of our interview, I asked two final questions. "Where do you wish to go from here? Where would you like your *Wholeness To* lead you?"

"My goals are not clear anymore," Ann hesitated, thinking, "where I wish to go from here ties in with that. I have all this information and experience, so what is the medium for doing that, aside from my work? I want to get to a place where I know what I am doing every day is the right thing...or being able to accept that right here, right now is perfect... or it is okay."

And then with the precision of a master artist deliberately shaping and delicately polishing the pieces of a *Wholeness To* canvas, Ann formulated the intricate designs of her portrait ahead, "I want to be the best person I can be. I want to be able to share with other people and give them hope—no matter how painful your childhood or your life, there is good which happens... and to believe that."

I waited, absorbing Ann's truths and admiring her integrity. She mumbled softly to herself, "Where would I like *Wholeness To* lead me?"

She lifted her eyes to meet mine. Her words spilled out and splashed over her canvass, creating a vision and a path.

"How do I give more back to the people and to the universe? There has got to be more I can give. I want to use all the information, gifts, talents, and all my experiences the way God wants me to use them."

The beauty of wholeness is that it cannot be contained. It demands to be shared. Ann's narrative—the pieces *From Brokenness To Wholeness*—are dancing and delighting around us, answering His first call.

Follow-up Reflection

It has been almost three weeks since my face to face interview with Ann. We have arranged our calendars in order to accommodate our follow-up or post interview phone conference. This follow-up session was designed to share anything which has come up for Ann since our time together. The post conference was also created to provide an opportunity for all daughters to add or amend their previous narratives, if so desired. And lastly, our post interview conversation offered daughters a platform to share any feedback about their experience in being a participant of "The Daughters Project." Placing the call, I felt my excitement grow.

After sharing some small chit chat and our most recent goings-on, Ann and I settled into our call. During the first part of our conversation, Ann disclosed a few life messages from her mom which were important parts of her *Betrayal Narrative*. She also reread several of her recovering journals and wanted to include a number of transformative insights which were integral in her moving *From Brokenness To Wholeness*. I committed to Ann that her messages and insights would be integrated into their rightful placements within her narrative.

Feeling a few butterflies dancing in my stomach, I calmed them and moved into our closing question. "Ann, how has this experience been for you?"

Ann jumped right in, "It's been really good! It has caused me to do more self-exploration of the positives I have made in the last twenty-five years. And, I've continued to do the work...." Ann's voice strengthened, "As I have gone back to read previous journals, I am so grateful that the messages I had back then are no longer with me. I know I am not responsible for people's feelings or their happiness and I have no power over them. I got that message! And I am very grateful I am in that place." Ann's confidence carried over into her truths today. "There are some self-defeating messages which I am still working on. I need work on self-care and self-love... and the belief that what I am doing is good enough. I still am struggling with being an over-achiever and how to have fun. Overall, this project has been a good review of my life and where I still need some work." She paused, then asked, "Is this what you were looking for?"

As I took in Ann's words, I was once again moved by her levels of openness and honesty. I, too, could relate to her journey of how life messages from our moms remain with us and how it is an ongoing process in healing from them. After dislodging the lump from my throat and sensing Ann's need for a bit of feedback, I spoke gently. "Today, Ann, for you to be in a place where you can step back and look at this process and look at your life and recognize not only your areas of recovering but also own your areas of ongoing growth …it is beautiful." I added, "Although you shared your narrative with complete transparency and truth a few weeks ago, your voice is in a different place today. It tells me that giving you the time to reflect and revisit your narrative is a critical piece of this process."

With an added strength to her voice, Ann eagerly interjected, "I may have mentioned this before but I am so grateful I did this work before my mother died. I have a letter I wrote the year after she died and several letters from 2009. Rereading them, I remember how I was shocked when I started having these feelings that I miss her…." Ann hesitated, "I'd like to read a bit from one letter from 2009…is that okay?"

Moved by the importance of this piece, I responded, "Yes, of course."

Ann refrained, just briefly. "I may start crying…." And then she began reading her letter.

> *I've been missing you a lot, Mom, the last years. I have felt your love more than I ever felt it. I respect all you did now as a mother and wife, and guess that your temperament was never having a minute for yourself. And I guess Dad was not the easiest to live with—being a perfectionist and wanting things done perfectly (for Dad?).*
>
> *I miss knowing you are here…or phone calls…or love or care that comes from you.* Ann's voice broke, heavy with love. *Forgive me for saying negative things about you in my shares and lectures but I do that to give hope we can't blame parents anymore. It is up to us to be a mature healthy adult. I appreciate all you taught me about the domestic side of life…..*

As Ann's voice tapered off finishing the last few words, she reiterated, "This shocked me!" Ann chuckled for a moment. Then, she spoke with calm, compassion, and conviction. "The last years, she did her best and I did my best. No, she wasn't the mom I wanted. She wasn't the mom my friends had. She wasn't all that, but there were some wonderful things she gave me, including the strength to do the work I do today."

Through the airwaves, a remaining piece of resiliency slid into place, adding its recovering touches to Ann's betrayal puzzle. Its messages were bold. They demanded to be heard.

"Holli, I am grateful you are doing this because it helps me…it helps me come to more resolution. I am very, very grateful I can see the positives." The words Ann had professed in our face to face interview, she now peacefully restated, "I am grateful I was able to tell my mom I loved her before she died, and I meant it."

As Ann's resiliency glowed from its position, her voice which was once silenced took on a formidable posture and passion, "I am out of the blame game. It is up to me to become a healthy human and do the things we do as healthy adults."

Our time together came to a close. Ann's canvas awaited her finishing touches. As we concluded our conversation, Ann requested to read a few words from a song which played a healing role in moving her *From Brokenness To Wholeness*. The pieces of Ann's puzzle still sing their truth today.

> It's a long road
> When you face the world alone
> No one reaches out a hand
> For you to hold
> You can find love
> If you search within yourself
> And the emptiness you felt
> Will Disappear
>
> And a hero comes along
> With the strength to carry on
> And you cast your fear aside
> And you know you can survive
> So when you feel like hope is gone
> Look inside you and be strong
> And you'll finally see the truth that...
>
> A Hero Lies In You

3   "I Made Me Who I Am" – Dawn

Reflection

In the Consent Form required for participation in "The Daughters Project," I have asked each daughter to plan and prepare for a thirty-minute pre-interview conference. Although the daughters have been given their interview questions for the comprehensive interview several weeks in advance, this is a time for us to check in with one another on any concerns or questions about our process and to establish a rapport and a rhythm with one another, especially given the subject matter we will be discussing. In addition, because my relationship with each participant is quite varied and unique—spanning from long-term friendships to professional acquaintances to unknown daughters whose paths were meant to intersect with mine in this project—the pre-interview conference is vital to crafting an environment of trust, safety, and equality.

Thus, on an unusually warm but beautiful winter morning in early March 2016, as I organized my notes and reviewed a few additional questions, I thought about how I came to know the extraordinary daughter I was about to call. Her name is Dawn.

In January 2015, I came across a written interview by Dawn—*Breaking the Dysfunctional Cycle of Growing Up Chaotic*—posted on the website of a well-respected professional friend of mine. Not only did the title resonate immediately with me, but its essence was incredibly informative and restorative. After reading Dawn's biographical information and learning that she hosted a podcast—*Growing Up Chaotic*—I reached out to her, pitching a show idea based on my recovery book—*Mountain Air*. Dawn replied promptly to my query and we set the date for our interview.

On February 3, 2015, Dawn and I had our first opportunity to speak together as we recorded *The Positive Possibilities of Relapse*. Although I had recorded dozens and dozens of interviews over the years, I was struck by Dawn's incredible enthusiasm and passion in serving her purpose; her intellect, integrity, and insight into our subject matter; and her authentic and genuine manner with which she approached her guests and her work. Needless to say, by the end of our interview I felt both honored and privileged to have connected with this amazing wellness advocate.

Over the past year, Dawn and I have supported one another with additional professional exchanges. While reading her weekly newsletters, blogs, and thoughtful posts and by watching her powerful video messages, I came to know that Dawn was a daughter who also experienced betrayal on a myriad of levels. As the universe would have it—almost a year exactly to the date I appeared on *Growing Up Chaotic*—Dawn, without hesitation, confirmed her desire to participate in "The Daughters Project."

With the required forms completed, we scheduled our pre-interview conference for 9:00 am PST. Because Dawn lives abroad with a seven hour difference in our time zones, I was a bit anxious hoping I had accurately calculated the difference. Using a landline, at 8:55am PST, I called Dawn's number. It immediately went to voicemail and I left a message. Thinking that maybe Dawn was on another line or busy, I waited about ten minutes and called a second time. Again, it went to voicemail. Just as I was hanging up, I noticed an email on my phone come through. It was Dawn saying that for some reason her phone was not ringing but she did receive my messages. She requested my phone number and within a few minutes, we were connected!

As soon as I heard Dawn's voice, we both started laughing. Dawn explained how she had never had any problems with her phone, and we both agreed that despite someone or something "across the pond" trying to interfere with our conference, we were not going to let it happen!

Moving into our check-in, I was quickly reminded of Dawn's gracious and generous spirit. She had prepared, even over-prepared, for our interview. As I did with Ann, I carried with me the intensity of the project and was keeping a pulse on Dawn's voice, listening for levels of strength and vulnerability. As I clarified a few items of confidentiality and of potential concern, she remained steadfast, strong, and secure to her commitment in moving forward.

After setting the date and time for our comprehensive four-hour interview, I thanked Dawn for her participation and for the valuable work she continued to do. And with levity in her voice and lightness in her heart, she joked about the phone issue and we discussed how to proceed if it happened again.

Thinking about the process ahead of us, I soaked in the moments filled with laughter.

Setting

Just as I did with the pre-interview conference, I called Dawn from my landline in my home in Arizona. Of the options I offered participants in "The Daughters Project" with whom I was not able to meet in person, Dawn chose to proceed in this manner. We set our interview time earlier in the day to accommodate the longer interview format. I organized my questions and checked the batteries in my tape recorders. I cranked up our heater just a bit more and refilled my hot cup of coffee. It was extremely cold out, so different from just five days ago.

As I continued to center myself and focus on this special daughter I was about to interview, I recalled parts of our pre-interview conference. As I had done previously with Ann, I asked Dawn a very important question regarding her "name."

"Dawn, even though you are a public figure, would like me to use your real first name or would you prefer to choose another name?"

Her response spoke volumes about her. "No, you can use my real name. That is fine." She continued, "I'm totally comfortable with that. I feel...you know in a weird way it's one of gifts of this whole situation. Because of my family, everything had to be secret and I didn't have anyone to talk to and now...as an adult, I don't have to hide that anymore." With more intensity, she added, "I don't have to hide and I don't have to keep secrets. So using my real name is kinda liberating to me... I can write about these things and I can talk about them. They are there. This is my story and you can't keep it quiet anymore." Dawn chuckled a bit, "Sounds pretty aggressive!!"

I joined in her laughter, still honoring the strength beneath her words.

When I asked Dawn about her age, she burst out laughing, hesitated, and then offered the guarded information.

"I don't mind at all... It's one of my biggest insecurities because I feel I should be farther along in my life. So when somebody asks me my age...it's like ooooooooughhhhhhhhh." She paused, then, jumped in, "I'm 38....and just saying that .....aaahhhhhhhh!!!" Returning to her lighter voice, she added, "It's something I have to deal with. It's my age, so get over it, Dawn."

I again thanked Dawn for her participation in "The Daughters Project" and shared how important it was to have a younger daughter's voice in the study. Over the past couple of years I have come across numerous daughters who have been betrayed by their mothers, the vast majority of whom were in their fifties or older. It was my desire from the beginning of this project to have a diverse sample of daughters.

In our pre-interview conference, I remembered chuckling, as did Dawn, when she referred to herself as a "mutt"—a mixture of Italian, English, and Irish ancestry. When I asked about any religious or spiritual influences, Dawn shared that when she was very young growing up with her mom and stepdad, she was raised Catholic and was made to go to Catholic schools.

Her voice took on a serious tone as she explained, "Being raised Catholic was a big influence growing up in my home situation and not being able to talk about things going on...." She continued, "I am not Catholic today...I don't go to church. I do get spiritual, but that is so broad...but no specific religion."

Although I believed Dawn was married, I wanted to confirm it with her. When I did, she spoke firmly, "I am and I want others to know because it is important for them to know how individuals can come from broken backgrounds and still marry and be happy." Dawn shared she had no children but with a surprise sparkle in her voice, she added, "I have a cat who is like my little baby."

I happily concurred, "Pets can be our children too."

Returning my mind to the present and checking the time, I made one last quick check of my materials. After pressing all fifteen numbers to reach London, England, the phone rang and Dawn picked up. I breathed a sigh of relief.

As is typically so, Dawn's voice was cheery and light. The intensity of the task in front of me was assuaged a bit by the bounce in her spirit. It was warm and welcoming. We eased into our conversation, recalling and laughing about the phone issues from our pre-interview conference. Before beginning with our interview questions, I checked in with Dawn, getting a pulse on how she was feeling. Not being able to look into her eyes or view her body language, it is my way of assessing her mood and keeping a pulse on her being.

"Dawn, I'd like to check in.... how are you doing?"

Without hesitation she responded, "I'm actually kind of excited. If this were...ummm...six or seven years ago, this may have been really difficult for me to do because a lot of what I was exploring was still very raw. And I feel like it is kind of an indication of how far I have come.... I am a firm believer that there will always something I have to work on or issues will pop up." With a seriousness in her voice, Dawn added, "I am by no means saying that I am a one-hundred-percent-wonderful person but I feel I have come so far to be able to speak about these things without the pain associated with it." Her bounce returned, "I was thinking about it this morning…it's like wow! I can't believe this is something I am doing… I couldn't have done it a handful of years ago. I am excited!"

My heart released some of its heaviness, but remained receptive to the process ahead of me. I believe regardless of the degree of healing daughters have done on their betrayals from their mothers, revisiting their narratives in their entirety requires much of them. Dawn's experience brings with it an added component. She has two betrayers— both a birth mom and a stepmom.

I took a sip of my coffee and moved into our first question.

Beginning

"Dawn, how do you refer to your moms? Do you use that noun or another? Can you speak to this?"

"Sure… with my birth mother, I do call her Mom. But, I don't think of her as my mom. I just say it because that is what she has always been referred to…like with my dad using the words *your mom*. With my stepmother, I refer to her by her first name because I try not to refer to her at all, as often as possible. I don't have any relationship with her. There was a point and time when I was younger…from about eight years old to eighteen where I called her Mom. I called her that to her face. I did it because I wanted to … I made a conscious choice to do so. But after she betrayed me so many times, I referred to her by her first name."

Wanting to dig a little deeper, I asked, "Dawn, in your thinking today or then, does the word mom carry any connotations, inferences, or meanings for you?"

Dawn paused. Her voice softened, "The word mom for me is a very empty word. It means disappointment. I have friends who I have had in my life for years who are very close with their mothers and there is such a huge difference in the way they think of their moms. And when I think of the word, I have nothing but negative reactions. However, I have come to accept that my relationship with my mother is not the same as people I know. It is just empty. When people think of a *mom*, they think of comforting…of the person they go to when they are upset. I don't feel that way at all. I wouldn't go to her…she would be the last person on my list to go to." Dawn further explained how foreign it was to her when her friends described how they looked up to their moms or admired them.

Her voice strengthened again, "When people say they don't want to be their mothers, I mean that. I don't want to be like her or speak like

her...or have her mannerisms. I just don't want to be her." Dawn
punctuated her sentence, "Just empty."

My mind absorbed Dawn's words. *Mom*—such a small word. And a
powerful one. I allowed the quiet space between Dawn and me to sit for
a moment before moving into the next question. The word *empty* floated
around us, containing the primary and poignant pieces of Dawn's
betrayal beginnings.

I gently asked, "How does it feel today to talk about your moms?"

Dawn hesitated. She shared that the day before was Mother's Day in
the UK and how knowing today was our interview, it was kind of a
weird feeling. Her voice lowered and softened, "When it was Mother's
Day in the states where such a big deal is made of it...it used to make me
sad. Really...really sad. But now, I just kinda accept it. And, I also see
holidays as sort of a joke anyway. Hallmark making tons of money on
it...really?!!" Dawn laughed, and I joined in. She added, "Maybe it's a
little bit of anger...so I joke about it?!"

I reflected Dawn's sentiment, noting the many triggers which can
evoke different emotions around our moms. Certainly, Mother's Day, is
a significant one. Tapping into the notion that our feelings and emotions
around our moms change and evolve over time, I moved into our next
question.

"Dawn, thinking about your relationships with your moms over a
larger span of time, is it different today than a year ago, five years ago,
other?"

Dawn took her time. Then she disclosed, "It has definitely changed. I
don't feel the same emotional pain I did before. Obviously, I still get
triggered by things... but it doesn't feel as painful." She elaborated,
"When you asked me the question, I was thinking about the fact that I
am married. And my husband has a good relationship with his mom. His
childhood is nothing like mine. On Mother's Day, it is hard... it is a
trigger for me. For so many years before I was married, I didn't have
that expectation on me. There's a part of me where the hairs on my back
go up...I don't believe in this crap...I don't believe in Mother's Day!!"
Dawn laughed, as did I, relishing a bit of levity.

Seeking clarification on her feelings, I asked, "It doesn't sound like it
is a personal issue with your husband's mom, but more around what the
day—Mother's Day—represents?"

Immediately, she replied, "Absolutely. Absolutely."

My mind shifted briefly to betrayal. It is complex and it is complicated. When we add *mom* into the mix, it becomes even more tricky and
tough. Understanding well the connotations of reverence and respect

with which many cultures view mothers, for daughters who are betrayed by their mothers, it often feels like an additional ambush by honoring those who injured us so deeply.

I segued into our next question.

"Dawn, although we haven't discussed the word *betrayal* specifically in our conversations, when you say the word betrayal, what does it mean to you? What connotations come to mind?"

"Ummm...when I think about the word betrayal with my mom... what comes to mind is, 'You were supposed to be my mother and you weren't.' My mom was an alcoholic and when my parents got divorced, I was only four years old. Very quickly afterward, she met my stepfather and they got married. And especially in that situation, I felt like she chose him over me. She chose that life as an alcoholic over me."

Dawn continued to describe how her stepfather provided well for her mom and her. And that, perhaps, it was sort of a way out for her mom, but it really wasn't. Dawn added, "I always thought we could have made it on our own together. I mean, it would have been difficult. She would have needed to work a couple of jobs...and my grandmother would have needed to help. But, we could have done it together. I feel like she betrayed me by not being my mom and giving in to this man. He destroyed our lives. He brought in so much pain. That is what I feel like with her..."

I could sense the roots of Dawn's betrayals from her birth mom were just the beginning. I waited for her to continue.

"With my stepmom....." Dawn let out a deep breath, a sort of raspy release, "She wasn't the person she pretended to be. And when I was a kid, she just played a really good game with me. As I got older and had my own mind and my own thoughts, I could see things more clearly. She just wasn't the person she pretended to be—the mother person...the one who went to bat for me—she wasn't that person. That massive betrayal." Dawn's voice strengthened and yet struggled for the words. Then, she concluded, "I guess, betrayal from my birth mom—you were supposed to be my mom and you weren't. From my stepmom, you pretended to be this person you were never....and I had to figure that out on my own."

Digging deep into the beginnings of one's betrayals is difficult, especially from the perspective of a young child. Betrayal does not make sense at any age, and certainly from a child's lens, it is hard to put into words what is happening or to describe it. I did not want to put words into Dawn's description; however, I wanted to check with her, to see if I was understanding her feelings of betrayal.

Tenderly, I moved into a clarifying question, "Dawn, from what I am hearing, would you say your betrayals from your birth mom could be described as rejection or abandonment?"

"Yea...absolutely. Yes...abandonment. For years [as a kid] I always...I never understood why my parents had kids if they were just going to abandon them. I can't say I was abandoned physically, but when my mom would get really drunk, she physically, at times, wasn't there. But the emotional abandonment and rejection.... absolutely. For whatever reason, my mom chose my stepdad over me and that was rejection. As a kid I felt like I wasn't good enough. There was something wrong with me."

Dawn briefly described her issues with trusting others, and then added, "I've always had this feeling...I am on my own. My husband is always telling me 'You have one foot in and one foot out' [of relationships], and I am constantly reminding myself that my husband is not my mom, he is a different person! He's not going anywhere! I wouldn't let him!" Dawn laughed, and I joined her.

We both relished the lightness of the moment. As I asked for clarification of Dawn's experience with her stepmom with regards to the connotations of the word *betrayal*, Dawn reframed it as one of lies—of her stepmom pretending to be someone she was not. Dawn explained how her stepmom, with disturbing manipulation, accused Dawn of lying, "without owning her own life of lies."

Listening to her words, I became more aware of how the field of Dawn's early betrayal experiences expanded into far-reaching places and postures. I paused for a few moments, allowing its magnitude to take hold while moving toward the last question of our beginning section.

"Would you refer to your two moms as *betrayers*? And how does that feel for you?"

With a steady and strong voice, Dawn jumped in. "The first thing that comes to my head is that both my mothers were the same exact woman but they expressed themselves differently. My mom was a raging alcoholic. Also mentally ill—she is bipolar. I can even say to myself—okay, that's why she betrayed me. That is why she did that. My stepmom wasn't an alcoholic. She has mental issues. She's never been diagnosed, but she definitely has them. But it is the same exact woman, almost like a continuation." Dawn spoke with conviction. "With my mom, I always knew what I was getting. With my stepmom, I didn't. But, they were the same person."

In my mind, I pictured a field of betrayal soil covering Dawn as a child. As I readied myself to dig into Dawn's background in more detail, I reminded myself of the tender territory we were continuing to explore.

Background

Over the years in speaking to audiences about betrayal, most individuals associated it with a specific person or persons. Of course, it is that. However, it has been my experience that although betrayal may emanate from a certain person or several persons, it germinates and grows in environments which are unhealthy. Without an arresting of its spread, a culture of betrayal becomes the norm of a family.

As I moved into Dawn's background, I was somewhat aware of the widespread toxins within her upbringing. Therefore, I remained sensitive to the depth and breadth of landscape ahead of us. "Dawn, how you describe your family growing up?"

Dawn broke out laughing, "We might need another four hours to get through this!" I laughed along with her, understanding all too well what she meant. Dawn continued, "Again, I can joke about this now because I have done so much work on myself, but, I joke and say I was born into a *winner's circle*." Returning to a more serious voice, Dawn added, "I say it sarcastically because anything that was wrong with a family was wrong with mine." She paused and explained, "My parents got married when they were really young. My mom got pregnant when she was sixteen with my older brother. I have two older brothers who are a lot older than me. I came along ten years after my younger brother. My parents are both alcoholics...and just really screwed-up people emotionally, really screwed up. My mom was bipolar and I only remember my dad as being chronically depressed." Dawn chuckled softly, "My dad reminds me of Eeyore from Winnie-the-Pooh...that's him."

Dawn described how she didn't have a lot of memories of her parents together. They divorced when Dawn was four and both parents remarried. Dawn's brothers lived with her dad and stepmom while Dawn remained with her mom and stepdad. Both her brothers were drug addicts and alcoholics, always in trouble, and spent time in juvenile hall. While her brothers were always in and out of her life, Dawn remained with her mom and her stepdad who was also an alcoholic and extremely abusive.

Taking in a deep breath, Dawn described her betrayal environment. "I've seen things most kids don't see...from guns to knives to [my stepdad] busting my mom's face open. Just a really, really crazy childhood. I don't know if my stepdad was mentally ill because I was too young," Dawn paused, "I lived with them until I was eight. This whole entire time this craziness was going on with my mom and stepdad— fighting all the time and they drank every night." With deep sadness in her voice, Dawn added, "This whole time, my dad lived about an hour away. He never did anything. He never saved me from them."

Betrayal environments can and do reach beyond a family's nuclear unit. As Dawn continued to describe the *craziness* in her households, she also explained how alcoholism was prevalent in her extended families on both her mom and dad's sides. She shared how there was not much support with other family members—no one to turn to.

As Dawn and I continued to wade through the thickening contagions within her betrayal environment, Dawn recalled a powerful and pain-filled incident. "I remember when my stepmom and dad got married. They got married in the backyard of my dad's house and my stepmom made my brothers and me get *married as a family.*" Dawn laughed nervously, "I mean my stepmom hated my brothers and she made them do this!" I sensed anger grow in Dawn's voice, "And my mom was pissed....so pissed about my dad getting married which meant she was going to get so drunk. After the wedding, my stepmom made me go back to my mom's house because she and my dad wanted to be alone, knowing my mom would be hammered and beat the crap out of me! I didn't understand how she could send me back after being in the wedding and knowing what was going to happen to me! That is a betrayal right there!" Dawn's voice softened, "I didn't say anything. I didn't have the vocabulary at the time to explain it...it was just the feeling I had."

The betrayal grounds we were treading through were messy and mucky, sticking to us both. While gently reflecting Dawn's raw releasing of her childhood pain, I gave us both time to honor her truths and allow the infectious particles to return to their respective spaces.

Moving into the last question, I remained sensitive to the enormity of Dawn's exploration into her betrayal environments. Two households. Two families. Double the territory to cover.

"Dawn, with both of your betrayal environments, how would you describe your role?"

Dawn spoke firmly, "I think with my mom, I was definitely the adult with her. I remember very clearly when she was really drunk and she would want another beer... I would go into the kitchen and get a beer, dump it out and fill it with water, and give it back to her. She would be so drunk, she would have no idea what I just did," Dawn paused, "The house was always a mess. After a night of fighting between my mom and stepdad, I would get up early to go and clean. So, I was always the adult. Always taking care of her…ummmm…always worrying about her if she got really drunk. Sometimes she would leave the house and go outside. I was the one who tried to bring her back in. I was the parent. Although I was the youngest, I had to be the oldest."

I listened, allowing space for Dawn to continue.

"With my stepmom, my dad was a doormat. My stepmother was always in charge. Whatever she said, went. For many years, from eight to about eighteen years of age, whatever crazy idea she had, that became the truth. So, I am not sure what that role would be with her. It was different."

Wanting to probe just a bit more, I asked, "Dawn, what do you remember thinking to yourself?" I paused and reworded, "How did you take care of yourself or keep yourself safe around her?"

With hesitation, Dawn responded, "I tried to please her…always trying to be extremely perfect for her. I wanted her to be proud of me, to be who she wanted me to be, which was impossible because her standards were just ridiculous. I see that now. I didn't know it then."

As Dawn concluded her thoughts about her roles in her betrayal environments, I reflected how it is only natural for children to default to those positions which make us feel safe, even when it means "trying to be extremely perfect" especially when we are children. Betrayers, whether sober or drunk, have power over familial grounds and those who reside within them. As I moved into our next section, I remained careful and thoughtful as to how Dawn's betrayals from both moms took residence within her.

Betrayal Narrative

Although it may certainly be very painful to do so, most adults who seek out wellness are willing to confront their injuries and injustices. Often, *naming one's pain* is the first step in healing. And even though betrayal is a word which is thrown around in many situations and circumstances, saying it and naming it and applying it to one's mom is extremely difficult. It doesn't feel natural or normal. It is hard to admit and to talk about. Add to these the complexities of growing up in betrayal environments which are sustained over long periods of time, it can be more challenging to unearth or piece together what is going on in one's surroundings.

Understanding the complicated anatomy of betrayal and the intricacies of it, I gently inquired, "Dawn, when did you first start thinking about your betrayal narratives with your moms. In other words, when did you make the connection between what was going on in your life, and perceiving them as being *betrayals?*"

Dawn spoke resolutely, "With my birth mom, it was very early on in my life because she was an alcoholic. She was never a sane person. There was a lot of pain there because she was constantly choosing my stepfather or the drink over me. I always felt that rejection from her...always. Also, abandonment from her at an early age."

Although strong, Dawn's voice sounded like a tumor had lodged its way into her being, choking her spirit. "A question that ran through my mind as a child was 'Why did you have me? If this was what you were going to do, if you never wanted me...why on earth did you have me?'" Dawn sighed, releasing a raspy sound. "I think the biggest betrayal from my mom was that she left me to figure it all out for myself. As a kid you don't understand, 'Your mom is an alcoholic. She is not in her right mind', but I had to fill in the blanks myself." Dawn paused and punctuated her truth, "She couldn't be my mom."

I waited. Forging through Dawn's betrayal territory was hard work. No solid ground. All cracked and broken.

Dawn described the contrast with her other mom, "With my stepmom it is quite different. It wasn't until I was a teenager when I started to see that her reality was not a healthy one. And my dad went along with her so it was two against one. It was very difficult to speak my truth." Dawn paused, then her voice strengthened, "By the time I was a teenager, she started to come undone. She was the liar. All these promises she made, she couldn't come through on them. After a while, I started to be able to put the pieces together. Again, I couldn't speak out. Who could I go to and talk about that?"

As we explored the breadth of Dawn's betrayal narrative, she shared how it was ongoing throughout her childhood. Although she had hoped for a reprieve when she went to live with her dad and stepmom at eight years old, the betrayal grounds were disguised at first, but then unveiled themselves over time.

Within a betrayal environment are the acts of betrayal themselves. These are poisonous behaviors which target innocent individuals within their path. Moving specifically into Dawn's narratives with her moms, I remained sensitive to her levels of strength and stamina, keeping a pulse on the toxins she was unearthing.

"Dawn, when you feel ready, please continue sharing your narratives—your truths."

"When I was very young and living with my birth mom, we were living on the second or third floor of an apartment building, and she was acting crazy one day. I don't know why she did it, but she picked me up and hung me outside of the window and she threatened to drop me on my head. My grandmother lived just around the corner and came over. Although my mom didn't drop me, I remember thinking, 'I am on my own', and wondering, 'Why did she have me?' And then it became, 'There is something wrong with me. I don't see any other mothers treating their children this way.' It was right smack in my face—the first memory I have of my mom. It just continued to build from there as her addiction to alcohol became more chronic and more intense."

Dawn described how things intensified after her mom married her stepdad. She paused for a moment and recalled a painful insight, "I have always had trouble looking in the mirror...I hate looking at myself in the mirror. I think a lot of it has to do with my mom, even though I take after my dad more than her...it is because I don't want to be her. I don't want to be that woman." Dawn continued describing the acts of betrayal—the intense anger in her home when her mom was drunk. Her mom would throw things at her and chase her around the house with knives...just constant betrayal that was in her face all the time.

Dawn took in a deep breath, "Because I couldn't speak to her, I started to hate myself. Really, from the moment I was born when betrayal is there all the time, not only was my relationship with my mom heavily distorted and not healthy but my relationship with myself became very, very bad. I don't know any other way to describe it but intense self-hatred. Perhaps it has more to do with my mom than with myself, but never having my questions answered, "Why did you have me if you didn't want me?' I questioned myself—if I was a better kid...if I was better behaved. As a kid, you just don't understand. You [mom] are supposed to be showing me the way, and I have to figure this all out on my own."

As Dawn plowed through her betrayal grounds, she reflected on some of the healing insights she gained as an adult helping her to come to terms with her mom's addiction and disorder. At the same time, she shared a powerful truth, "That betrayal of a parent—of my mother—who conceived me and gave me life ....it is such a deep betrayal. I don't think it is something you can figure out in a lifetime. Even if I live to be one hundred years old, I think it will always be there."

Listening to Dawn's words, I thought of the importance of identifying specific acts of betrayal, and yet I was reminded of the foundational premise from which "The Daughters Project" was conceived—"mothers who betray." It is hard to get our minds around a betrayal which runs so deeply though our core being and runs against the natural flow of mother-daughter bonding. I thought of Mother Earth who carries within her all the innate nutrients, particles, and formations to create and sustain a planet. We never question or doubt her ability to be there—to provide for us—to take care of us. We trust Mother Earth. We are born to trust our mothers. Betrayal takes that from us.

Thinking about the broken bonds of trust in Dawn's life, I wondered how that felt for her as a child. Dawn's voice softened, then strengthened, "I remember when my stepdad would take me out to buy me things after being abusive. When we would be in the car on our way to the mall to go shopping, I would be sitting in the backseat. My mom would throw her arm over the front seat and wiggle her fingers like she wanted to grab my hand and hold it. I think that was her way of acknowledging that something was bad...and maybe that she loved me. For a long time, I would grab her hand, and it would make me so sick to my stomach. I stopped doing it and she would get angry with me." Dawn continued, "I didn't talk to her about it. There was already enough craziness going on that I knew we couldn't talk about it."

I gently reflected Dawn's sentiments, honoring her powerlessness over her betrayer and her betrayal environment. As I was getting ready to move into her narrative about her stepmom, Dawn sifted through her betrayal soil and shared another poisonous particle.

"I remember when my mom was still very active as an alcoholic and my stepfather was still alive. One year out of nowhere she sent me two little porcelain dolls—one was the mother and one was the child. The mother had her hands wrapped around the child. I don't know why she sent it to me...but I threw that thing out." Dawn let out a soft gasp, "I thought, 'What does this mean? Do you think this means anything to me?' I was only about ten years old. I threw it out."

Betrayal, even when it is chronic in nature, can still emerge as underground quakes to our souls. Unexpected and unwanted gifts from a betrayer can shake us and throw us off course. And living for a period of time in a pretense of normalcy, only to be awakened by a virus of lies, shatters fragile truths and further contaminates weakened grounds.

Dawn described in more detail the landscape of her betrayal grounds with her stepmom. For several years, Dawn's stepmom painted a portrait of safety and non-judgment, such as inviting Dawn into "mother-daughter" talks around safe sex and sexuality. However, by the time Dawn was fifteen or sixteen, her stepmom had changed completely.

Dawn recalled her stepmom's crazy words, "If you ever get pregnant, I will disown you." For the first time in our conversation, I could feel Dawn's pain through the phone. Her voice cracked, "All these attacks from her… 'If you start having sex, people at school will think you are a tramp.' I didn't understand. I wasn't even sexually active. I didn't understand how it was even a possibility. It all started to unravel with her. And it kept getting worse from there. My dad was depressed, not in the picture. He was off drinking."

I waited. Dawn's composure returned. Her strength fortified.

"I'll never forget the day where I started questioning my reality, but then I started questioning her. I would question her on what she said two hours previously, and she would deny it. She would call me a liar. I would start writing down everything she said to me, the date and the time. And the next time she tried to deny it, I would whip out my little paper." Dawn took in a deep breath, "It is what I had to do to protect my own sanity."

Dawn described a final incident with her stepmom, which validated her betrayal truths and was a turning point for her. After high school, when Dawn was going to college but living at home, her stepmom met a man on-line and had an affair with him. Her stepmom left Dawn's dad and her, moving with her lover to another state. During the time she was away, Dawn had the opportunity to share openly with her dad about the lies, manipulation, and unfounded accusations by her stepmom. Although her dad listened, two weeks later, Dawn's dad moved her stepmom back home. From there, Dawn knew she had to get away—from them and from her birth mom.

Within the fragility of her world, Dawn recalled how she grabbed hold her truths from within and gave them a voice, "If I don't get away from these people, I'm going to be so mentally screwed up. It is going to be irreversible." Shortly after the incident, Dawn moved out. She was on her own.

As I began to weave together Dawn's betrayal narratives from her formative experiences, I asked Dawn if she felt there were any distinct differences between her birth mom and stepmom. Dawn's response was both raw and real. "With my mom, the physical abuse was right there. If she punched me, there was a bruise. There was the proof. With my stepmom, the emotional and psychological abuse could be hidden well. There was no one to witness it, but the scars were still there."

Taking in Dawn's powerful words, I visualized her betrayal grounds with two distinct surfaces—one filled with diseased debris, dangerous cracks and crevices, and deadly slippery boulders waiting for the opportune time to crush what lay underneath. And the other—a smooth field filled with deceptive traps, deceitful camouflage masking wild animals, and destructive triggers calculating when to go off—without warning.

With my mind absorbing it all, Dawn's voice broke though. "I'm not sure what is worse—betrayal from the very beginning by my mom the alcoholic, or, to have someone come into your life and pretend to be someone they are not. Which one is worse? Should one hurt less than the other?"

Dawn's thoughts hovered between us. We acknowledged them with quiet and calm. There is no answering to betrayal. I thought about betrayal and its connotations—forms of rejection or abandonment, violations of trust, shattered beliefs, and truths turned into lies—all are formidable forces. Acknowledging our experiences, in whatever form, honors our truths.

Brokenness From Betrayal

Changing the tape again in my old-fashioned recorder provided Dawn and me with a brief respite. Although her unwavering courage and conviction about sharing her betrayal narratives assuaged my concerns regarding her stamina, moving more intimately into Dawn's *Brokeness From Betrayal* meant navigating through delicate grounds of past pain.

I listened carefully to her breathing. After checking in and hearing the resiliency in her voice, I began.

"Dawn, in recalling your betrayals from both moms, how were you affected or impacted? What do you remember thinking, feeling, and doing? And, also, Dawn, as you alluded to earlier in talking about some of your life messages, could you expand upon those as well?"

"Ummmm, as I think I said it before, with my birth mom I can definitely make the connection between her and my relationship with myself...this intense self-hatred. I mean I've gone....uhhhhhh....I'm a lot better now but I just remember hating myself so intensely thinking there were things wrong with me not even God could understand. Just feeling that if I could be somebody else, or if I can't be someone else entirely, then I don't want to be here anymore. If my own mother did not even want me...or whatever...ummm."

I listened and waited, following Dawn's pace.

"I remember a long, long time ago when I would get really angry with myself, which was quite often because I hated myself, because everything I did was wrong, I would get physical with myself. I would literally punch myself in the head or smack myself or pull my own hair. And those are things that my mom did to me, but I didn't realize at the time I was doing them to myself…even after I had moved away from her."

Dawn exhaled, releasing another raspy pocket of air. She explained, "I think because everything happened when I was so young that my whole entire world got so distorted- my view of myself—who I was in the world." She paused, recalling some of her life messages, "Is the world a safe place? Is it not a safe place? I don't fit in this world. I shouldn't be here. I should have never been born." She sighed and added, "All having to do with my relationship to myself. Somehow I took responsibility for it."

I kept a pulse on Dawn's lead, as she transitioned quickly to her stepmom.

"With my stepmom, it was just more of the same. It was just more subtle initially, and what I had already felt about myself—that broken-ness which was already there—my stepmom fed off of it. And, she continued to feed it."

I pictured in my mind Dawn as a young child, and the core of her being poisoned by the very persons charged with its care—her mothers. As Dawn's breathing became a bit more labored, I waited as she unearthed more brokenness.

"Ummmm… I may have felt this way for a very long time, which I probably did, but it wasn't until I was in my early teens that I look back now and see I was incredibly depressed. Sickly depressed. I remember thinking 'If I can't reach out for help, even from my parents, there must be something wrong with me.'" With pain flowing from her past, Dawn gave voice to her messages, "There must be something terribly wrong with me. More self-hatred. I didn't do very well in school because I had all those problems emotionally. What is the point of trying? I am stupid anyway. I'm not meant to be here anyway."

When betrayal has been embedded into the formative years of a child, the degree of injury is widespread. The life messages which emanate from early years take hold and remain with us, transforming our image of ourselves and our perceptions about life. Absorbing the impact of Dawn's life messages on her being and remaining sensitive to their significance, I checked in with Dawn. I sensed she was ready to continue.

"Dawn, can you speak to other short-term or long-term implications you experienced from your betrayers—your moms?"

"Umm…I can remember a handful of times when my birth mom would tell me, 'Don't ever get married…don't ever trust men…they are no good for you.'" Dawn explained, "My stepfather was a maniac. He was crazy. I…ummm…remember for a very long time, I hated men. I hated them. I can't even explain it. I really thought they were the scum of the earth. And it took me a really long time to realize that my mom's choice to be with my stepdad, who happened to be a maniac, was not a reflection of men. The message I got from her was, 'Don't ever trust men…they are bums. Don't ever get married.'"

Dawn elaborated, describing how her betrayals were compounded. One mother. Then, the next.

"From my stepmom, she fed off of these things…. uhhhhhh… it was just more of, 'There is something wrong with you'. She would compare me constantly to my friends. I had a friend name Tracy, and my stepmom would say, 'I bet Tracy would never do something like that. I wish Tracy were my daughter.' So the message was, 'You are bad…you are not right.' She would not say these things out in the open, just when it was the two of us. The long-term implication was of course more self-hatred. I'm not good enough…I'm not Tracy….I'm not this, I'm not that."

Dawn paused for just a moment and then shared an incident with her stepmom which occurred after Dawn had graduated from high school. Dawn returned to her high school to put together a fundraiser, helping to support the sports programs at her school. She worked hard, obtaining a lot of media coverage for it. Her stepmom showed up, uninvited. Dawn explained how it was quite traumatic, especially when her stepmom approached her saying, "I'm going to take credit for all the good things you do in your life." Dawn thought for a moment, and reflected, "It is interesting because growing up, I was never good enough…and now she would say something like that to me after years of telling me I was not good enough. So, I guess I am okay now? And you are going to take credit for it?"

Although there was a nervous chuckle in Dawn's voice, I sensed it emanated out of memories of long-standing confusion and chaos.

I connected with her feelings of exasperation, and the words, "*craziness… just craziness,*" slipped from my mouth.

Dawn sighed deeply, and then a little burst of laughter lightened the moment. "Yesssss……," she concurred.

Wanting to probe a little more deeply into additional areas of broken-ness, I reminded Dawn that any question I asked which she did not feel comfortable answering would, indeed, be respected. She acknowledged she was ready to continue.

I referenced a previous area of brokenness in my next question. "Dawn, you talked about your depression and your debilitating life messages of self-hatred. Are there any other pieces to your brokenness which are important to share and how they manifested in you, or showed up in you or in your relationships?"

Dawn jumped in, "Definitely in relationships. I was the stereotypical girl—someone who grew up with alcoholic parents. I always managed to find the guy high on coke all the time, or drank…or I continued to be attracted to people like that. But then there was a part of me that said, 'Don't do it…stop it!' But a lot of that came from not feeling equal to or worthy of a partner."

Dawn's voice softened but remained strong.

"Depression and anxiety have always been huge for me. I can manage it today. But at the point when I was extremely ill…..I actually had a suicide attempt." Dawn breathed in and out. Calmly she disclosed, "I was in my second semester of my second year at college and just got to the point where I didn't care anymore. At this point, all my parents are out of my life with barely any contact with my family. This was a choice I made …I could not have them in my head anymore. I was so completely numb…just the numbest I've ever been in my life. I did not care anymore. I did not care. The voices in my head from years of conditioning, 'You are not good enough. You are a tramp. You are a disgrace…' I just couldn't take it anymore and do anything to stop it. I thought it was my only option." Remaining composed, Dawn added, "I understand now it wasn't, but at the time that is what I felt. When people say, 'This is the only way out,' I understand that because that is how I felt, 'It is the only way out.'" And then with a surprise bounce popping back in, Dawn's voice lit up, "But, it didn't work, I'm still here!"

The brief moment of levity was relished by us both. A serious tone replaced it.

"I'm joking, but I've come to an understanding where I know I haven't been that low since. And it is because I have done a lot of work on myself. I understand I have a tendency to get depressed and anxious so I need to have things I can rely on to make myself feel better." Dawn chuckled, "Legal things."

We both laughed but respected the seriousness of her disclosures. And without further exploration on my part, Dawn shared a profound insight from her broken background.

"It is interesting because even though I removed myself physically from my family, they were still in my head. I remember thinking, 'If I just remove myself from my stepmom, because she was the dominant mother figure in my life at the time, I'll be okay.' But, really…the work was just starting."

Meeting Dawn in a place of unconditional positive regard, I joined with her, taking ample time to honor her feelings and respect her disclosure around her suicide attempt. It is my belief that regardless of the degree of healing we have done on ourselves, sharing deeply personal pieces of our brokenness can stir up or cause other painful parts to surface. Unearthing her seeds of betrayal and exposing their ensuing injuries within her was a testament to Dawn's commitment to wellness for herself and her courageous desire to help others move toward wholeness.

Before leaving the section of *Brokeness From Betrayal,* I asked Dawn if there was anything else she felt like sharing.

"I think I started to talk about this before with my stepmom and I think it could go back to my birth mom. It [betrayal] had an impact on the basics of my being. Did I have a right to be on this planet? It [the betrayal] attacked the very root of who I was....ummmm....and who I am. With my stepmom, the betrayal attacked....." Dawn searched for her words. And with renewed focus, Dawn described her broken core, "I am thinking of a tree and the roots are in the ground. These betrayals ate away at the roots of what I was and who I am." She continued, "For example, my stepmother and her ideas of sex...of what is right and wrong. And her saying, 'You'll be a tramp...and if you do this and you do that', that is attacking something that is very personal." And with a piercing poignancy which resonated through the phone, Dawn repeated, "It is attacking the root of life."

While absorbing and processing Dawn's disclosures, I was moved by her metaphor of betrayal. I expressed out loud to her what I felt, utilizing it as a means of affirming her experiences. Visualizing her vast betrayal grounds with layers upon layers of toxins infiltrating the soil and making their way into her core—into her essence—I validated with Dawn how her use of, "attacking the root of life" brought forth the image of a struggling tree, suffocated and left to survive on its own.

As I prepared to move into *Brokenness To Wholeness,* there was an unusual quiet between Dawn and me. I let it be, knowing how clearing away of past debris and damaged particles is necessary in order to make room for honoring new growth.

Gently, I checked in with Dawn. "How are you doing? Do you need to take a break? Get a cup of coffee? Other?"

A forest of wholeness filled the space, in its center a thriving tree. Dawn pronounced, "I'm good. I'm with ya."

From Brokenness To Wholeness

In moving into this section, Dawn and I both commented on the heaviness which was behind us. However, exploring the paths of Dawn's journey to wholeness also carried with it the raw reminders and re-occurring residual effects of chronic betrayal. While Dawn was eager to share her healing pathways, we both remained mindful of the broken grounds which led her there.

With sensitivity, I asked, "Dawn, as you think back to your broken-ness in relationship to your moms, when did you first consider addressing your injuries and your wounds?"

Dawn quickly responded, "I think it all came to a head with my step-mom when she had her affair and that was kinda like my opportunity to make a decision for myself, not really caring what anybody else thought. I was no longer under the rule of my parents. It was like, 'I am cutting out of here and doing what is right for me.'" With a marked firmness in her voice, Dawn added, "My whole life I knew I had problems about my moms to address. That was a given, my whole entire life."

I listened. Dawn continued.

"In terms of when I really started to realize I needed to really start addressing all of this....my guess is my early twenties when I sought out therapy on my own, 'cause I started to see I was repeating some of the patterns my parents had been working through their entire lives. I wasn't an alcoholic...thank God I never became an alcoholic or drug addict, but mentally and emotionally I started to see I was a lot like them. I realized I didn't want that. I wanted a different life. I wanted a home I could come home to and not worry about what I would find. I wanted a safe place to come home to. I wanted all these things. And so, I needed to start addressing all these problems."

Dawn moved further away from her betrayal environment. She chose to move to Manhattan because she loved the city so much. Days before September 11th, she was on her way to work and she had a massive panic attack. Although she never made it to work, she saw an ice cream truck on the corner and she bought about five ice cream sandwiches. Dawn explained, "I didn't even know what I was doing except that I was trying to calm myself down. One of the ways I did it [calm herself] was to eat. I went home and opened up the yellow pages [before the Internet] and found a therapist who had a sliding scale. I remember walking to my first appointment and looking up at the sky and it was the weirdest thing...I don't know if this will make sense." She paused, then spoke, "I thought to myself 'I don't know if I can trust that that's the sky. I don't know if I can trust that right now I am walking.' That's how messed up I was." Dawn laughed softly. "I knew I was doing the right thing. I needed to get help!"

Dawn's words of self-questioning illustrated vividly how profound violation of innate trust between a mother and a child can and will shatter perceptions of what is real and what is not. When mothers (or primary caretakers serving in a mother's role) have misused, manipulated, and masqueraded trust to serve their own hidden agendas, selfish desires, or unhealthy patterns of behavior, children have no anchor from which to tether themselves and no way of gauging what may or may not be true in their world.

Without minimizing the importance of Dawn's turning point in seeking out a therapist, I needed to seek clarification on a prior area of brokenness—her suicide attempt—and see if there was any kind of intervention or recovery work at that time. I asked Dawn for permission to return there briefly and I explained why.

Without hesitation, Dawn responded, "No, I didn't talk to anyone. I didn't have an intervention and wasn't seeking therapy at that time. I never told anybody about it. And I remember when I first moved to New York, I started to have those feelings about it again...very intense feelings about ending my life. I was afraid to tell anybody because I was afraid of how they would react to me. So, I found this on line group. I could email them when I felt suicidal. They would email me back and help me through it. I remember I was temping at an advertising agency at the time, emailing with this random person I've never met in my life about how I wanted to kill myself. And they would walk me through it. That was like the only help I had before." Dawn's voice returned to its bounce. "It actually really helped me quite a bit. It really did. Having this anonymous person who really cared."

As Dawn shared a little more about her appreciation for the online group and how it helped her, I thought about how healing comes to us in all kinds of ways. In spite of her brokenness, Dawn trusted in the anonymity of a caring person and took her first step on a path toward wellness.

Returning to our conversation about her therapist in New York, Dawn quickly picked up where we left off, "I started therapy and started working with a woman who used a sliding scale. I had no money. She was incredibly helpful. I remember a lot of tear-filled sessions...I punched pillows. I did a lot of work with her for years." It was during this same time, when Dawn was in her early twenties, that all her friends were getting married and having kids. Referencing a session Dawn had with her therapist, she spoke solemnly, "I didn't have those things. I moved to New York and that's a different life. But I had to save my life. I couldn't think about those things. And one of the things my therapist said to me was, 'Your life depends on this. You've got to work through this stuff. Your life depends on it.'"

Dawn's voice strengthened, "That was the beginning for me. And from there, I also began taking self-development courses...courses I would hear about from friends, like women's groups where you go once a week and do exercises and connect with other women. I was also going to Al-Anon meetings." While sharing her different venues for healing, Dawn returned to a previous issue of significance to her. "Depression still came up and over those years I was learning how to manage it. I always thought I could get rid of it, but once I realized that I could *manage* it, I started to feel better. I would go to depression support groups at hospitals. It was only a $10 fee. It was actually at those meetings where I realized that with depression, what I was feeling actually paled to what others were dealing with. It was extremely helpful to see how others struggled. It was really eye opening for me."

Listening to Dawn's words, I was reminded of the healing concept of *shared suffering*. Because of the stigma, shame, and secrecy surrounding numerous mental health issues, we are often fearful of speaking about them. Being part of a group or connecting with others who know and understand our experience adds layers of comfort as we give ourselves permission to acknowledge our pain and to reach out for healing. Along with her transparency in *sharing her suffering*, Dawn continued sharing her recovering.

"That started my whole journey. I read self-help books. I used to go to bookstores and when I felt sad or depressed, I would just find a book. I'd get a cup of coffee and sit there.... I realize now that was a huge part of it as well!" With a burst of laughter, Dawn voice bounced again, "Barnes & Noble doesn't know, but it was part of my healing process for me!" I joined in with her, enjoying the visual of a young woman cozily situated in a comfy bookstore, pouring over a recovery book and embracing the healing words of a caring author.

Exploring a bit further, I asked Dawn about the kinds of books she sought out. She described self-help books covering subjects around self-esteem and alcoholic families. She stressed the importance of learning about codependency and when she read *Codependent No More* (Beattie, 1986), she shared excitedly, "My whole life changed. It was something I didn't even know existed. I started to make sense! Everything I was feeling that I thought was wrong with me...I started to say 'wait a minute....no! I make sense...this makes sense! This is why I am this way.'"

In *naming her pain,* Dawn discovered a gem along her wellness path. With her knowledge of why she felt the way she did, Dawn's understanding deepened as did her healing. Wanting to explore a bit more about Dawn's work with her therapist, I inquired about Dawn choosing to work with a *female* and how and if that was important to her.

Dawn responded openly, "Ummmm, for me any therapist I've ever had or any doctor has always been female. I don't know if that has any connection with me not trusting men. This particular woman, she was like grandmother, almost. Over time, I began to have those feelings toward her. She was caring, very gentle. Her voice was very gentle and soft and when I couldn't afford to pay her that week, she didn't yell. She just kept the bill going and I paid it as I could."

Wondering about the *kind of therapy,* I asked, "Dawn, do you remember if she utilized a certain method of therapy? Did she have you keep a journal, role play, other?"

Dawn paused, then recalled, "Our therapy was just talking. We just talked but we focused a lot on the past and my life at that moment." Her voice strengthened, "We did role playing...I punched pillows. I kept a journal. I did some screaming!" We both laughed.

Dawn described that after about three to four years with her therapist, she started to feel better. She explained how she still attended any support groups she could find. As Dawn continued her journey, she sought out another female therapist, but expenses prevented Dawn from continuing with her. During all this time, Dawn continued reading self-help books and attending Al-Anon.

Dawn continued, explaining how she decided to go back to school about five to six years ago. She recalled how things started to become difficult again, "I started having really strong suicidal thoughts. They had a clinic at the university and I started working with a therapist. That is when I started taking medication for depression. I worked with a girl [intern] who was doing her training. I worked with her for about a year. Because it was through the school, I was limited on how long I could work with her."

I listened. Dawn continued.

"After school had finished, right before my husband and I moved to London which was about three years ago, I started working with a psychiatrist. I worked with her for probably about a year. It was actually quite helpful because I was going through another..." Dawn paused to clarify her situation, "It was at a time when I had started talking to my mom again. I had not spoken to her in decades. And then she got sober and I reached out to her. She was in my life and I was having issues with it, so it was good that I had that therapist in the picture at the time."

Reflecting on Dawn's healing narrative, I was both moved and touched by her transparency and her honesty regarding her journey. Doing the hard work with her therapists was critical to her wellness path, and yet she remained open to supplementing her recovery with medication, under the careful watch of her psychiatrist. *Moving from Brokenness To Wholeness* does not mean we necessarily follow *one path*. It often requires exploration into to a variety of treatment methodologies and a willingness to remain receptive regarding their healing properties.

While validating Dawn's authenticity regarding her recovery work, I moved into a related question. "Dawn, it sounds like your work has been ongoing. However, would you say there have been *stages* within that? Or other? How would you describe it?"

Dawn thoughtfully explained, "I was always under the impression, like with depression, that I would get over it one day and life would be great. Through the process of learning that this whole thing is a process...there is always something that is going to pop up because my roots are deep. These wounds—these psychic wounds—are deep and it's an ongoing process...and my therapy or whatever is it that I do is constantly changing because there is always something new coming up. But, I have these tools that I have constantly been collecting in my little box that I can go back to." Her voice intensified, "I think it's a misconception that you just go to therapy for a year and you'll be fine. I don't know, maybe that's true for a few people, but not for me!" Dawn's bounce returned, filled with laughter.

Although I joined in with her, I was struck by Dawn's use of the word *wounds*. I steered our conversation back to that word, "Dawn, I am interested in your thoughts around your wounds." I explained a bit more, "I think identifying wounds are important, especially with betrayal from our mothers. We've talked about their depth and breadth and how they can smother the core of our beings." I paused for a moment, then questioned her, "As you think about your healing journey, are there any wounds that you would say have been carefully tended to? Are there any which you can speak to where you have experienced a pronounced sense of healing?"

Firmly and insightfully, Dawn responded, "My understanding and my acceptance of who these people were...who they were before I was even thought of, and making that connection." And then like a judge delivering a verdict, she proclaimed, "Understanding that *I* wasn't their problem. *I* was never their problem! They already had those problems! Even recently, this has been huge for me...*knowing* it. And not just knowing it, but *knowing it*. I was never the reason my mom became an alcoholic. Never the reason she felt the need to hit me. Never the reason for the issues my stepmother had...it was never my problem. Now, I *know* they were not my fault."

Dawn took in a deep breath, "With that said, it doesn't mean that I am still not untying the knot of liking myself. I know it's not my fault...and there is still a lot of work to do. But that *knowing* has been critical—it was *never my fault*."

In my mind, I pictured Dawn traveling down her recovery road. She had taken time to scour her landscape, taking inventory of her betrayers and of their injustices. She sifted and sorted through mounds of toxic debris. Bravely, she dug down deep underneath the layers of her betrayal grounds and unearthed massive boulders of burdens she had carried within her. And most importantly, with a solid level of recovering soil in place, she released the giant rocks of responsibility for her past, and began recognizing and reclaiming her healing truths.

We both sat quietly, relishing the freeing of Dawn's feelings and honoring the space as they floated around us. A welcomed lightness moved in. I waited a few more moments before leading into our closing questions in this section.

"Dawn, you've traveled so far. You've come such a long way. Looking back on your journey, is there anything else you could point out which really helped you? Any path that led you further down your road to wellness?"

Dawn's bounce returned, renewed and reenergized, "Being able to write about my experiences and share them with people has changed so much for me. I don't just mean writing in a journal. But I mean writing and having it published." She paused, then added, "Even get paid for it! And I know that might sound kinda awful, but for all the years that I was never able to talk about what I was feeling...what was going on or what was happening....and having extended family members look the other way." The bounce took on new heights. "NOW, I can write about these things and other people read it, but I also get paid for it. It is incredible!" Dawn grabbed her breath, "I don't mean revenge...it is almost like taking something awful and using it for my advantage. Turning my experiences into assets! And yes, there is always something to work on, but it does get easier!" Dawn's bounce was bursting out of her. "It does not have to be the end! It is a choice! It is huge for me! I can actually use this!!"

Basking in Dawn's words, I realized I was hearing a familiar voice—the voice I first listened to when I tuned into one of her podcasts on *Growing Up Chaotic*! Vibrant! Fun! Strong! Empowered! I was jolted back to the present as Dawn poured out her truths.

"My mom, when she was drunk would say, 'You are never going to be anything…you are never going to be anything…' And my stepmother would say, 'You will never be able to take care of yourself. You are never going to be able to do this, that, or the other thing.'" Dawn's bounce took on more and more resilience. "*I* was the one who did the work and see that I could use it in a positive way. You [mom and stepmom] thought you were going to bury me! You didn't!! It makes me happy to think that!"

And with the majesty of a giant sequoia, Dawn's wholeness burst forth. It could not be contained. Her words spilled out, spreading across acres of healed landscape. And then with a quiet calm overflowing with conviction, she voiced her decree, "*They thought they were burying you, but little did they know you were a seed.*"

I remained speechless, honoring Dawn's journey and soaking in her words of wellness. I thought about *this daughter*—I thought about how the odds were against her—not one betrayer but two. And the betrayals, not doubled, but compounded year after year. And yet, Dawn made the decision to *right herself*. She fought for herself and for her recovering. She reclaimed herself and revived her truths. Dawn was living proof—*doing good work restores the good.*

I took in a deep breath and returned my focus to our last section. I was excited to discover where Dawn's wellness path was leading her next.

Wholeness To ...

As we moved into *Wholeness To ....,* I asked Dawn to describe her current relationships with both moms. Dawn explained that after her mom became sober, there was some contact through phone calls and visits. Because her mom still lived in the house were Dawn was raised, it was very difficult. When Dawn married, her mom was invited and attended. Although Dawn recalled how great it was to have her there, she described how certain "feelings came up" when her mother pushed to have a "mother-daughter" relationship. When Dawn's husband received an opportunity to move abroad to London several years ago, they decided to move. Although Dawn's mom pushed for her to send postcards and to say, "I love you" back to her, Dawn declined, standing her ground and remaining strong in her boundaries with her mother.

Dawn described her feelings from the recent past as well as from present day regarding her mom, "I have my life now, and you [moms] are not in it. I've created this life for myself... I think of my life as being my cat and my husband. Just the three of us. I'm very protective of my family and of my life. I felt as though my mom was trying to come into that without inviting her. I haven't talked to her since [for three years] and that was my choice. I just don't think she was getting it."

Dawn moved into her relationship with her stepmom, explaining that they had not spoken in at least a decade. After her mom's affair, Dawn explained to her dad, "I don't want this ...or her [stepmom] in my life." Dawn's relationship with her dad became more "screwed up" after that.

Prior to all contact ending, Dawn agreed to have a planned phone call with her stepmom. Dawn recalled her stepmom's words, "'I'm no longer going to allow you to hurt me'....meaning I was hurting her!" Dawn realized at that moment nothing was going to change and, until it did she did not want to hear from her stepmom. Reflecting on the conversation, Dawn added, "This woman gave me all the information I needed. She has never apologized, she has never addressed the issues, and she is blaming me still." Dawn let out a burst of laughter and continued. "This is me telling you [stepmom], I am done. I am not ten years old anymore. You can't play these games anymore. I can choose. I can't have you in my life. That's where I am with the two of them now."

Although boundary work can be challenging, when betrayers express little or no responsibility for their actions and/or claim to be victims themselves, implementing strong boundaries is essential in protecting and safeguarding our healing spaces. And even if there is some measure of accountability, strong boundaries message others what we will or will not accept from them, and who or what we will or will not invite into our lives. Thinking about how Dawn's boundary work was supporting and serving the wholeness she was creating for herself and her family, I moved into the next question.

"Dawn, where are you today with yourself...and why?"

"Ummmm.... I definitely feel a lot different about myself than I did in my early twenties. I'm starting to realize that I had more strength than I had before to have gone through what I've been through and to be the person I am today. Some people would say, 'Well, your experiences made you who you are...your parents made you who you are.' I don't like that, personally." Dawn's bounce took on a familiar intensity, "I feel very strongly that *I made me who I am.* I had a choice. Things happen to you. You are born into a family. There is not much you can do about it. But *I* chose for my life to be this way."

Dawn's words—"*I made me who I am*"—hung in the air like a banner between us. Pensively, she described her observations, "I think we have a tendency, in our culture or in our society to kind of give our parents—and I'm not a parent—but when I think about my family—my mothers—we give them a lot of leeway. We don't hold people responsible for what they have done." Dawn's voice lowered slightly, "We put so much pressure on kids…to get over it…to move on. So when people say, 'Your parents made you who you are'.….no, no, no, no… you are not giving them credit!" Dawn chuckled softly, "I've worked really hard and continue to work hard to create the life I want to live which is different from what I had. I *have* to take credit for this!" Standing solidly on her healing grounds, Dawn spoke as if she were concluding a keynote address, "You do the work…you take the time…you do what is best for you. You don't give that away to anybody. I feel like I have already given up too much. I am not giving that up!"

Dawn laughed loudly and I accompanied her. Soaking in the strength from her words, I continued my questioning, "Dawn, what life messages do you say to yourself now?"

"Ummmm…. I guess I would say one of the big things for me right now is—I don't have to be perfect. This is huge for me because my stepmom expected that from me and with my mom 'there was something wrong with me,' so the idea was, 'I had to be perfect.' The message I am working on now is 'It's okay for me to do my absolute best. If that is what I am going to do today, that is what I am going to do today. It's okay…it doesn't have to be perfect. It's okay to make a mistake…it's okay to mess up. It's okay to have to start over again." Dawn paused, and added, "This has been a huge lesson for me lately."

Reflecting on the importance of this life message for Dawn, my mind returned to a former struggle of Dawn's and I asked her permission to revisit it. She agreed. "Dawn, do you look in the mirror today? And if you do, what do you say to yourself?"

"I have to say the mirror is still an issue for me today. It is not as intense as it used to be at all. But I know when I started to talk to my mom again, the issue got worse. It started to flare up again. I think a lot of it had to do with this anger that hadn't been resolved. My husband will often say, 'When you look in the mirror, your view of yourself is so distorted. You are not seeing yourself.' It is something I have to work on…but being able to look in the mirror and say, 'It's okay…you're okay....your body is okay.' Just every time I step in front of the mirror to say, 'It's okay...you're OKAY, Dawn.' I can't do it every day. I can't. Some days are harder than others."

As Dawn continued to describe her work in this area, her strengths surfaced as did a more personal experience she was willing to share. "This may sound ridiculous but when I go to the hairdresser...you have to sit in front of the mirror for however long it takes to cut your hair. It is really hard for me to do, but it's something I do for myself and at the same time, it is something which can cause a lot of discomfort. Because that mirror is right in front of me, I can't get away from it." Dawn bounced back, "Sometimes I come home from the salon and I'm great... and sometimes I'm crying." And with a familiar burst of laughter, she added, "My husband will say, 'What's wrong? Did you get your hair done today?'"

We laughed in unison, enjoying the lightness of the brighter days in her journey. I waited. Then asked, "Dawn, as you continue to work on your wellness, what areas are important to you, or perhaps more important than others?"

"It is so important to me to discover my potential. Because for so long I feel I've had to work on these things. I had to or my life would have been a major mess. But now, I want to discover my potential. What could I be...who could I be...without that [past]? I'm not who they said I was. I'm not that person. So who am I ...and what can I do?"

Dawn's bounce was filled with excitement and enthusiasm. She added, "My husband and I agreed when we first met each other that we didn't want to have kids. We have different reasons for that. But one of the reasons I don't want to have kids is because for the first time in my life, I can focus entirely on myself. I wouldn't be able to give that child what it needed. I would hate to do that to someone. So, it is not right for me. And at the same time, anytime I want I can go to a museum...I can explore things... it is freedom! And, I am at a place that whatever comes up for me, I can deal with it. But, I still have all this freedom I've accumulated for doing all this work."

Resolutely, Dawn added, "It's OKAY to be selfish! Not everybody's relationship with their mother after a betrayal is going to be like mine, but it is important to realize that in anyone's journey, you have a choice." Dawn punctuated her truth, "Your choice is okay whatever it is, and... it can change!"

Listening to Dawn, I again visualized the majestic sequoia. When wellness is given the time and space to settle in and to grow, its legitimacy is strengthened. Not only were Dawn's roots taking hold, but as she continued to nourish them by honoring her healing truths, her core was also fortified.

Picking up on her life messages which were shining through her branches, I asked Dawn to speak to those.

"It's kinda what I was saying. No matter what, I have a choice. I've chosen not to have a connection with both moms. And there is kind of an independence in that. I appreciate that independence, both physical and emotional. I do not have to answer to anyone. I do not have to be pressured to have kids or to give my moms grandkids." Dawn reiterated, "There is no one to answer to. Again, it's OKAY to be selfish!"

I sat quietly, honoring her messages.

"You have to trust yourself. We don't get that message in our society or culture. It's part of what my journey has been. I really believe that no matter what it is in your family, you have to trust yourself because it's your life! It's *your* life. At the end of the day, you are a separate person, and you have to trust yourself and accept that too!"

Towering high above the rest of her forest, the sequoia stood solidly in her wholeness. Understanding that in order thrive in fertile soil, it is essential to separate from betrayal environments and their inhabitants. Believing in her process and trusting in her choices, the sequoia crafted protective boundaries around her spaces and surrounded herself with healthy seedlings, feeding them with healing rays of light.

Examining her growth and looking beyond, the sequoia spoke of her journey ahead.

Dawn's core opened and her truths flowed, "Personally, I still have a lot to learn. In this phase, try things. Have faith in my ability to do things and showing up and not having to be perfect. Give myself room to make mistakes and be okay with that. You fail, you make mistakes. It's about getting back up...and learning from that."

I listened, intently.

Dawn's branches reached out and swayed in the breeze, "Professionally, with the Internet I have the ability to connect. If I can take my experiences and help somebody else who is in a similar situation I was in, that is really what I want to do. If I can help somebody else not to experience it alone, and help them through, give people the help I didn't have, I'd like to do more of that."

This majestic sequoia's expansive forest has heard her calling...and waits for more.

Follow-up Reflection

It has been a day or two past the three weeks since my phone interview with Dawn. Although I preferred not to go past three weeks, with both of our busy schedules this was the first opportunity to connect. What I have learned in this process, once again, was to trust the process!

Preparing myself for our call today, I have been thinking about Dawn. As was true in the writing of Ann's narrative, I also found the process of writing Dawn's story extremely heavy work. Transcribing her words by replaying my tape over and over again in order to get the words down accurately, I was acutely reminded of the toll it took on a daughter to share her betrayal narrative in one lengthy interview. I wondered how Dawn felt over the past three weeks.

After organizing my tape recorders and notes, I placed my call to London hoping there were to be no hiccups in the call going through! Moments later, Dawn answered and her familiar bounce popped through the lines. We exchanged a bit of small talk and settled into our call.

I began, "Dawn, how have you been feeling since our interview and how are you feeling today?"

"Today, I am feeling good. I was excited to talk with you again. But I have to admit that after—not immediately after our session—but trickling on after our session a lot of weird feelings started coming up for me which is not unusual, I don't think. I might read a book and it might trigger something...or I might start journaling and it will trigger something, or I will meet someone who will share a similar story and it will trigger something. I think it just goes to show you that you are never done with whatever work you do, there is always something. There is always another level. There is always another layer to peel back. I continue to learn that you just have to keep an open mind about it and trust that this is just another step on your path. Every lesson which shows up is meant to be there for a reason."

Taking in Dawn's words, I spent a few moments validating her responses to our process. Revisiting a betrayal narrative in its entirety demands incredible strength and stamina. At the same time, it is only natural, in fact, it is to be expected that after doing so "triggers" can emerge from any source and tending to them takes additional work and energy.

I continued my questioning, checking in on other emotions Dawn experienced, "Dawn, did you feel a heaviness afterwards? Or other feelings? Would you like to speak to that?"

Without pause, Dawn responded. "Heavy is definitely a word I use a lot. Sometimes it can feel like this massive knot of things. It's like when you pull a necklace out of a drawer and it is tangled up and you sit there on the edge of your bed tearing your hair out trying to untangle this thing! It can be frustrating at times 'cause I think, 'I sort of dealt with this already!'" Dawn's voice lowered slightly, "But, then it is okay because I don't personally buy into the idea that it [my betrayal work] is done. Things are going to keep coming up in different ways."

Dawn described how she was continuing to utilize her recovery lessons in her professional work, writing a recent article on her "double betrayal" by her two moms. Listening to her words, I kept visualizing the tangled necklace—the knot within Dawn. Having experienced the frustration myself of unraveling a single necklace crumpled up in a jewelry box, I found myself honoring Dawn's experience even more as I imagined two necklaces, intertwined and mangled, and her remarkable work of unraveling them both.

I listened, sensing the steadiness and strength of her voice. I waited and then continued to check in, "Dawn, any other feelings which have come up for you?"

"Yes, I was taking to a therapist friend of mine. I mentioned to her that this whole process, whether it is a mother or a really important family member, is almost like you are grieving a death. This person did not quite agree with it, but I made it clear it is not like an actual physical death of someone. But I do think the grieving process is very similar and I don't think it is something we talk about." Dawn paused and continued, "I think back to my twenties and saying to myself, 'I have a mother, but I don't.'" Dawn's voice deepened, becoming much more serious, "And how in our society we 'honor our parents no matter what.' I don't buy into that either. I think that idea kinda blocks people from acknowledging their recovery." Dawn added strongly, "I don't *want* to be in recovery because I don't have a mom, but it is something that happened to me. I think it is important to give people permission to grieve and to look at it as a grieving process."

Dawn voiced an important truth for herself. And as I listened, I was reminded that betrayal is a "loss" issue. Many times, betrayal is a loss of trust in someone or something, but it carries other connotations of loss as well. When we are betrayed by our mothers, we feel significant loss in several areas such as the erosion of personal, relational, and inner-personal dynamics (i.e., understanding intimacy, developing a positive identity, establishing a sense of worth) characteristic of a healthy mother-daughter experience. At the same time, betrayal by a mother may also come to represent the more traditional and literal meaning of loss—death of the relationship. Therefore, blending in grief work along with our betrayal work is essential.

After affirming Dawn's words, I felt the heaviness lift a bit. I tenderly moved ahead, "Dawn, how are you feeling today?"

"I no longer look at the things that happened in my childhood as things that *happened to me*. I look at them as things that *were given to me*. Today, as I am sitting at my desk working and taking my experiences and trying to use them to help other people, I realize it's not *all* that bad. I say that because I have done a lot of work on myself..." Dawn's bounce returned, "On a good day, like today, that is what I try to remember—these are gifts now that I can use. I wouldn't be able to do now what I do if I had not gone through my experiences. And that makes it all worth it in a way, well, not worth it. I mean if you were to ask me if I would change anything, I would say 'No, because this is the only life I've known.' Today, being able to talk about these things and to use it to my advantage now...to be able to call the shots now, it is soooo valuable."

The image of the sequoia suddenly reentered my mind. Absorbing Dawn's words, I pictured how her branches have reached out to others all over the world. Yes, there are days when she turns inward to tend to triggers or wounds which have resurfaced, but Dawn's primary focus remains outward which is an indication of her level of her hard work and her healing. And each time the majestic sequoia utilizes her growth to help others, she strengthens her core and validates her experiences. When she gifts others, she gifts herself.

Sensing we had reached a peaceful place in our conversation regarding Dawn's emotional responses to our interview, I moved into the next area, "Dawn, is there anything from our prior conversation which you would like to amend or change?"

Dawn briefly described how she has become more aware of her need to do some work around her mother-in-law and the feelings which surface from that connection. Because her husband and her cat are the two most important relationships in her life, Dawn acknowledged the importance of looking at her relationship with her mother-in-law and negotiating it on a more healthy level. Dawn closed her comments with her usual bounce, "It's always something!" And we chuckled together.

As we began moving toward the close of our conversation, I shared with Dawn, as I have done and will do with all the daughters I interview, several important pieces in the writing of her narrative. The most significant one was explaining how each daughter's name at the beginning of each chapter is followed by a tagline and why that tagline was chosen. I shared with Dawn what I chose for hers—*I Made Me Who I Am*. Before I asked my final question, I asked Dawn to share anything else she was feeling.

With an emotional tidal wave in her voice, Dawn's words came splashing out, "When you said the tagline—*I Made Me Who I Am*—I probably say that a lot. I don't realize it." She took a breath. Words continued to pour out, filled with shiny particles, "But it is just different when you hear somebody else say it to you. Ummmm...it just kinda struck me because I never heard it said to me. I just found that to be powerful!" Dawn's familiar voice surfaced once again. However, her bounce reached extended heights, "Wow.....it just kinda took be back for a second! I'm just excited to be part of this, and to see what the final outcome is!"

Trusting in the confidence of the sequoia's core strength, I asked permission to read the closing section of Dawn's narrative. With each daughter, it was very important to me that she had the opportunity to hear a portion of her story. And although the writings were still in rough draft form, with the sampling I read for each daughter I was confident she would glean a sense of how her words we were treated with respect and responsibility, and how her truths were tenderly cared for and crafted into this special work. Dawn agreed enthusiastically.

I cleared my throat and began reading. Although emotions welled up within me, I focused strategically on each of Dawn's words, like moving carefully through a field of sunflowers taking time to touch each stem and tending to the significance of each blossom. At the end of the passage, I paused and took in a deep breath. I waited for Dawn.

The sequoia sighed slightly and then spoke softly, "I'm like....there are tears running down my face. I guess because all anyone really wants is for someone to witness your situation and to validate it, and that is what I feel like now." She lowered her branches and wrapped them around her being in a loving self-embrace, "I don't know...I think it is so important for everyone who grows up in these dysfunctional relationships...you just want someone to hear you and validate it. That is what has happened. Even physically, as you were reading it, I just felt this warmth in my chest. This warmth of like *wow*. I mean not *wow* at myself." Suddenly, the sequoia became silent and remained still. Then, unfolding her branches in a full spread, a thunderous bounce echoed throughout the forest, "But *wow*- all this has come together to be this!"

Dawn's words soared across the landscape like a solid stream of shooting stars. They came back around forming a perfect strand of six pearlescent lights, circling the tall sequoia. From miles away, they could be seen...

I Made Me Who I Am

4   "The Power Rests Completely Within Me" – Robyn

Reflection

It has been about six weeks since completing the interview process and the writing of Dawn's narrative. Never before having experienced anything like this, as I moved through unfamiliar territory of conducting a qualitative study, I found I needed ample space to tend to myself as well as scheduled time for honoring each daughter's voice in the quietness of my spirit. Thus, I have kept a pulse on my emotional stamina and strength while pondering who the next daughter might be and when I might approach her.

When I began planning for "The Daughters Project," I had several daughters in mind who I already knew to varying degrees, who I felt might want to participate, and who met the criteria for the study. Ann was one of them. I contacted a few other daughters who initially expressed interest but then later declined. Although Dawn did not come to mind until I actually began my investigation, I discovered how this process was leading me. I was not leading it. I have learned to trust in the process, in the daughters who come my way, and whose narratives bring another voice to my findings.

Therefore, I was not surprised when the next daughter's path crossed with mine and with this study; however, I never planned on it. I met Robyn at a social gathering a couple of years ago through mutual acquaintances. On the few occasions I have had the pleasure of seeing her since, it has always been in social settings and around our common connection. Therefore, there was never a reason for or an opportunity to get to know Robyn on a deeper level.

With each ensuing encounter, as I observed Robyn I noticed how easily she moved through a room and how comfortable she was engaging others in conversation. Her warmth radiated throughout every setting and her laughter sprinkled across the table when we dined at different venues. Upon first hearing Robyn's voice, I noticed how her still-evident New York accent added rich flavors to her already colorful personality. I took notice of Robyn's depth of intelligence equally matched by her compassion for all living things and her regard for the rights of others. Each time, as I have been a part of the circle in which we both find ourselves in, my respect and admiration for Robyn has grown, and I certainly saw why others were drawn to her.

However, it was only recently when I learned through our mutual connection that Robyn's background, in particular her relationship with her mother, might interest Robyn in participating in "The Daughters Project." Not wanting to compromise friendships or boundaries, I did not pursue the conversation further except to share that I appreciated the trust placed in me regarding Robyn and her mother. Within a very short period of time, I was able to connect on a more private basis with Robyn about "The Daughters Project," sharing just the basic purposes and intentions. Robyn readily expressed interest, noting she would welcome additional information before making a commitment to the process.

By the end of April 2016, Robyn read through the Informed Consent, reviewed the Interview Questions, submitted the required documents, and we scheduled our time for our pre-interview conference. Mindful of the preparation required, I organized my materials, revisiting the forms and process of interviewing for "Daughters Betrayed by Their Mothers." I again felt my enthusiasm begin to swell as well as the responsibility it carried with it. With Ann and Dawn, we shared much more of a personal and professional history together. I knew of them and about them, and to varying degrees, of their respective journeys with their mothers. This prior knowledge, by no means, diminished in any way their experiences and their powerful recovering narratives; it provided me with a foundational backdrop from which to navigate their interviews. As the interviewer, I felt like there was a safety blanket around me—anticipating what was ahead, being able to prepare for it, and perhaps most importantly, it assisted me in being fully present for each of them.

As I thought about Robyn, I noticed a few butterflies fluttering around inside. Without having any prior knowledge of her betrayals from her mom, I would call upon my therapeutic skills utilized during the intake and ensuing sessions with a client—being acutely aware and present; being finely tuned in my reflective listening; and being able to provide unconditional positive regard with an openness to experience. And, as I have done with the other daughters, I would be mindful of Robyn's pace and her need for pause, and keep a pulse on mine.

I rearranged my notes, one last time, for our thirty-minute or longer pre-interview phone conference. In my mind, I replayed Robyn's New York vibrancy and anticipated its emergence on the other end.

Setting

On an unusually cool second week of May 2016 in the later part of the afternoon, I called Robyn at our designated time. Reviewing her background, I was reminded of what an incredibly accomplished daughter she is and how in demand she remains in her professional circles.

Robyn is in her early forties. She is Caucasian, born and raised in New York. Although her family is Jewish and she has a strong sociocultural identification with Judaism, from a religious standpoint, Robyn has shared she is an Atheist. Her levels of education include a BA in Psychology; JD (Doctor of Law), and an MA in Organizational Psychology.

In her short written biography for participation in "The Daughters Project," Robyn stated, "I began my career as a lawyer, but after two years, decided it was not for me and went back to graduate school to pursue organizational psychology. I am very interested in the inter-personal and intrapersonal domains of leadership and I work with executives to help them gain greater mastery in these domains of organizational life. I have had my own consulting business for fifteen years and do assessments and coaching of CEO's and C-level executives."

Not knowing much about Robyn's personal life, I learned from her biographical sketch that she identifies her sexual orientation as bisexual and her current relationship status as single. And from Robyn's statement as to why she would like to participate in "The Daughters Project," I was touched by her words:

"I would like to participate because I have done a significant amount of work to heal from an extremely difficult relationship with my mother, and would be happy to share my journey and lessons learned if it could help other women on their healing path."

Another daughter's path has intersected mine. I placed the call.

Robyn answered the call with a professional poise which provided an instant calmness to our conversation. We settled into our rhythm quite quickly. I began with a question which I had not anticipated asking Robyn regarding her name. In Ann's narrative, it was vitally important to her that I use "name substitution" in the writing of her story. Aside from being a best practice for a study such as "The Daughters Project" in which the protective clauses regarding anonymity for each daughter were clearly delineated in the Informed Consent, Ann had numerous personal and professional reasons for not using her real name. In Dawn's narrative, it was equally important to her, for the reasons she disclosed, to keep her real name. As has been the driving force behind my study, it is paramount to me that I honor the voice of each daughter and the integrity of her being. Thus, I checked in with Robyn regarding this important aspect of confidentiality.

Robyn answered pensively, "It has to do with more of my professional life. It's like more of a boundary thing for me. I think a part of me would rather not expose that. But could I think about that a little bit more? Maybe once I go through the actual interview and see what comes up. Do I need to decide right now or can I feel my way into it?"

I responded, "Of course, Robyn. Take your time. Up until the time we conclude with our final interview, please know you can amend, add, or change anything. This is your truth. This is your story."

Sensing a mutual ease settle in, I moved into a question which Robyn and I, unlike the other daughters, had discussed only briefly prior to our pre-interview conference. And because of its thematic implications for my study, I wanted to pursue it a bit further.

"Robyn, in the Informed Consent I have delineated several explanations or definitions of "betrayal" for this study, but I would like to hear from you about your thoughts around the word betrayal. When you read the Informed Consent and the connotations around betrayal, what came up for you? Could you speak to that?" I paused and added, "What did or what does the word betrayal mean to you?"

Robyn responded, "Even when we first started talking about this, when you mentioned the word betrayal with moms and daughters, I thought I wouldn't be really good for this because my mother didn't *betray me.* In my sort of definition of the word, it was much more narrow I would say than in yours." Robyn spoke firmly, "There is something that automatically comes to mind when I think of *betrayed...* like violated....violated some sort of basic principles of trust and protection. And she did not do that. So that's where I think it was helpful to see your bigger definition because when I wrote the words down—what does betrayal really mean to me?—it means, you know, you didn't act in my best interest, you broke trust, you didn't protect me. My mother did not do any of those things, so there was an initial reaction to the word like when, excuse the word, but betrayal is like when someone *fucks you over.*" We both broke out in laughter. Robyn continued with a serious but lighter tone in her voice, "They lie, they cheat, they don't show up for you if you are being abused. My mother did a lot of awful things, but she never did any of those things." And then her voice lowered and strengthened, "But when I thought about the way you were defining betrayal as any profound disappointment as to how we expect mothers to mother, I was like, 'Oh yeah'...... I got plenty of that!"

A softer laughter between us sprinkled though the airwaves. I gently reflected Robyn's perceptions and interpretations of the word betrayal, reminding myself of the broadened lens from which betrayal is viewed and of the importance of honoring each daughter's unique experience with it. I checked to see if there was anything else Robyn wanted to add or share.

With a mindfulness in her voice, Robyn spoke, "I thought of something else. It has been a while since I have been down this path. I feel like I have deconstructed it down to molecules and put it back together, but I have not done so in many, many, many years. And I am actually, sort of in a weird way, I'm kinda looking forward to revisiting my narrative with my mother, *now*. I did my mother work before I did my father work, and so chronologically I did the mother stuff sort of first, I think. It has been a long time since I have been in dialogue with these issues. I think there is something that I am looking forward to....sort of coming back to it. Especially now, everything that I have behind me."

I thanked Robyn for the additional insight into her background with her mom. And I found myself intrigued by the initial pieces of her narrative which were starting to emerge.

Almost two weeks have passed since our pre-interview conference. As was true with all the daughters, my excitement and enthusiasm grew in anticipation of this process. Because the distance between our home environments was extensive and we wanted to connect face to face, Robyn and I agreed to utilize video Skype to conduct our interview. Having organized my questions and recorders, I placed the video call.

On a breezy warm May morning, I eagerly awaited the narrative of another daughter. Another voice. Another journey.

Beginning

Within moments after connecting through our mutual screens, we settled into our conversation with a bit of familiar chat. I soon learned that after having time to reflect upon the use of her real name, the name *Robyn* was chosen to use as a pseudonym for "The Daughters Project." It is one which held meaning for this daughter. It is one which provided a protective level of anonymity while still honoring her authenticity. I moved into our first question.

"Robyn, how do you refer to your mom? Do you use that noun or another?"

"In a way the story I am about to tell you will encapsulate the remaining three hours and forty-five minutes!" We both laughed. "It's funny because when I saw that first question and my response was well, I call her *Mom*, but that is actually not true. So, the way that we refer to her—my sister and I and even my friends...and she has even started to refer to herself this way—is *The Womb*. And literally like in my contacts, it comes up as ...*The Womb.*" Robyn's laughter filled the space and I joined in. "So how did that come to be?" Robyn's rhythm slowed slightly, "When I was in law school, she was coming to visit me and I was talking to a friend of mine and I was sorta anxious about it saying 'my mom is coming to visit and it is very difficult with her....she is not the most presentable person.' And my friend said to me, 'Well, you don't have to tell anyone she is your mother, just say you rented space in her womb for nine months.' And the name was born. That was twenty years ago. We all call her 'The Womb'—my sister, Jennifer (my ex), and even my mother has taken to signing cards—'Love, *The Womb.*' That is what I call her."

Again, we giggled in unison. I sensed an ease with Robyn which led me to my next question, "What about before the name—*The Womb*—how did you refer to her?"

With a softer and lowered intonation, Robyn replied, "Mom." And then added, "She gave birth to me and sort of gestated me, but when you think about a relationship that the word mother connotes versus a sort of storage facility for nine months, that tells you a lot about how I think about my relationship with her."

Keeping a pulse on the territory we were covering, I felt a calm strength take hold. I moved ahead. "How does it feel to talk about your mom in this interview?"

"There is not a lot of new material for me with her. It feels fine. It doesn't feel particularly charged. It is what it is. It is very sad. And I think if anything when I talk about her it is just a reminder of how different my relationship is with her than what many people have...what daughters have at this point in their lives."

Wanting to explore this questioning a little more deeply, I referenced a part of our conversation from our pre-interview conference, "Robyn, although we are going to talk about this more when you share your betrayal narrative, you alluded earlier to doing your work around your mother first, so I am wondering if talking about your mom has changed over time. And if so, how?"

"I would say it hasn't really changed over the last eight years. It really flared up around my sister's wedding which was nine years ago." Robyn paused, "Just a little bit of background. When Jennifer and I got married, my mother was like, 'I'll come as an invited guest but to me it is not the same as if you were marrying a man.'" Robyn took in a deep breath and exhaled slowly. "It was not that whole thing for me like, 'My daughter is getting married, and we'll plan a wedding, and I'm going to pay for it!'" Robyn continued, "When my sister got married, she pulled out all the stops, and did way more than she could even afford, honestly. That was like the moment when I think a lot of my anger coalesced, and it was very raw for me. That was nine years ago. I remember I had to do some work around that. But in the last six to eight years, the story has not changed very much." I waited, allowing room for further disclosure.

Robyn's voice took on a warm resolve, "If anything, Holli, I would say my compassion for her has probably grown and while I haven't renegotiated the boundaries in our relationship, with her I've just developed more compassion and more empathy for her—and her plate and how limited she was."

Sensing the strength in Robyn's voice, I reflected its presence. "What I am hearing is that this change has more to do with you and your work than any changes in the relationship."

Robyn's voice remained steady, "For sure."

Although we had discussed the connotations of the word betrayal in our pre-interview conference, I checked in with Robyn regarding our last question, "How does it feel to use the word betrayal in our interview today and in relating it to your mom? Any additional thoughts? Can you speak to that?"

"It's funny; it's still a word for me that has a connotation of *deception.* And I feel like my mother did a lot of bad things, but she was never dishonest, deceptive, or deceitful. Betrayal still has the idea for me that you are doing something *covert.* I think it is just semantics, honestly." Robyn's voice became reenergized, "My mother did very horrible things to me, but there was nothing covert about it!" Robyn's laughter broke out and I joined in. "It was right out there! And I think that is why the word betrayal didn't instinctively fit, but when I thought about it more broadly—as a mother not showing up in the ways in which a child needs her to—if I define it that way, then, of course, it fits much better."

Understanding well the difficulty in identifying our mothers as our betrayers, I probed Robyn further about her feelings around talking about 'her mother not showing up for her.'

Robyn's voice remained secure, "The substance of it doesn't trigger anything new. My basic affect with her is sort of resigned disappointment at this point."

I paused, allowing Robyn's truth to fill the space. As I moved into the closing of the first section of our interview, I reminded myself how unique each daughter's experience with betrayal is as is each one's disclosure of it. From our first half hour together, I sensed a flame in Robyn—not a fragile, flickering spark, but a steady, strong stream of strength. With contained intrigue and heightened interest, I moved into the next section wondering how and under what conditions this remarkable daughter found her source.

Background

Knowing very little of Robyn's background, I tenderly moved into the first question, "Robyn, how would you describe your family growing up? And any of your background which you feel comfortable sharing?"

"Suuurrre….," with her flavorful accent, the word seemed to roll off her tongue in song. Robyn's vibrancy returned, "I grew up in New York. My parents were 15 years apart so my dad was forty, I think, when they got married which was kinda old for that generation. I am the older of two girls. My younger sister is Megan, and we are very close. I don't remember a ton about the first five or six years of my life, but it was probably the most normal those first years. My parents were married and my mother was, like, *contained* more, and then they separated when I was six and divorced when I was seven or eight.

"And, unfortunately, that was like a real turning point in my life because without the confinement of my father….she just lost it." Robyn paused and added, "My mother probably has Borderline Personality Disorder with a lot of depressive and anxious features. She was very angry, very verbally abusive….physically abusive certainly by today's standards—even by the 1970's standards. She was truly easily triggered so anything could set her off. She was very volatile. My house was very chaotic. And because we were struggling financially, my mother went back to work. My parents did not have a lot of money. But my dad lived five minutes away and he was very involved and very supportive. He paid his child support and all that, but there just wasn't a lot of money. That was also a hardship."

Regardless of the levels of healing a daughter has integrated into her life or of the healthy detachment a daughter has embraced with her mother, I consistently kept a pulse on the pace of conversation allowing space for each daughter's disclosure to unfold. Viewing Robyn on my screen, she resettled herself and took a sip of her refreshing drink.

"Right after my parents divorced, I remember basically hating my mother. I don't remember any time in my childhood of having any feelings of positive regard or of love for my mother. For as young as I can remember, all I wanted was to go and live with my father. I was very close to him. I saw him every weekend." With solemnity in her voice, Robyn continued to describe how financial resources as well as her father's own inhibitions prevented him from doing something which was unconventional for the times. She added, "This was the 1970's and men did not take their little girls away from their mothers. So it was really hard. I had this crazy mother who was abusive and I got the brunt of it more than my sister. I had this father who I loved so much, and I felt like he could have so easily changed the course of my whole life."

Robyn paused for a moment and continued, "My mom remarried when I was about ten. He was a very good man. In fact, he probably reined my mother in and kept her contained, and he did stuff for us because my mother was very low functioning as a mother. Like, he would take us grocery shopping." Robyn's voice reflected its usual vigor again, "They are still married. They have the most dysfunctional marriage!" With her sophisticated humor, Robyn joked, "I think he is the perfect masochist to her sadist! They have a great thing, psychodynamically!" I joined in, appreciating the therapeutic insight!

As we continued exploring her background, Robyn returned to more difficult territory and disclosed a very painful time in her life. "My dad got lung cancer when I was thirteen and died of lung cancer when I was sixteen. It was pretty horrible. He was the parent that I sort of pinned all my hopes to. Luckily, when he died I was only about a year away from going to college, so thank God he hung in there as long as he did." A profound longing permeated the space between us. "But from about age fourteen, he was in some stage of being ill, so he really stopped functioning as a father for me from about fourteen years old."

Honoring her experience, I gently reflected, "Robyn, there is so many levels of loss and hardship laced with heartbreak which you experienced. I am so sorry."

Robyn's response came forth in a whisper, but it carried with it a haunting sadness, "Yes....heartbreaking...."

Allowing time for the softened flame to find its source, I paused and then continued. "When you feel ready, would you speak to what your role was in your family?"

With a parental tone, Robyn responded, "I think about my role, vis-à-vis, my little sister. And I would say I was the first line of defense against my mother. Partly being the oldest, partly being my personality. I feel like I absorbed most of my mother's abuse. I protected my sister from it. I just felt like I needed to protect her, so I took the brunt of it. That was probably my role."

Unsure as to the role Robyn's stepfather played in the family, I probed a bit further, "Did your stepdad ever intervene or did he take on a parental role in protecting you?"

"Ummm... that is a good question. I am sure there were times where my mother literally could have beaten the shit out of me...put me in a hospital...and I'm sure that he stepped in. I don't remember. I have a vague sense that he probably kept her from going over the edge a few times. He tried to calm her down...step in between us. To his credit, my stepdad was really good at trying not to pretend he was my father. He just really tried to keep my mother from killing me, basically," Robyn added, "so I feel pretty grateful to him for that."

Robyn described in more detail how her few happy memories with her family revolved around a period of time when her stepdad was doing well financially. There was more calmness in her home, but as Robyn qualified, "It was all relative."

Reaffirming her role as protector in the family, I wondered how else Robyn viewed herself within her family.

Robyn's voice lit up, "I don't know if this is so much my role, but when I think about where did I get my self-reliance, my sense of independence, and sort of on my darker side—my needs for autonomy and to be self-directed, I feel I got that for having to be that for myself and for my sister because I didn't really have a mother. And so, I learned very early not to need anything and it has played out in my life in some very positive ways and some more unfortunate ways."

Knowing we would explore the impact of Robyn's betrayals more thoroughly in our next section, I paused briefly, honoring her truths. In closing our section on background, Robyn added how her relationship with her maternal grandparents was very important to her. Although her grandmother made her own mother look like "the pinnacle of sanity" and her grandmother's background role as a mother explained why Robyn's mother was the way she was, Robyn shared how her grandparents were "the most stabilizing force in my life."

Needing to clarify how an unstable woman could serve such a positive role in Robyn's life, I asked Robyn to speak to that. Robyn added, "My grandmother was very loving and supportive of me, and she also knew why my mother was the way she was. She was a sounding board for me. She understood me." Robyn explained further, "My grandfather did very well in business. Money was not an issue for them anymore. My grandmother just like mellowed out...you know you hear of people aging out of mental illness," Robyn's soft chuckle filled the space. "I think my grandmother just aged out of it! She was like a different person than my aunt and my mother (to a lesser degree) described her as. I loved her very much and was very, very close to her."

Sensing we had touched upon one integral source within Robyn, I waited for her words.

"I attribute being halfway intact when I made my way into the world, to them and to the role they played in my life."

The steady flame filled the screen with a warm glow.

Betrayal Narrative

After taking a short break and refreshing our drinks, Robyn and I resettled ourselves in front of our respective screens. As I moved into the first question, "When did you first start thinking about your betrayal narrative with your mom?" I wondered if its wording would pose a bit of a stumbling block given Robyn's contextual references and connotations of the word betrayal and given its newly applied application to her experience. Checking in with Robyn, I found this to be the case and so I reworded the question just slightly.

"When did you first start thinking that, 'What I am getting from my mom is not what I need?' Or, 'This isn't right for me?'"

Robyn's tone was solemn. "I have to say I feel like that at a very early age I knew that this is not how it is supposed to be. I knew my mother was crazy even as a little girl. I was even able to talk about it to my dad—how irrational and difficult and volatile and abusive she was. I remember thinking about it almost immediately after my parents were divorced. I can't remember a time I wasn't thinking about it."

While Robyn paused, I asked if she experienced any of these feelings before her parents' separation.

Pensively, she disclosed, " I don't have any real memories before I was five; my first real memory of my mother was sitting in the public library right after my parents got divorced and she was reading us a story about parents who got separated. I remember sitting there thinking, 'I hate you....I don't want to be here with you right now.' The feelings of disgust that I had about her, that was my first memory of my mother."

As I had with the other daughters, I was consistently being mindful of the pace of the interview and taking my cues from each daughter. Although Robyn was moving into and sharing her painful past, her voice remained strong. She had not waivered thus far, and so, I too moved forward matching her pulse and her poise.

"Robyn, when you think about your betrayal narrative with your mom, is there a pattern, or stages, or a specific chronology from which you reference it? How would you describe it?"

Unwavering in her strength but with increased intensity, Robyn vividly detailed her experience, "So I guess the way I think about it.....it is like living in Israel. Like getting bombed every day or living on high alert. Like you live with violence or the threat of violence. It was a chronic story. Some years were better; some years it was worse." She paused and added, "I would say it probably got to its worst when I was twelve...when I wasn't a kid anymore. My teenage years were very hard with her. Once I got out of the house, there was distance with her. I wasn't as vulnerable to her anymore. A very big turning point in my relationship with my mother was when I went to college and even more so when I went to law school. And when I was no longer dependent upon her for anything, I felt like I redefined the relationship on my terms."

I listened intently to Robyn's words and yet my mind was still replaying the visual of Israel being bombed—of Robyn living with ongoing violence or the threat of it. Before moving into the next question, I joined in with Robyn's experience by reflecting its chronic, invasive, and expansive nature. Robyn slid her fingers through her silky hair, a soothing gesture she repeated often during our interview. Although she resituated herself into her white cozy sofa, relaxing more fully in its comfort, Robyn's voice never vacillated from its truth and she remained securely positioned in it. I moved into our next question.

"Robyn, when you are ready, will you share your betrayal narrative? And if you need to take any breaks, please just let me know."

"I cannot remember that time when I felt like ...'I love my mother.' Every feeling I can remember I have about her is anger, and hatred, and disgust and disappointment. My earliest memories of her are right after my parents got divorced." Robyn paused and continued, "There are these funny memories I have. I remember when I was in third or fourth grade, we had to bring a recipe into school. We had to make something. I made ambrosia—the food of the Greek gods. I remember mine looked like dog food. The bananas were all rotten...nobody wanted to eat it in class," Robyn chuckled. I waited as a quiet moment of reflection moved in. Her voice warmed and softened, "And then I made it with my father, and it was, like, beautiful."

Although I knew that Robyn has also done extensive recovery work around her father and the losses she endured with him, I did not want to dishonor her memories of him by moving too quickly through our betrayal questions or returning the focus to her mom too abruptly. Thus, I remained present with her, keeping a pulse on her being. Within the quiet space, the flame soon found its source. Her voice, once again, re-energized.

"It was like living in a war zone with her. She was full of rage, full of anger. She had very low self-regulation. So, anything could set her off. Her anxiety and depression were externalized. So it was all in the form of rage and violent outbursts. She wasn't a loving, nurturing mother. She just wasn't. She was trying to survive herself. That is the piece where I have developed the most compassion: she was fighting for her own survival. She was probably doing the best she could, but it just wasn't enough."

Robyn continued to describe how financial stresses worsened her mom's volatility, which she experienced on a daily basis. With an understanding of how her younger years were being experienced, I asked Robyn if there was any change as she moved into her adolescent and teen years.

"Adolescence made it even harder. It is a time where you assert your own independence and I was already an independent person." Robyn added, "And if I think about some of her better qualities, she was very overprotective, but yet very suspicious. Her irrationality just made it so hard to deal with as I was trying to individuate."

As Robyn continued to describe incidences of volatility with her mom, I wanted to remain cautious about putting labels on any of her experiences. However, I explored a little more deeply with Robyn around her insights into human behavior and their relationship to her mother.

Firmly and calmly, Robyn responded, "She was abusive. I think that she inherited my grandmother's rage and volatility and re-enacted with me a version of what she endured with her own mother. My father never ever raised his hand to us. My mother could not self-regulate and she would lose control. She was physically abusive. She was verbally abusive. Screaming, uncontrollable rage. Screaming diatribes. It was like the dam would open for her. Her thresholds were so low." Robyn's voice took on a quiet but strong resolve, "That is the story of my mother. It is remarkably consistent."

Absorbing Robyn's words and respecting the precision with which she described her narrative, I moved forward in my questioning asking Robyn if she responded to her mom or how she protected herself. Robyn described how she would react in one of two ways: "Either I would get in mom's face where I risked further retaliation," or "I would not show any emotion and just stared at my mom with a steely-eyed look."

Although Robyn instinctively took care of herself with regards to differing sources of neglect, I wondered if this carried over into other aspects of her life, "Did your mom take care of your basic needs? Did she cook, clean, and that sort of thing?"

"No, some of it was financial, and I understand that now. And some of it was checking out. It was very hard to get her to go grocery shopping. There was never enough food in the house. And, she did not really cook very often. She didn't pay any attention to our nutrition: a lot of frozen dinners, pizza, Chinese food." Robyn paused, then continued, "She was a slob. She just wasn't on top on those things."

Robyn stated that her needs were met at a very minimal level. However, her voice became elevated as she explained, "She had to have done something right! Because look at me!" With contained optimism, she added, "Holli, I think the best mothering she ever did was in her first five years. And they say how those years are very important to development. She was a good-enough-mother during those first years. And after that, at a very minimal survival level."

Wanting to explore a bit deeper before leaving this section of our interview, one final question came to my mind. "Robyn, during all your formative years, what do you remember feeling?"

With her calm strength, Robyn replied, "The first word which comes to mind was 'hatred.' I couldn't stand her. So that is the first one." Robyn reflected, then added, "I was afraid of her. So, I lived in fear a lot, never knowing what was going to set this woman off," Robyn paused, "I remember thinking—what was this? This was not normal. I was also very envious as a child because I saw other mothers who went grocery shopping and who loved them [their children]. I've lived with a lot of envy and this perpetual state of longing to be with my father. I lived with a constant fear of, 'Get me out of here....this is not a safe, happy place for me'."

Robyn's words tugged at my core. I found myself needing to tap into my inner strength and re-center my being. I paused and then reflected Robyn's painful emotions back to her, acknowledging them and validating their presence in her life.

Robyn's voice remained steadfast and her tone secure, "I'm in a very resigned position." Her words carried her truth. "Yes, it is such a shame. I look at your relationship with your daughter and others with their mothers. I don't have that and I've never had that. I don't have a mother."

The flame within Robyn did not flicker. It did not spark. Its essence encompassed warmth and compassion. I've witnessed how it consistently carries with it a healing light which constantly fills her being and, in turn, spills out onto others. Again, I wondered about its source. I wondered how it served her as she navigated through her brokenness.

Brokenness From Betrayal

In moving through this experience of conducting interviews, I've learned how one section of questions can easily overlap into other areas. While allowing the process to guide me, I also want to be mindful of repetitive questioning which might subject each daughter to unnecessary revisitation of painful experiences. Therefore, because Robyn addressed her *feelings* to her betrayals from her mom in the previous question, as I approached the first question in *Brokenness From Betrayal,* I broadened it to suit this section more appropriately.

"Robyn, in thinking about how your mom's betrayals affected or impacted you, can you speak to all areas of your life?"

With unwavering self-compassion, Robyn spoke, "As a child, I had a very hard time socially, making any friends until I was about thirteen years old. I think a lot of that had to do with kids thinking that I was from the wrong side of the tracks in a way. I was not very well cared for. I was angry and I was not being nurtured at home. And nobody wanted to come to my house and play with me. I think because she was so neglectful of me it affected my ability to make friends. I felt very socially isolated until I was a teenager. I felt very alone. I felt different, like there was something wrong with me. Like I wasn't acceptable. Ummm....I felt very jealous and very envious of kids who seemed to have good families. I'm getting a little into my psychology but I was very vulnerable to idealization." Robyn chuckled softly, "I over idealized people and I lived with a profound feeling of inferiority my entire life. As I child I couldn't name it, but I felt it acutely my entire childhood. The only thing that pulled me out of that a little was school. I was known as one of the smartest kids in school. That boosted me a little bit in terms of my self-esteem. But, that came much later in my adolescence." With a shyness to her voice, Robyn added, "I carried around a lot of shame as a child. I felt like 'Pig Pen,' liked I walked around with a cloud of dirt everywhere." Her warm laughter sprinkled across the screen, "That was me!"

Interested in how school played a role shaping her life, I asked Robyn to expand further.

"Starting in junior high school and definitely by the time I got to ninth grade, school was my savior. I loved school. It was structured. It was stable. There was a very linear relationship between doing something good and getting something good. That equation did not hold up in my home, so, I loved school. I loved to learn and I did very well. I used my academics as a bootstrap for me. I knew my education was going to be my ticket out of this horrible life."

While validating Robyn's intrinsic survival mechanisms and their external rewards, I moved back into other arenas in her life which impacted her either positively or negatively.

"I sensed very early on that nobody was ever going to take care of me. I was going to have to take care of myself. So, I started babysitting when I was eleven or twelve years old. So when all my other friends' parents were buying them Guess jeans, I was out there hustling, earning money." Robyn's gracious giggle filled the space. She continued, "My sense of independence and self-reliance was a direct result of not being taken care of. And that started very, very young."

Noting that we were already moving into an extremely important part of the questions, I followed Robyn's lead and asked if she would speak more about her *life messages*—not only the ones she said to herself about herself, but also others which she perceived from her environment.

Robyn jumped right in, "The one which is very pervasive for me...is... hmmm...what is the right way to say this? People are easily angered and uncontrollable. I am one of the most conflict-avoidant people. I have to rehearse in my head having to ask a taxi driver to slow down...I do it several times because I am scared. I think I walk around believing that everyone has the same threshold that my mother had in terms of getting triggered and then being filled with rage. I am very scared of people being irrational or unpredictable in their behavior. And having forty plus years into this, I still have a really hard time. The message is—people are easily angered, so don't make them angry even if that means denying your own needs. There is a very adaptive component to that where I can figure out very quickly what I think people need from me and be that for them. But there is also a shadow to that which I can be very split off from what I need...very afraid to assert myself when I am not getting my needs met. That is a big one. I am scared of people because I have my mother as a template. Obviously, the volume has been turned way down on that. But, it is a big life message."

Robyn's life message carried with it a heaviness, and yet, it did not deter from her steadiness. Monitoring the pulse between us and sensing her strength, I waited for her to continue.

"This is an unconscious message… and it influenced my decision not to have children. For me, there is no positive association with the notion of mother-child relationship. It is like, 'That is something you don't want to get into…it is something you want to get out of…as quickly as possible.'" Robyn's laughter broke through and I joined in. "I don't have a positive association to the idea of a family. I don't like to be in groups. I find them falsifying. I don't have children of my own, and I think there are legitimate reasons for that. Why would I voluntarily want to sign up for something that was so horrible?" We laughed together, more outwardly. Robyn returned to her inner constant source and reiterated, "Another life message is, 'Families are something you want to get out of…not get into.'"

I, again, found myself connecting to Robyn's life message on a very profound level. I reflected her words, containing my emotions and mirroring her strength. I moved into a question which I had been holding onto until we reached this section on life messages.

"Robyn, I think earlier in our conversation you made reference either to *not having enough* or *not being enough*? Am I remembering that accurately and would you speak to either one, if it is indeed a life message?"

Robyn's voice took on an extremely tender tone, "I felt unworthy and inferior. I was like in a caste system…in the very low end. It was conflated with our financial situation. But it was like an emotional caste system. And I felt at the very bottom of that…like the untouchable."

Just as she had shared throughout our entire interview in her more painful disclosures, Robyn's voice was couched in a calm resolve. Her life messages could not and would not douse her source. It was like her flame was turned down to a lesser flow, but it remained in a full and complete formation.

Before moving into Robyn's life messages as a young adult and older, I asked Robyn if there was any physical affection demonstrated in her home and how that might of impacted her or her life messages. Robyn described how even though her father was very affectionate and loving, there was none shown to her by her mom. In her words, she described how she, "recoiled at the thought of it." Robyn shared how her life messages around sex and sexuality were healthy. She never received any bad messages from her mother about sex, and attributes some of her healthy attitudes about sex to her mother.

Moving into more of her life messages, Robyn shared how they presented themselves in her years after she left home.

"The first thing that comes to mind is that I have a very strong need to control my home environment. I have created, or in some cases, recreated in every place that I have lived a *haven* for me. It is the antithesis of the home I grew up in. It is calm and it is peaceful. It is serene and immaculate, not cluttered. All that is good. But at the same time, the darker side of that is I don't do very well when things are messy or out of place where I can't control my environment. I get very uncomfortable.

"When I think of why I am not drawn to having kids, I don't think I could handle the chaos. I couldn't handle the inevitable disruption to order...that happens when you have little people!" Robyn's familiar chuckle resurfaced, then subsided. "That is definitely a long-term impact. I need to control my home environment. My environment needs to be a certain way. It gives me such a sense of peace, and it has an upside and a downside, for sure.... When people are here, they feel loved and nurtured. The downside is that it is almost a compulsive need, to have control over my environment."

Reflecting the messages Robyn has disclosed thus far, I asked about other areas of her life and their respective impact upon her. Robyn readily responded.

"I'm definitely conflict avoidant and scared of anger. I don't do well in personal relationships with anger or professional relationships with anger. I have to be mindful, being what I do for a living, that something I share might make them [clients] angry. But, that is my piece of it. And that is true of my personal relationships as well."

Robyn described in more detail how she handled anger in her relationship with her ex-wife, Jennifer. Although she was never abusive, Jennifer had no problem getting angry. Robyn disclosed how she avoided talking about things with her because she was scared. As she has grown and worked on herself, Robyn shared how she is now more drawn to people who have their anger under control. Professionally, Robyn is more discerning about taking on clients who may trigger her as well as being able to say things without fear of angering them.

Tapping into her prior life message as a child feeling socially inadequate, I asked Robyn if and how those messages may have impacted her adult life.

With the flame turned up on high, Robyn's voice took on even more vibrancy, "I don't want to say I have overcompensated in my life, but I am so acutely aware of my need to belong and other people…and other people's plates and vulnerabilities, it has become a top priority in my life. And I have friends that are like family to me! I think some of it is that I don't have children…some of it is that remembering on a cellular level how painful it is not to have friends. It is a driving force in my life and that has been true since high school." Hearing her fullness coming through, I listened intently. "Holli, it is a bit of a mystery for me, but somehow I was able to figure out the secret recipe. And, I think some of it is my personality. I am an empathetic person. I am a loving person. I care very deeply about the people in my life. I am very on top of my relationships."

The warmth from Robyn's flame emanated from her being. I had witnessed it in person. Now, it flowed through our screens. We sat quietly for a moment. Then, I moved on.

"Any other important life messages to share?"

"I am a very discerning person. I don't let people easily into my life. I think my filter is very sensitive. But the people I let into my life, I trust them very much." She paused, then, continued. "It's not really an issue of trust… It's more that is hard for me to meet people because I'm not convinced that people are really going to be there for me. I learned I had to take care of myself…this is as much from my father as my mother. It's harder for me to be vulnerable. It's hard for me to ask for what I need if it is going to inconvenience someone or put upon them."

Robyn's messages were filled with humility and honesty while remaining rooted in strength. She continued to describe how her messages of an idealized life presented themselves as a young child in the form of *envy* and how for many years she devalued her own life, comparing her life to others whom she believed came from "superior" families. She felt, "There are good people and then there are people like me. There are worthy people and then there are people like me'."

Robyn's words touched my core deeply. I asked, "Did those messages along with their accompanying feelings help propel you to be successful or serve you in positive ways?"

"It served me and it didn't serve me. Yes, it fueled me to go to a top law school…to work in a big law firm, to decide that wasn't for me and get into this other successful career. Yes, I think I was trying to build my life from the outside in, instead of the inside out. But, it also means I made life choices trying to build a façade. For example, my relationship with Jennifer was about wanting to bootstrap myself up into a life that I didn't have as a child, instead of staying with what was actually emotionally real for me. The negative side is that it colors my judgment sometimes about people and choices. I have to work hard to not let my judgment be colored in that way."

Robyn's flame surged, glowing with embers which emanated from her life messages.

"In my relationships, I am very caretaking. I am very attuned to the people in my life who matter to me. I am very nurturing. I am very maternal. I just think I have such a sensitivity to that depravation which allows me to be that way with the people whom I care the most about. It is a joy for me. It is almost like I heal my own unmet needs by giving that way to other people." A momentary flicker interrupted the steady flame. "It's funny...this is what is making me emotional. I can tell you all about my mother beating the shit out of me without shedding a tear. But when I think of how essential it is for me in my life to give and nurture the people who matter to me—that is a defining force in my life."

We both remained quiet, encircled by Robyn's deeply fueled sources of warmth, compassion, and kindness.

The flame within Robyn lowered slightly, but remained pure in intensity. "If there is anything about what I said that makes me sad... it is how it [life message] has influenced my decision not to have kids while keeping intact a very deep ability to love. I think if things had been different and I did have children and I wasn't so blocked in my needs to control my environment, I would probably be a really wonderful mom. I'm not beating myself up about the choices I've made in my life. However, I can also hold the idea that if I had more available to me and didn't have the limitations I have, I would have been an amazing mother. And, that makes me sad."

The flame dimmed slightly, never diminishing its truthful essence.

From Brokenness To Wholeness

Robyn and I took another short break. Conducting our interview via Skype, I found that it felt very natural and comfortable, quite similar to being present for her in person. After refreshing our drinks again, we returned and settled into our rhythm.

Looking over the first question—*When did you first starting thinking about your brokenness in relationship to your mom?*—I was wary of its repetitive inferences. Thus, I reworded it slightly stressing the connection between Robyn's full awareness of her brokenness and its genesis with her mother.

Robyn responded, "You know, I've always blamed my mother." A hearty chuckled filled the space. "She was not right...and maybe I over-attributed the things which were going wrong in my life to her. I, one hundred percent, attributed them to her and her lack of parenting ability and her abusiveness. I always thought, 'This was because of her.'" In her compassionate resolve, Robyn added, "The more sophisticated insights—that took therapy and distance and the mind of an adult."

Utilizing her reference to therapy, I segued into the next question, "Robyn, when did you first consider addressing your injuries, wounds, or brokenness? And what was that like for you?"

"I had some women in my life. I had a couple of teachers. I had a couple of women whose kids I babysat for who were like surrogate moms and who I could really talk to, and also, I could use as female role models for 'what is like to be a woman, and what is it to be a mom, and what is it to be a wife?' I had some very strong identifications with some very strong women in my life. I don't think of them as therapists, but they were definitely serving a very therapeutic purpose for me." Robyn paused, then added, "I first went into therapy when I was sixteen. My father was dying of cancer."

Robyn hesitated briefly. There was a noticeable shift in her tone. Still calm and still reflective, and yet there was in intense privacy to her intonation, "One thing.....another very important part of my story....it might be a little surprising for you to hear so buckle up your seatbelt." I listened and waited. "When I was fifteen I started babysitting for a family and they were an example of one of these perfect families—attractive, loving, a great marriage, a beautiful home, and I was very close to them. And when I was fifteen years old, the husband who was thirty-one at the time came on to me. And....I had an affair with him for two and half years. So, from the time I was fifteen until my mother found out and I went away to college, he was my first love, the first person I hold all of my sexual experiences with. Ummm...and all along I was babysitting these children and *very* close to the wife, very close to the family." Robyn took in a deep breath, "It was really a very horrible....as an adult I'm like.... '*That was really fucked up!*' At the time I didn't think it was. I was trying to get a lot of needs met. My father was dying..." Her honesty surged, "It is hard to talk about my life without that piece of the puzzle."

Wondering if Robyn disclosed her affair in therapy, I asked Robyn about it. She explained how she shared it with a trusted teacher who knew Robyn's mom was not a safe person to turn to. Her teacher kept her confidence with the condition that Robyn would go into therapy, which was the beginning of her work around her mom.

Wanting to clarify Robyn's perspective around the affair, I probed a bit further into the "consensual nature" of it. Robyn described how as a fifteen year old, she felt she was an equal participant in the relationship and how she was in love with him. As an adult, Robyn felt like a strong argument could be made that anytime a thirty-three-year-old man comes on to a fifteen year old girl whose father is dying of cancer, she "wasn't sure how voluntary it was." Robyn concluded, "At the time, I didn't feel like I was being abused at all. Those were some of the best years in my life, honestly. It was an emotional rollercoaster. There were highs of having his love which were pretty significant." She paused, "We didn't actually have sex until about a month away from my seventeenth birthday." Firmly, Robyn added, "But, if any thirty-three-year-old man told me today he had sex with a sixteen year old, I would say, 'There is something wrong with you...you need help.'"

Gently, I expressed my appreciation for the trust Robyn placed in me by sharing such an intimate and inner-personal part of her journey. I joined with her in compassionate understanding of the deep voids created from mother-wounding and of our desperate need to fill them with love from unexpected and often unconventional sources. I waited for the space to clear, giving us both time to honor past pain.

Sensing we had covered the critical pieces to Robyn's story, I transitioned to the questions back around to her therapeutic journey.

Robyn voice reclaimed its familiar resonance, describing her experience with her first male therapist, "We talked about my mother...we talked about my father, and we talked about the affair. I do remember it helping. I remember feeling like almost relieved, that there is another adult who knows about how my father is not going to help me. So, it was a comforting feeling, like there is an adult in my life who is consistent and stable and accountable."

Robyn, utilizing her training and insight in psychotherapy, shared how as an "analyst," her therapy with this doctor was probably not the most affective with a teenager. She described how she needed somebody who was more interactive and more parental. Although she said it was better than nothing, she noted that she wasn't sure if she really started healing anything about her mother in that therapeutic relationship.

When Robyn went away for college, she was able to leave New York, get out of her mother's house, and become independent. She stressed how it really set the environmental conditions for her to start healing, to reclaim herself, and to go out and create a life which was full of the things she did not have from her growing up.

Robyn described how meeting Jennifer was also a turning point for her. "My relationship with Jennifer had a very protective component to it. I wasn't as vulnerable to my mother because I had a partner. We had a life which had boundaries around it. I just didn't need my mother. I needed her less, and less, and less. The final nail in the coffin was when I met Jennifer, which was when I was about twenty-five. I had my *person*. Jennifer was my *person*." Robyn's familiar chuckle surfaced, "It's almost like I redistricted my psyche in a way! My mother was on the outside of that, and I was in therapy working on the trauma of her abuse and her neglect."

Tapping into her recovery work, Robyn spoke further about her therapy.

"I did have a wonderful therapist in my twenties until I was about thirty." Robyn breathed in deeply, then exhaled slowly, "I was never anorexic or bulimic, but I definitely had very disordered eating patterns and exercise patterns, and a very distorted body image and a lot of rules. He helped me with a lot of that. It's a little hard for me to remember, to deconstruct everything after eighteen years of psychotherapy." Robyn reflected, then continued, "It was really where I started to work on my idealization of other people, my devaluation, and my need to have my life look a certain way…to compensate for what I didn't feel what I had inside. I really worked on that with him. He saw me through leaving my job and going back to graduate school. He was also with me through my first few years in my relationship with Jennifer when I was very conflicted about it. I would say he played a critical role of, like, a parent. My dad was dead. My mom was crazy. Dr. B was, I would say, like a holding environment for me. He was that for me. He re-parented me in a way, during those seven years I saw him."

I empathically connected with Robyn's words, commenting on the safety and comfort she felt with Dr. B. Wondering about her choice of gender preference, I asked Robyn if having a male doctor was of importance to her.

She exclaimed, "Yea, I don't like female therapists!" Robyn's laughter burst forth. "I have a very strong transference with them. I have a little bit of bias that males are a little more analytical and consciously or unconsciously less influenced by their emotions, which I actually think is helpful to the therapeutic process. I do better with male therapists!" Robyn's laughter continued and I joined in.

After several years of working with Dr. B, Robyn described how he became very ill and was not able to see patients any longer. Robyn disclosed how she felt "abandoned" by him, just like she felt with her father. Approximately six months later, Robyn began seeing another male analyst, Dr. S. It was with him where she started to unearth the roots with her issues around her mom as well as the dilemma [conflicted feelings] with Jennifer.

Waiting for Robyn to settle in to the next significant piece of her journey, I again kept my pulse on her being.

With a spark in her voice, Robyn giggled, "Dr. S was almost a caricature of a psychoanalyst.... So old school, very Freudian! My joke is like, 'The man rarely said a word for eleven years,' which is not true!" Picturing the scene in my mind, I joined her in uncontrollable laughter. It took several moments to contain ourselves. "He just embodied all conventional and traditional ways of operating as a psychoanalyst—neutrality, self-restraint, not warm and fuzzy."

A serenity descended upon her, much like stillness in the evening sky after the sun has disappeared. Her flame was steady; her source well-fueled. Robyn's voice softened, "And yet, my life changed because of him. So, whatever he did, he did it right. He saved my life. There is no question. I would not have the life I have today if it weren't for him."

Robyn's healing truth floated between us—*my life changed because of him ....he saved my life.* We both honored it, sitting in silence until it felt right to proceed.

Robyn elaborated, "Trying to remember the chronology of my treatment, I think we started with my mother. You start at the surface—my crazy mother. I wish, Holli, I remembered the details but I don't. I feel like in the course of my analysis I made peace. I think about the arc with my relationship with my mother. The early years—my childhood all the way into my twenties—were just about hating her and about individuating and being the opposite of the way she was, almost on principle." Robyn breathed deeply, "But a lot of anger. A lot of intense negative emotions. Dr. S once said to me, 'You are more tethered to the people you hate than the people you love.' I really started to metabolize those feelings with Dr. S, and really worked through that anger and hatred and disappointment and....shame. I feel like I really, really processed that with him and metabolized that with him. And found a way to neutralize it so it wasn't eating at me where I could have the kind of relationship with my mother during the past eight years where I am not reacting. I am not reacting in a negative way. I am not reacting to her. I am deciding what actually makes sense for me, but not from a place of anger or hatred. Just like you would make a decision about any relationship."

I waited, respecting Robyn's truths and allowing their recovering properties to unfold.

Paraphrasing the arc in her healing journey with Dr. S, Robyn added, "At first, the tail was wagging the dog when it came to my relationship to my mom. That was dragging me along and I was almost a prisoner to it. And with Dr. S, the dog started wagging the tail. It was on my own terms. I wasn't a prisoner to my hatred of her anymore. I could see her for what she is and not have my emotions control me as it related to her."

Sensing we had touched upon the critical pieces to her recovery work with Dr. S around her mom, I recalled Robyn mentioning feeling conflicted in her relationship with Jennifer during the same time period. I asked Robyn if and how this intersected with her recovery work. Robyn described how as she healed, tending to her needs and voids, she discovered how Jennifer wasn't meeting her very core emotional needs, not out of neglect but because of what Jennifer was and wasn't capable of. And, Robyn was becoming more acutely aware of her own personal needs and how to care for them.

Before leaving this section of our interview, I asked Robyn if there was anything else to share from her time with Dr. S, or if there were other pieces to her journey from brokenness.

With a marked resurgence in her flame, Robyn added, "Actually last year in the Hoffman Process, I did a weeklong psycho-spiritual retreat in Northern California." Unfamiliar with the Hoffman Process, I asked Robyn for a brief explanation. I learned that it was a weeklong retreat of transformation and development for people who feel stuck in one or more important areas of their life.

Robyn continued describing her experience, "With group dynamics and the spiritual pieces, I just got to access my compassion and my empathy for her [mom] which is different than just being neutral, right? I haven't walked around with a lot of compassion or a lot of feeling like, '*She actually did the best she could.*' I just made peace with it and that we [my mom and I] will agree to disagree." Robyn's voice lowered, "But it was actually in the Hoffman Process where I got a picture of the limited resources she had, and she gave a hundred percent of that to my sister and me." And then, her more heightened tone returned, "But, one hundred percent of zero is still zero....right?" She paused, then continued, "But that was a new insight for me. It opened up some compassion and some spaciousness that did not exist before. I do look at Hoffman as my last milestone of healing for my mother."

Moved by connotations and implications of the word *milestone*, I asked Robyn to explain further.

"I think it's all an ongoing journey. There may be something else. I don't know what is going to happen when my mother dies. There is a part of me that thinks that it will not even register emotionally for me because in my mind she died soooo many years ago. The thing that one does when one loses a mother, I have done that already. And so, there is a part of me that believes when she dies it will be a psychologically insignificant event for me. But who knows? I could be very wrong about that."

Robyn's words resonated deeply within me. Her feelings mirrored many of mine, as I had pondered very similar thoughts and emotions. Recentering myself, I moved into the spiritual piece of the Hoffman Process and asked, "Robyn, would you term any of what you experienced during the retreat around the principle or practice of forgiveness?"

Without hesitation, Robyn confirmed, "Yes, that was something that came out of Hoffman for me. And there is a difference between making peace with something and a sort of resignation to a set of circumstances. I would say Hoffman gave me the first sets of actual forgiveness for her." Her voice remained steady, but softened, "It doesn't change any choice I make today to the kind of relationship I have with her, but it is just another level of healing and of peace about the whole thing."

Because of my work in betrayal recovering of any kind, and because of my own interpretations and connotations around the word *forgiveness*, I wanted to explore it further with Robyn. I was curious to the meanings it held for her and its implications with her mother. "Robyn, what does forgiveness mean to you?"

Her voice was full, brimming with warmth, "For me, it means having real empathy and compassion. Allowing myself to let those emotions figure into the mix when I think about my mother. It's not saying something to her; it's not doing something differently. It's not trying to have any closer of a relationship. It's allowing me to think about her with more empathy and compassion. It's more humanizing. That is what forgiveness means to me."

I felt Robyn tapping once again into the powerful source within her. Wondering what else she was wanting to share, my closing question to this section was very open, "Is there anything else which has or continues to be a part of your journey to wholeness?"

Her flame surged and remained constant. "This goes back to what I was saying earlier. My friendships have taken on the emotional significance of a family." Healing embers emanated in her and through her. "I don't have a family. I have my sister and I would cut my limbs off for her. But I don't have a family. I don't have a mother. I don't have a father. I don't have children. I don't have a spouse. I do not have a family. So, my friends are truly my family. And, what you get from your family, I get that from my friendships. I give that to them and I get it from them. And that is part of my wholeness, one hundred percent."

Reflecting upon Robyn's words and her journey, I recalled how painful particles of past brokenness had been dislodged and discarded. Then, over time and with intensive therapy, how those empty spaces had been replenished with new sources of wellness purposely created and mindfully crafted to fuel her unique being. My eyes returned to the warm, nurturing flame before me, wondering where this daughter's wholeness would lead her next.

Wholeness To ....

Checking in with Robyn, I found she felt ready to move into our last section without another break. I proceeded with the first question.

"Robyn, where are you today in your relationship with your mom?"

Robyn's energy remained strong, "So, the way I think about my relationship with my mother is, 'I don't have a mother.' I have this mental patient that I have some custodial responsibility for." Robyn's familiar laughter lightened the space and lingered for a moment. I found myself joining in, but felt a sadness inside. Robyn's voice softened, reflecting a mixture of feelings, "It's hilarious and heartbreaking." She continued, "Because I do not have a mother. I have this woman who I know gave birth to me. I know raised me, but in no sense of the word as we understand it as between a forty-four year-old-woman and a seventy-one-year-old-mother....I do not have a mother." More resolutely, Robyn added, "I have somebody in my life who I want out of my life. I do feel some sort of custodial responsibilities for her and ummm... It is on my terms. I do what I can. The best way to say it is, 'I know she did the best she could....and I am doing the best I can do.' And, it is not out of anger; it's not out of revenge. I don't want to hurt her. I'm just doing what makes the most sense for me because I have to put myself and my own needs first. And, I don't feel conflicted about that, at all."

I waited. I listened.

"So, we talk on the phone. She's very low functioning. She's very ill. She has many lifestyle induced problems: obesity, emphysema, diabetes—all could have been avoided if she has taken better care of her physical and emotional self." Robyn paused, and added, "Sometimes she is very good on the phone and actually very engaged. There are these moments of sanity with her where she is a normal human being, but most of it is just listening to her bemoaning her lot in life. And, I tell her what is going on in my life," Robyn's voice tapered off a bit, but remained steady.

"I don't see her very much. She lives about a two-and-one-half-hour drive, on a good day, from Boston. So, I try to keep it to about once a year. And if I never had to see her, I would be okay with that just because it is so painful for both of us. She just sits there and drools like sort of a decompensated mental patient and I try to have a conversation with her. She is very anxious around me. I am very anxious. We don't enjoy being together." Robyn further described how her mother no longer calls her, ranting about their lack of contact or threatening to take Robyn out of her will. Robyn added, "My mother has learned that kind of behavior will drive me further away."

Sensing the finality of Robyn's response, I moved into a related question. "How do you feel about all of that?"

The flame held steady, its source fueled by integrity. "I feel completely at peace. I don't want any more. I don't need to have any less. It's fine."

Although I felt we had touched upon the next question to some degree earlier in our interview, because of its importance, I revisited it, "Robyn, today...where are you with yourself? How do you feel about yourself and why?"

Once again, the glow from within Robyn filled the space between us. "I feel like ......I never thought I could live with this feeling of joy and contentment and delight that I have the life I have built for myself. It took me twenty years to heal and to be able to have a relationship with myself that I have and have an experience of my life which feels so joyful and so peaceful....and that is intrinsic." Robyn took in a deep breath, refueling her source and its accompanying truths, "It took me forty-two years to realize that happiness cannot be given and it cannot be taken. It comes from inside and it can be found in the most mundane of moments. And that's how I live every day."

The flame dimmed slightly, but held its intensity. "Holli, you did not know me back then, so you do not know the contrast to how I lived the first forty years of my life where happiness and self-worth and validity was like chasing a cloud. It was external to me. I was just trying to chase it and then every time you get underneath a cloud, it moves out in front of you. It is elusive and that's how I lived all my life....certainly twenty years of my adulthood." The flame opened up, truths flowing out. "So, I've never been happier. I've never been more content. I've never been more at peace with who I am. I've never enjoyed the minute by minute unfolding of my life as I do, and I never ever had as much to give as I do now."

Touched by Robyn's words, I reflected, "It's amazing how that works."

A humble tenderness emanated from Robyn and yet a powerful surge came from within her, "I can't even contain it."

Instantly, I recalled the times I was in Robyn's presence. When she entered into a room, it was like the lighting of a candle. Her flame brought in light and love, and its essence filled the space with a sense of safety and positive regard. And for those of us around her who are drawn to her, it is her unconditional source which we want to invite into our lives as well.

Returning my focus to our interview, a quietness remained between us. I waited a few moments and moved to the next question. And, although many of Robyn's life messages were inferred in her prior response, I asked her to speak to those more fully.

Her voice remained soft but steady, "Probably the biggest message I live by is 'The gift is in the giving,' whether it is in a friendship or kindness to a stranger. If nobody ever says anything about me other than I was kind to everyone I met, I would have lived a very successful life. So that is a defining value and human virtue." Her tone unwavering, but her pace slowing, she added, "And the rewards in that for me..." Robyn paused and took in a breath, "it brings tears to my eyes sometimes because you don't expect it. But, then there is something that comes back to you...comes back to me." Her voice strengthened, but held its gentleness, "A big life message for me is to lead with kindness. Let that be the first way I am experienced by another person. And to be non-discriminatory about it and be as kind to people who have nothing to offer me as I am to people who are very close to me."

Absorbing the authenticity and rarity of Robyn's life message, I gave us both time to relish its implications and applications.

Robyn reflected and added, "I think there is a very important life message for me—'It is okay to be so independent, self-reliant, resourceful, and self-directed, and I have to compliment that with my vulnerability and my soft side. I'm not sure if that is a message, but it is definitely a theme for me. I know I am really working on that."

She paused and shared another life message, "Contentment, happiness, and joy cannot be given and they cannot be taken away. That was an epiphany for me. It just changes everything for me. We get to choose the relationship and the interpretation we have to the events which unfold." From the parable *The Old Man and The White Horse*, Robyn disclosed a lesson which has held importance for her, "It's a story where there is this idea that something is neither a blessing nor a curse. It just is. And then life unfolds and we get to interpret events in our lives in whatever way we choose." Her voice strengthened, "How we show up in the face of them, that *is* where the real answers are. That's a very important life message for me."

The flame across from me remained erect and steady. I thought about betrayal and how so many individuals tether themselves to their betrayers or others, waiting for them to make it right. Robyn's path to wholeness had taught her how to turn inward, choosing her responses purposefully and *righting herself* in the process.

I moved into our next question, wondering how Robyn saw her wellness journey unfolding, "As you continue to work on your wholeness, what areas are important to you?"

With precision, Robyn stated, "I need to see my brokenness as actually a part of my wholeness. Right?" Her laughter gushed forth and then subsided. "I really need to see my vulnerable, needy, dependent, fragile side of myself as part of my wholeness...as a part of me to be celebrated and brought forth, particularly in my intimate relationships with men."

Visualizing the polished broken pieces sparkling within Robyn's widening circle of wholeness revealed an empowering, self-affirming, healing perspective on Robyn's inner source and inner strength. I waited and she continued.

"The lesson I am learning is that I think about my independence as my biggest selling point. But the truth is...it is not. It's nice, but it is not what forges strong connections between people, friendships, romantic relationships, or even my clients. It is the vulnerability, the humanizing behaviors which create intimacy in relationships."

Robyn paused for a moment, and disclosed, "I'd like to find a life partner more than anything. All the love I can give to my friends, I can give that one hundred-fold to a partner. I've got everything else in my life I could possibly imagine needing or wanting, and this is the only thing that continues to elude me. So, that is what I am really trying to work on."

Because we were addressing life messages and had covered much of what was being asked in the next question, I reworded it just slightly to complement our conversation. "From your betrayal experiences with your mom, are there any other life lessons which have served you well and continue to do so?"

Robyn eagerly explained, "So, I don't think I mentioned it but it is an important one. I don't think my mother—and I know some of it was not her choice, but I think she could have altered the course of her life had she gotten better help." As Robyn qualified her thought, her voice strengthened, "I want to bracket the fact that she didn't have the money to get better help, but a big lesson for me is, 'You cannot allow your childhood to determine your fate.'" The flame surged again, signaling its strength. This time, however, its message revealed the core of its truth. "Ultimately, *the power rests completely within me* to have the life I want to have. And, that is a *very* important life lesson. In a weird way, I feel like my mother was, unfortunately, a prisoner of her childhood her whole life. And the lesson is, it does not have to be that way."

As I listened intently to Robyn's life lesson, I was struck by her words—"*The power rests completely within me.*" For as long as I had known her, I wondered about her source—her power which supplied and sustained the flame within her. By unearthing, harnessing, and honoring her truths, Robyn chose not only to douse the burning embers of past childhood pain, but she crafted a circle of wellness from which her healing first sparked. And through years of deliberate mindful tending, her truths solidified and strengthened, fueling a purposeful path *From Brokenness To Wholeness.*

As we prepared to conclude our interview, I moved into our final questions, "Robyn, where do you wish to go from here? What is beyond wholeness for you?"

Robyn acknowledged, "I think it is too late for me to have children." Her voice remained tender, "However, I think it would be wonderful to find a man who has kids who are older and to be able to love them and to mother them in a way that gives me an outlet for all those feelings, but doesn't take too much from me." She giggled and added, "Yes, I am hoping I wind up with a man who has kids...not young kids! But college-age kids who are just beginning their lives and who will go on to have kids. I'm excited about that. I think I could more than handle that. I have a reservoir of maternal love that I could bestow on stepchildren and step grandchildren at some point in my life."

Affirming her capacity to give, I reflected her thinking. I paused and waited.

"I feel like I am in a wonderful place in my life. I'd like to meet some-body, and I'm trying to ask myself all the right questions about my role in that. My life has been sort of euphoric, not in an outside way, but in a way that I don't have to tell anyone about it." The flame skipped, just for a second, then returned, "The euphoria I live with on a daily basis, I never ever imagined one could enjoy one's life as much as I have and so....I don't know what is beyond that...."

A few tears surfaced, revealing *their* truths. Robyn gently wiped them away. As I observed the candle of kindness glow unceasingly in this remarkable daughter, I couldn't help but wonder who else in Robyn's journey would be so graciously welcomed into her circle of light and love and so generously warmed by its flame.

Follow-up Reflection

On an extremely warm June mid-afternoon, I organized my notes and questions in anticipation of my Skype follow-up interview with Robyn. Because both our schedules were quite busy, a little over three weeks have passed since our intensive interview. As I discovered with the other daughters, I really looked forward to speaking with Robyn. Although I was mindful of my role in this interviewing process—maintaining an objective perspective as interviewer—I found that it was impossible to feel the same toward each daughter as I did before our four-hour interview. I have also discovered that even though this process was similar to that of a therapist, where professional distance (boundaries) and healthy detachment were an integral part of the ongoing therapeutic relationship, I felt a tremendous bond form with each of the daughters. And so, I was both excited to speak with Robyn, and yet, I was sad our time together was coming to a close. I held the rough draft of Robyn's narrative in my hands and glanced down at her name with her tag line below it—*The Power Rests Completely Within Me*. While composing each daughter's narrative through the transcription of their interviews, I was mindful every *word of the way*, honoring their voices and their truths in the process. As I have done with the other daughters, I prepared to share a section of Robyn's narrative with her. My heart felt full.

Within moments, the video call came through and once again, Robyn and I joined together in this unique experience, connecting as though our conversation was moving from one stream smoothly into another. After a few minutes of casual chit-chat, I explained to Robyn that I would be checking in with her about her post-interview feelings as well as her current feelings about our process. I also explained how our time would involve clarifying and/or amending any parts of her narrative, if she so chose to do so. And we would conclude with me reading the last section of her narrative—*Wholeness To.* With her usual vibrancy, Robyn awaited my first question.

"Robyn, how did you feel after our interview?"

"Ummmm....I was definitely exhausted after. It was very intense. I mean therapy is about an hour. So to be talking about that stuff for three or four hours, it was very intense. I blocked off the whole day. I wasn't working the rest of the day. I went afterwards and had a really nice lunch outside and took my dog, and, I felt fine." She paused and stressed, "But it was definitely intense."

Because Robyn used the word "intense" several times, I was curious if anything else came up for her, "Did any new feelings or thinking surface? Did something old come up which surprised you? Anything else?"

Pensively, Robyn responded, "Ummmm....no, not really. Not really. It was just a reminder of...." She paused and continued, "I think there is a way that I just normalized the situation with my mother because what choice do I have, right? And, talking about or going back to a time when things were arguably still embryonic and sort of thinking about all the things that shaped the relationship that we have today....it is just a disappointment. And, it is easy in my day-to-day life—out of sight, out of mind. And I don't really deal with her. Yeah, talking about it was like...not a pleasant stroll down memory lane." Robyn chuckled softly and added, "But, it was a good thing to do also."

Robyn described in more detail how she took the remainder of the day to practice self-care and to surround herself with friends. The tenderness in her voice revealed their importance to her, "That night I had dinner with friends and their little girl who I am very close to. I usually do gymnastics with her...." Robyn's lovely laughter filled the space, then subsided, "I got to hang out with her. It was very sweet." As Robyn's voice surged with its customary strength, she concluded, "It is like a good reminder that you are not just stuck with the family you are born into."

I moved into the next question. "How are you feeling today?"

The familiar flame I remembered returned. "I've been feeling really good, actually." Recovering from a foot injury, Robyn described, "Physically, I was able to start some weight lifting the past couple of days. So, that is good. And emotionally, I feel fine. I really do."

Matching her pace, I moved right into our closing questions, "Can you think of anything you would like to add, change, or amend in your narrative?"

Robyn responded, "I would think, and I can only tell you from my own experience, that the benefit of doing an interview with somebody like me who has put all of this under the microscope already is like, I've got it pretty well put together." Her voice remaining strong, she added, "Whereas I can imagine if you are asking people these questions and it is their first time even thinking about it, it is hard to think about it and express it coherently in the same time." Robyn's laugh gushed forth. "No, I feel like you got the whole story!" We chuckled together.

Thinking about Robyn's words "I've got it pretty well put together," my mind reflected back to the narratives of former victims of all kinds of betrayal. Many times, survivors of betrayal asked me how they would know when their work was done or when their healing from betrayal took hold. And I often replied, "Our work never really ends. We are always refining ourselves. However, when we have betrayal recovering tools under our belts, we can embrace our healing more readily and effectively when we are triggered or something arises. At the same time, I believe we are able to have a clear sense of when our healing from betrayal takes hold because we no longer are retelling our betrayal narratives or allowing them to define us. Instead, we become refined by our experiences." As I thought about the evenness and steadiness of Robyn's voice and of the consistency and continuity of her wholeness narrative, I was reminded of the final chapter in *Breaking Through Betrayal*—"Reframe and Refine." After committing completely to her recovering work and integrating newly adopted healthy ways of being into her circle of wholeness, Robyn not only reframed her betrayal by her mother as "a disappointment" but she ceased allowing it to "define" her. Instead, Robyn has continued to "refine" her life—honing interests, cultivating opportunities, and embracing nurturing relationships in order to become a more energized, effective, and elegant being. No wonder her flame burns eternal.

As we moved into our final question, I reworded it just slightly to suit our interview, "Robyn, is there anything else you would like to share, either about your narrative or about this process?"

Robyn paused. Her voice was tender, "Nothing really about the narrative. Ummm... the process. It makes me feel closer to you...so it was very....it was like a secondary benefit to all of this." As Robyn continued, a glow filled the space between us. Her warmth radiated through her words. "First of all, I told you things which I don't tell everybody...and I just felt very 'held' by you. So, thank you very much for that," her voice tapered off, but held its core of kindness. "Thank you...this was a beautiful gift."

I swallowed and gave myself a moment. I took in a deep breath and responded, "Robyn, thank you for sharing that. It was paramount to me that I make this process safe for the daughters." I paused and added, "I, too, know how you feel about a closer connection. I'm not sure how anyone could do something like this and not experience a shift in emotions." Both of us sat quietly for a few moments, just cherishing the connection.

When I sensed we were both ready to move forward, I spent several minutes checking in on a few questions of clarification on Robyn's narrative. Then, taking in a couple more deep breaths, I composed myself as I got ready to share Robyn's last section—*Wholeness To* .... Although the narrative was still in rough draft form, it was critically important to me that it be read with the levels of integrity and authenticity in which her words were first delivered to me. Before beginning, I explained to Robyn how her tag line—*The Power Rests Completely Within Me*—was chosen and why the metaphor of *the flame* was created to represent her.

Robyn relaxed into her sofa and I began. Although I had read and reread Robyn's narrative many times—editing, rewording, rephrasing— as I read it aloud seeing Robyn across the screen, the words flowed like clear plumes of purpose and promise, filling the space and forming wholeness messages around us. The more I read, the more they accumulated and hovered over us, a testament to their legitimacy and their longevity. As I came to end of Robyn's narrative, her white billowy truths remained steady and strong, suspended and supported by its flame. As I looked up, the candle before me was glowing. One sparkling crystal plume signaled its source ~

The Power Rests Completely Within Me

5   "I Have More Work To Do On This Topic" – Kiersten

Reflection

Summer 2016 was a strange one. As with most of the country, our weather was extremely moody and unsettled. Although we typically have monsoons plummet our mountainous terrain during the months of June and July, the thunderous angry skies shouted at us throughout the month of August and pounded us with mothball-sized hail. My unintended ten-week break from "The Daughters Project" at first brought with it feelings of an unsettled nature. I felt strangely anxious about who the next daughter might be. And yet, I sensed I needed to give myself permission to relax and to indulge in a few planned pleasures of summer: a visit from family members, a trip to Utah spending time with a dear friend, and an opportunity to entertain a mix of close friends escaping the trappings of their busy lives.

As the summer unfolded, a familiar calmness settled back in and I once again reminded myself to trust in this extraordinary process. As breaks from other writings or work presented themselves, I revisited my slightly torn but treasured two-year-old folder containing my "Daughters' Project" notes. In it was a list of names of daughters with whom I had shared, to varying degrees, the ideas behind "The Daughters Project." I had made notations of those who expressed interest along with their contact information. Within the year since I had begun my investigation, a few daughters' names were given to me by trusted females who knew of "The Daughters Project" because they felt these daughters might be a good fit. I placed their names on my list. In my folder were also the names of several therapists of diverse backgrounds whom I knew from different projects we were connected with or worked on together. It was my hope that through these contacts I would be able to include daughters of differing races and ethnicities.

Beginning in the order of my list of names, I began making initial contacts to the daughters and to a few therapists. In reaching out in a sort of cold call, I remained extremely sensitive to the tone and posture of my introductory email or phone call. While positioning myself in a professional manner, I also wanted to approach each potential daughter or conduit to a daughter in a gentle and caring voice. Where possible, I attached the "Letter of Invitation" to "The Daughters Project" to provide more information. I was also very mindful of the spacing between my initial contacts, concerned I may receive more responses than I was able to handle or tend to in a timely way.

June passed. Then July. I continued to send out invitations. Aside from one tentative response, no others came in. In mid-August, I revisited my list of daughters' names again. As my eyes focused in on the next name, Kiersten, a warmth filled my spirit and an ease settled in. We had known each other for a few years, mostly professionally but we had developed a personal connection as well. Eagerly, I reached out to Kiersten who responded enthusiastically, and we began the process in late August. However, after our pre-interview conference and shortly before our scheduled four-hour interview, Kiersten withdrew from the study. Reading Kiersten's words of explanation reminded me of the complexities of each daughter's journey is and how brave it was of her to acknowledge areas which were still unhealed or recently reinjured.

> "Holli, your project has been on my mind as I talked with my mom a couple of times last week and her hostile behavior and angry tone with me is starting to affect me again. Perhaps it's due to thinking about a lifelong of betrayal and with that said, when I get to your notes about how I have journeyed *From Brokenness To Wholeness*, I can't answer without breaking down. I don't feel whole and with that said, I don't think my story will be of benefit for your project. There are times I feel as if I've conquered the pain, the betrayal, and all the myriad of emotions; however, as of late, I'm struggling to get my sense of it again.
>
> It goes without saying that I have more work to do on this topic about breaking the cord and the bonds. I'm sorry to say that I have decided that going through four hours of this pain will not be of benefit to me, or to your project. I hope you understand as I truly did want to be one of your 'daughters', but I have yet to reach the pinnacle of wholeness when it comes to the damage done at such a deep level."

Because I felt Kiersten had much to offer "The Daughters Project," I noticed a significant level of sadness around her departure. However, as

I collected my notes, placed them in Kiersten's folder, and then locked them in a secure place, that sadness was immediately replaced with unconditional regard and immeasurable respect for Kiersten. By acknowledging her level of pain and the need for more work around the betrayal wounding from her mom, Kiersten courageously put her wellness first. She chose to take care of herself. She chose to continue her journey toward wholeness.

Kiersten was exactly where she needed to be.

6 "I am Vulnerable ~ I am Enough" – Alexandra

Reflection

While moving through the extensive interviewing process for each daughter and adhering to the protocol of "The Daughters Project," I felt the intensity of being heavily invested in and attached to each daughter's experience. As a result, I discovered how very important it was to give myself time for additional reflection. And, of course, I was mindful of the enormous responsibility with which I was entrusted—honoring each daughter's voice and respecting her truths. Thus, after giving myself a period of rest, by the end of October 2016, I felt renewed and re-energized, more than ready to resume "The Daughters Project."

Perusing the names of daughters listed within my well-worn manila folder, I noticed I had come to the end of possible participants. I knew this day would arrive and I was prepared. Two years after moving to Arizona, I joined several service and professional organizations. It was an opportunity for me to meet other individuals in the health care field and also connect with like-minded women through their community advocacy. Through a select number of closed online forums, I sent out "The Daughters Project" Letter of Invitation to the members with a request seeking participants for the qualitative study. My hope was that with the number of members along with their contacts, I might find one or two interested participants.

To my pleasant surprise, within a couple of days I received a response. Her name—Alexandra. Although I did not know Alexandra personally, I knew she was an active member in one of the communities to which I belonged. In addition, in the early spring of 2016 I sent out a request through one of the online forums asking for reviewers of my newly published 2nd Edition of *Breaking Through Betrayal*. Alexandra generously offered to review it. Our only contact at that time consisted of a short in-person exchange and several email messages regarding the review. What I learned about Alexandra from that brief encounter was that she was incredibly professional, completing the review with quality and integrity and in a timely manner. And presently, once again, around the topic of betrayal, Alexandra's path would intersect with mine.

As part of the Informed Consent, I asked prospective participants to submit a brief biographical sketch. At the same time, they were free to keep private any items which breached their anonymity. Within a couple of days, I received Alexandra's. As I read through her background, a feeling of calm and contentment swept through my being confirming how trusting in this process was vital. Allowing it to lead me was paramount. Alexandra's presence and portrait would bring an added layer of diversity to "The Daughters Project." I felt my excitement build as the process began to unfold.

Setting...

With Thanksgiving holiday plans nestled into our respective calendars, Alexandra and I set our time for our pre-interview conference for the end of November. On a chilly afternoon following an early dusting of snow, I reviewed Alexandra's biographical information before placing my call to her.

Alexandra is in her late thirties. She is Latina, born in Columbia. She is of Columbian descent; her mother is Columbian and her father is Caucasian, Euro-American. Identifying as bicultural or multicultural, Alexandra's second language is English and she is fluent in Spanish. Alexandra is a heterosexual female and is married to a heterosexual male. Although she has no specific religious identification, she "engages in daily spiritual practices such as meditation, mindfulness and spiritual readings."

Although I knew of Alexandra's professional career as a therapist, I was not aware of her levels of education and her status as a clinical psychologist. She holds two master's degrees—Master of Science in Leadership and Management and Master of Arts in Clinical Psychology. In addition, Alexandra has a doctorate degree in clinical-community psychology (PsyD) with a specialization in pediatric psychology. Alexandra's own words added meaning and depth to her accomplishments and provided an opening into her compassionate character, "I enjoy working in the helping profession, especially with children and adolescents and would like to continue in this field, perhaps helping create an Intensive Outpatient Program (IOP) for adolescents who are struggling with significant mental health issues."

Reading over her words, I was, as I have been with the other daughters, humbled by the degree of Alexandra's accomplishment and authenticity. Achieving so much, both personally and professionally at such a relatively early stage in life, I found indeed remarkable. While ordering my paperwork and double-checking my recorders, my eyes reviewed Alexandra's explanation as to why she would like to participate in "The Daughters Project."

> "My desire to participate in this study is both personal and professional as I strongly recognize the clinical value of the research topic you are investigating. I have spent the last decade delving in both formal and informal self-exploration and healing, [with] much of my therapeutic work stemming from childhood issues, specifically my interaction with my mother. I feel that my self-work has helped me live a more engaged, authentic and content life than I otherwise would have if I had not chosen to understand and heal through my childhood attachment trauma.
>
> Additionally, as a fellow researcher, I appreciate the benefits of qualitative research in understanding one's lived experience and acknowledge it is ideal for 'digging deep' with people to expose thoughts, actions, opinions, and possible connections that might otherwise not be articulated using a quantitative method. I feel truly honored and excited to be given the opportunity to participate in this important topic!"

My stomach started to tingle a bit, intrigued by this daughter and all she had to offer. I excitedly placed the call. Once the phone rang, a calm settled in. It was important to me that each daughter felt safe and that each daughter felt warmly welcomed into this process.

Within the first few words, Alexandra and I connected comfortably and naturally. After checking in briefly on holiday events and activities, we transitioned into our pre-interview questions. Clarifying a few issues around confidentiality, we then moved into a question which I have asked of each daughter—one which is referenced in our lengthy interview and one which is foundational to our study.

"Alexandra, when you think about the word *betrayal*, what thoughts, perceptions, beliefs, or connotations come to mind?"

Alexandra responded resolutely, "When I think of *betrayal* specifically in my own life, I think of my own kind of personal safety...my emotional safety being compromised. I think of the foundation of feeling that things are cyclical and safe and then they are all kinda turned upside down." Alexandra paused briefly and added, "Being exposed or vulnerable, but not in a healthy way, in a really awful way or in an unsafe way. That is what I think about when I think of *betrayal*."

I waited for a moment to see if Alexandra wanted to add anything. Her connotations of betrayal brought a heaviness into the space. I let it lift, giving us both time before moving ahead.

"Alexandra, do you have any questions or concerns or anything else you are feeling as you think about this process?"

With a lightness in her voice, her words danced, "I am just really excited and I am honored that you allowed me to me to participate...I am like, 'Oh my gosh how fortunate...' I am so excited and plus I can tell by just the few interactions that we have had that you have just a wonderful way of interacting with people and making people feel calm and supported. Right away when you first started speaking, okay, I feel good...all these things about participating in qualitative research. I feel open and excited!"

We both chuckled. And then, I added, "Thank you, Alexandra, for sharing that. I believe that this is a difficult topic and a tender one. I think it is extraordinary that daughters are willing to step forward and talk about this and share their narratives." As I had with the other daughters, I spoke briefly to Alexandra about the enormous responsibility I carried with me through this process—to care for and to hold each daughter's truths, voice, and narrative in the highest regard."

I paused. I revisited the same question, making sure we covered any additional questions or concerns.

With a serious tone, Alexandra commented, "No....no concerns. It is absolutely a tender subject but it is no longer a raw subject for me because I have done so much work. I don't feel...'Oh my gosh...can I deal with talking about this?' It's kinda like exciting for me because of look how far I have come to be able to talk about this because there was a long time I was not able to emotionally.... I did not have the emotional strength and fortitude to talk about it." And then, Alexandra's voice lifted again, "It's exciting!"

We both chuckled softly. As we set our time for the four-hour interview, my mind returned to the steady strength in this daughter's voice. I was filled with heightened anticipation about exploring and discovering how it came to be.

Beginning...

Just one week has passed since our pre-interview conference. The sun finally made an appearance, brightly casting its much-needed warm rays onto a frosty morning. During the last hour or so, I neatly organized my materials on my dining room table, tidied up the living room, turned on the gas fireplace, and set up an assortment of teas and an array of pastries for Alexandra and me. Because we live in the same area, we have decided to conduct our interview in my home. Thus, it was my intent to make the environment as warm and inviting as possible. I glanced over at the clock—8:45 am. I quickly checked my recorders one last time and arranged my notes for the fourth or fifth time!

I smiled as I looked down at my pre-interview notes focusing in on Alexandra's name. It is a name which she has chosen for "The Daughters Project," one which held personal meaning for her. The rhythm of its pronunciation seemed to represent Alexandra so well— fluid, serene, and purposeful. A knock at the door interrupted my momentary reflection. As I scurried downstairs to welcome her, the familiar excitement of interviewing another daughter started to build. Opening the door, I was greeted by Alexandra's gentle presence. I invited her in and we proceeded upstairs where the warmer air welcomed us.

We chatted briefly about the chilly December air, filling our teacups to the brim before moving into the dining room. Alexandra and I settled into our respective chairs next to the flickering flames of the fireplace. Making sure she felt comfortable, I briefly checked with Alexandra about the four-hour process ahead of us. She nestled herself into her chair, smiled, and indicated she was more than ready. I moved into our first question.

"Alexandra, as we begin our time together, I think this is such an important question. When you refer to your mom, do you use that noun or is there another word?"

"Sure….I remember when I was reviewing your questions, I thought that was interesting. Yea, I refer to her as *mom*. And I think there was a time when I didn't call her by her name. I just didn't talk about her for years."

Wanting to follow up further, I asked, "Did you ever use another word like 'mother' or was there another word in your primary language that you used?"

Softly, Alexandra added, "When I was younger I used 'mommy.' And then, ummm… No, I just referred to her as 'mom'."

"How does it feel to talk about your mom today and how has that changed over time? Is it different today than five years ago?"

Without pause, she explained, "Talking about her is still a little bit uncomfortable for me. But it doesn't elicit the same pain it used to. So I would say even five years ago it was a little more uncomfortable. It would be very hard for me to talk about her without having some sort of pain....emotional pain."

I probed a bit more. A question came to mind I had not previously asked of other daughters. I hesitated for a moment, then proceeded, "In a sort of related question, when you would hear other daughters talking about their mothers in a very loving way or affectionately, was there anything that came up for you?"

Alexandra's stream of words flowed, "When I was younger in high school and people would talk about their moms when they would go shopping for prom or things like that...I guess normal daughter stuff, I would be very envious. And then when I was a young adult, I would seek out mother-like figures—an aunt, my uncle's longtime girlfriend, and just other friends' parents and even my mother-in-law—and sometimes I realized it was almost inappropriate because I was trying to get this motherly need met."

Alexandra took in a deep breath. She elaborated, "I think, being a mom now, that's been healing because I get to nurture and have some of the aspect that I didn't have, and I am also close to my nieces and nephews. As so that is very healing... That is going to make me tearful already," Alexandra's eyes watered and her voice quivered slightly. "Even though I didn't get those experiences in my home...and I still wish I could. And, I accept that is not ever going to happen." She dabbed her eyes with a tissue and quietly added, "It's still uncomfortable, but I am much more in a place of acceptance versus anger."

Alexandra's words carried both a heaviness and a lightness. I was reminded of how the word 'mom'—simple and succinct, yet powerful and poignant—can evoke a quake of emotions and feelings. I gave them time to linger between us, honoring their respective truths.

After a few moments, I gently questioned Alexandra about being a mom, "From your bio, I didn't know that you were a mom. I'm wondering if that is something you want to share, or is that something you wish to leave out of your narrative?"

Excitedly, she responded, "No...no....Oh yes.... It has been instrumental in my own healing." Joyfully, she added, "I have two children. My first one is a child I adopted and I became her legal guardian when my husband and I got married. She was three when my husband and I started dating... then five...and so she has her own issues from her mother leaving when she was a child. And she has been a very challenging child to raise." Alexandra's voice quieted again, "And so my own mom issues have been activated...it has caused me...it has forced me—and I am grateful although it was been tremendously painful—to work on my own mother issues. Having a daughter and not raising her since birth and then just so much of my own pain was activated through her." Alexandra breathed more easily and sighed, "It is very different from my relationship with my son who...we're kindred spirits....the same person." A light laughter sprinkled between us. "So much fun together. So easy to get along with." Returning to a more somber tone, Alexandra added, "So my daughter—she is a teenager—has caused me to address my own mother issues....for the last ten years or so."

Alexandra described in more detail how her daughter was instrumental in her healing process. Alexandra explained how being a mom pushed her to look at milestones and transitions during her own growing-up years when her mother was not there for her. Alexandra disclosed what she would learn years later in therapy, "I was trying to get my mom needs met through my daughter."

Not wanting to breach any issues of confidentiality, I thanked Alexandra for sharing about her children and confirmed their inclusion within her narrative. She reiterated their importance in her life and to her healing journey. We moved to our next question.

"In our pre-interview, we talked about the word *betrayal* and its connotations for you. How does the word *betrayal* feel for you today, and how does it feel to use it in referencing your mom today in this study?"

Alexandra's voice was intense, "It's a word which really solidifies the relationship. She wasn't able to show up as a mom for whatever reasons. And she just...." Alexandra breathed in deeply, "...she just ended up injuring us so badly, that the worst thing that could ever happen is she lost her ability to have us in her life. And so, for the ones where you are supposed to feel safe, supposed to be predictable, and [they] are supposed to be consistent...for her she was incredibly unsafe and hurtful and causing a lot of harm." Alexandra's voice softened but remained strong. "So the opposite of what a parent is supposed to be... and not to the level she inflicted on me and my siblings."

Alexandra's explanation of betrayal in connection to her mom, "It's a word which really solidifies the relationship", brought with it an all-encompassing level of depth and breadth. It felt like a formidable fence surrounding a vast open field, defining its past existence but not determining its present reality. As familiar as I was with the many connotations of betrayal and their respective injuries and injustices, I was further moved by Alexandra's choice of words. Wondering if there might be more she wanted to share, I segued into a related question.

"Alexandra, when you read the Letter of Invitation for "The Daughters Project" with the broad definitions of betrayal, were there any other connotations to the word betrayal which connected with you or any other thoughts around betrayal?"

Confidently, Alexandra spoke, "Not so much the word betrayal, but the idea that you can move through this process and not necessarily be stunted...and that you were looking at how people can show up...and be whole! So that is what drew me... 'Oh yeah...I love it!'" Her soft laughter lightened the space between us. She continued, "What is going on that some people can move through these situations and some people are stuck...that these experiences have negatively impacted your life so much, that you can't have a full life, you can't have a whole life. So I guess that is more what struck me than the word betrayal!"

Basking in Alexandra's enthusiasm, I was taken aback by the contrast of "betrayal solidifying her relationship with her mom" in comparison with the wide-open field of wholeness displayed before me. What was in it? How did come to be? The exploration continued.

Background...

After checking my recorders, Alexandra and I transitioned smoothly into her background. "How would you describe your family growing up? How many siblings, parents in the home, other family?"

Alexandra eagerly responded, "So my family is a little bit unusual. A lot of time when people say, 'Where were you born and raised?' that is a very challenging question for me to answer. Because I was born in Columbia; my mother is Columbian. My father is American but he speaks fluent Spanish. And, he wrote a series of love letters to a number of women in Columbia. He and his friend went to Columbia and were visiting all these women...this was in the 70's. My mother was like number four and he stopped. She was the one. He didn't want to see the rest of them. So, he decided he wanted to marry her. They were in their mid-thirties. And so, they moved to Arizona for a year or two and she decided she wanted to go back to Columbia. They went to Columbia. And my mother had a child..."

Alexandra's voice slowed, "An older sister of mine died shortly after she was born. She had my mother's name." Alexandra took in a short breath and paused, "And then, I was born in Columbia. My mother's sister, whose husband was a resident, delivered me. He would often say, 'Oh...that's my baby.' That was kinda neat!" The sweetness of the memory brought forth a light laughter. "So we lived in Columbia for a year. I don't remember that. Then we moved to Venezuela for four years where my sister and brother were born. There are three of us...I am the oldest. So, then when I was about six, we moved to Hong Kong and that is where I learned English."

For the next few minutes, Alexandra recalled important pieces of her language acquisition. She explained how learning to speak Spanish in Venezuela as a young child was different from her mother's Columbian Spanish. Alexandra spoke with an accent which would be the equivalent of a British accent when speaking English. Alexandra explained the nuances of this as we continued to explore her background.

"And so we went to Hong Kong for two years. My dad was an engineer assistant [for a large American company] and also a farmer. I have really good memories there, and that is where I learned British English. And because I was in kindergarten in Venezuela and I didn't know enough English, they held me back. That was hard for me," she paused. Then continued, "Although I was young for my age, I graduated at 18, it was hard that I got held back in kindergarten.... So, I learned English. And then we moved to the United States. But we moved all over. And when we came to the United States, I did not speak English correctly because I didn't speak American English. It was this huge transition. And then we ended up....I don't know...we ended up in California for a while."

I listened intently as Alexandra explained how she lived in several different towns attending different schools. She disclosed how she was a poor student, not being able to read at grade level. They placed her in what was termed as ESL (English as a Second Language) classes. As her words flowed, Alexandra revealed an important piece of her childhood, "I just thought I was really stupid." Although education was really important to her family, her mother did not acquire much. Alexandra's family worked very hard, and many of her cousins earned advanced degrees.

Understanding the depth of value placed on education within Alexandra's family brought clarity to the foundational roots of Alexandra's background. She returned to her family describing other elements which contributed to her development.

"During the time we lived in California, my parents...I always knew they were unhappy. As a child, the messages I learned where: one, adults lie. They do not tell you the truth. I caught my parents lying all the time." Her narrative moved swiftly, "Two: marriage on TV where you see happy families was a façade. People don't actually live like that. Nobody does..." Alexandra's voice broke and softened to almost a whisper, "They just do that to give you a break....because my family fought so much. There was so much anger...and then so much love. I didn't know what to expect." Her voice strengthened again, "There was no substance abuse... no alcohol...neither of my parents drank or anything, but I recognized much later that my mother was a victim of some kind of sexual trauma at some time in her life."

Alexandra focused in on her mom and the strange messages she received from her. "I love you...I believe in you. Oh and then she...was very spiritual in metaphysics. She was always believing she could cure people and do these kind of things I thought were weird. She was very healthy and made everything from scratch, organic, at a time when that wasn't the norm. She fed us almost no meat. This was in the 80's. My dad would sneak us off and take us to McDonald's and buy us hamburgers." Alexandra's voice lifted a little, returning quickly to a serious tone, "There was just this.....weird conflict. They were never on the same page."

Alexandra disclosed how her parents' marriage worsened. Her mom accused her father of cheating and resorted to cutting his ties. Although her father did not touch her mom, she scratched him and pushed him. When Alexandra came to her father's defense, she described how her mom started punching her, scratching her, calling her names, and throwing away her clothes. Alexandra described how she felt like she was betraying her mom because she was on her dad's side.

Digging deeper into her field of experiences, Alexandra revealed her inner turmoil as a child, "I felt very torn. I felt like...I wanted to love her very much. I was about twelve years old, but she was so violent and mean to my dad." The intensity in Alexandra's words increased, "She couldn't keep any friends! She had no friends!" Her voice held its conviction, "She was a beautiful, beautiful woman, very charismatic, very talented... an incredible artist, but couldn't keep people in her life because she was so volatile. What I remember is being on edge. I knew when she would be home because I would hear high-heels clicking. And for many years as an adult when I heard high-heels clicking I would have a physical visceral reaction. Of course, I don't anymore obviously."

Listening to Alexandra's narrative and the mixed messages within, I thought of how confusing life can be, especially for a child. I thought about the anatomy of betrayal with its degree of occurrence; in other words, the frequency of betrayals is a reliable predictor of the depth of harm sustained. And compounding the chronic nature of her mom's betrayals were the inconsistencies between what was real and what was not. As we continued to explore Alexandra's background, I visualized a young fawn, bewildered and startled by its uncertain and unsafe environment. I remained focused on Alexandra's voice and her truths as she unearthed more from her vast field.

With a soft but firm tone, Alexandra explained, "What I remember of my family is that we had to pretend that everything is okay to everyone. No one was allowed to know about our financial issues. My parents overspent. They had very lavish incomes and always overspent. They [others] were not allowed to know about our emotional issues. Nobody was allowed to know about anything, except that we were perfect. We always had a façade…and the adults were liars. Those are the main messages I remember."

I waited for Alexandra, sensing there may be more. "I do remember my parents loved me. I never felt unloved from my mom but I felt it was conditional. She would always say, 'After all I have done for you, why don't you do the dishes for me'….or whatever it was. I wasn't a kid who liked negative attention. No matter what I did, it was never enough. I ended up getting the brunt of her anger, her physical violence, and her emotional violence. By the time my parents got divorced in seventh and eighth grade, the courts gave her no parenting rights in that you could have visitation if you chose. My sister and brother chose [to have visitation]—they were younger. And I chose not to. And I pretty much only saw her for a handful of times until I was about twenty-three or twenty-four. For about ten years."

The young fawn's separation from her mother at such a tender age brought with it another level of pain. I gave it time for release, respecting the significance of her truth to choose safety…to choose herself.

Before moving into our next question, I reflected back to Alexandra several of the messages about her childhood, making certain we had covered the critical pieces of her background. Returning to the concept of feeling loved but that is was always conditional, Alexandra added, "If I didn't get straight As, if I didn't do extra activities, if I was involved in everything I could do including volunteerism, I [still] didn't feel good enough. I felt like I was a bad person and constantly trying to prove to everyone that I wasn't." As Alexandra's truths had flowed throughout the interview to this point, they continued, never wavering in their steadiness or strength, never overcoming her or overwhelming her. A gentle resolve fueled her spirit, "I did feel loved, but I couldn't handle being around my mom…and it was heartbreaking because I wanted her in my life so bad. But at that stage, it was really black and white. She was a bad person, and I had to say, 'She cannot be around me.'"

As I replayed Alexandra's words in my mind, 'She cannot be around me,' I once again envisioned the young fawn wandering amidst a field of forces which ran contrary to the wellness of her. At the same time, I pictured an intuitive fawn with the instincts of a mature doe. Amazed by the fortitude she carried within her, I asked about how she viewed her role in the family.

With an elevated rush of words, Alexandra gushed forth. "Oh my gosh, so my role was to make sure everyone was okay. I was the peacekeeper. I was the one, if people were fighting I had to solve the situation. I initiated to make sure everything was clean...everything was done for my siblings before my mom got home, because anything could trigger her rage. I was the oldest, so I was in charge of all that."

I reflected her words in a question, "The parentified child?"

"Yes, yes, and I also took on the role of making sure my dad was okay because I felt bad for him to be married to someone who was volatile. She was mean and she would hit him. And he would just take it. I mean it was just....awful." Alexandra's voice quieted again, turning to a whisper, "I would take care of them [younger siblings]. When my mom was at her worst my brother would hide. We had horses and a tack room." Her words flowed more slowly as a heaviness descended upon her. Alexandra allowed her tears to speak, "He would get dressed and everything and hide there [tack room] because my bus would come first. We lived in the country so it was about a mile walk to the bus stop. His bus wouldn't come for about twenty more minutes. So I would make sure everything ready...his lunch. So he would hide there until he could walk to the bus stop so he didn't have to be alone."

Alexandra took in a deep breath, returning to her poised position while explaining more of her role. "It was expected that I would take care of everything that needed to be taken care of. So we had horses; [I had to] take care of the animals, take care of the siblings, making sure that they would do their chores. I had to get very good grades, and help them with their homework." Alexandra described how her dad commuted to his work and often traveled for work. Because he was gone all the time and her mom attended beauty school, Alexandra took on additional responsibilities.

Moving into a related question, I asked, "When your dad was home, did you feel safer?"

Without hesitation, Alexandra responded, "Yes, yes, absolutely. And I missed him so much. I begged him to divorce my mom. We all did. He would say, 'I can't because if I do then I will lose you guys...' I guess that was what typically happened at the time—usually the mom got the children. But then, [it was] because of the circumstances and maybe the time that it was." Alexandra paused, weaving her truths into the situation, "It was extreme, no it was very extreme." With a hint of sarcasm, she questioned, "Resolution? Try to reintegrate the family?" Then, like a jury delivering its verdict, Alexandra stated, "No, she's bad. Out of here!"

The finality of Alexandra's words reverberated between us, punctuating her strength and her spirit. This time, an image of a fearless fawn, standing her ground and saving herself, flooded my mind.

Gently, I inquired, "Before we leave this section, Alexandra, is there anything else you would like to add?"

Pensively, she concluded, "I think my role has always been...my family always described me as...'You have the most ambition in the family,' because my sister was the rebellious one. My brother was the quite serious one. He was the one who was not seen. He was invisible. And my sister was rebellious. I was just the responsible one that they always said was a crybaby because I felt too much...like too emotional." Alexandra's voice softened, almost to a whisper, "That was the label I got as a child from my family."

In contrast to her background narrative, Alexandra described briefly how there were fun times, especially during the summer. She recalled, "Feeling free-spirited, riding horses, and being with friends". As I pictured those lighter experiences, I imagined the fawn running freely in a vast open field providing a safe space to grow and trust her strengths while nurturing her sensitivities.

However, segueing into our next section, I knew there was more to uncover in the betrayal fields before us.

Betrayal Narrative...

Preparing for our first question, I reminded Alexandra that there may be some crossover between the various sections of our interview and their respective questions and responses. I encouraged her to share what came up naturally for her.

"Alexandra, when did you first start thinking about your betrayal narrative with your mom? When did you first remember connecting the word *betrayal* to your relationship with her? What was that like for you?"

"I think....by the time I was eight and a half, we had probably moved [so that I had gone] to nine different schools. I had been to three different countries. So, I remember just feeling...I just wanted stability and consistency. I don't remember exactly what happened but I remember my parents fighting. My mom did something mean...it was around Christmas time and I remember thinking, it's so weird that I would think this, but I remember thinking, 'I just don't want to live anymore.'" Alexandra's voice quivered, then broke. Tears followed. "And it's the only time I ever did anything like this but there was this cologne I got my dad for Christmas. It was in a boot kind of thing...a little green boot stocking. And I drank the whole thing...'cause it was the first time I was so incredibly unhappy with my life because I didn't know how to deal with my life circumstances." Her voice remained soft but steady, "The fighting and the chaos. I don't know if I necessarily thought it was all my mom but I just couldn't deal with it." Alexandra took in a deep breath. She paused and began, "And then, I ended up telling on myself and I threw up and I was fine."

Unearthing the pain of her past, Alexandra's roots of betrayal lay exposed between us. I remained quiet, allowing their truths to speak.

Alexandra's strength surfaced again, "But I do remember I was around eight and a half. It's the only time I've ever wanted to do anything like that where I wanted to take my life or have that kind of intention." Her voice spiked with emotion, "I was young! It wasn't until later [when I was older] that I realized, 'Wow! That's pretty significant!'" She paused, lowering her tone to its natural level, "But I think it was when we moved to California when I was in third grade, when I really started realizing my mom is not like everyone else's. And I was not only really embarrassed, but I was like, 'Don't do anything bad...don't do anything wrong' because she will blow up at people and they won't want to be your friend. 'Cause she would also like...when my friends would do something...like kids do...and then she would go off on their parents. She would call their parents and then I would be ostracized at school." With resignation in her voice, Alexandra added, "She would just do these crazy things. She would misperceive people all the time...their actions. So I was really embarrassed of her."

Alexandra explained how additional mixed messages added to the confusion and chaos of her upbringing. Although her mom would spoil her siblings and her by giving into their temper tantrums when they were younger, as they got older and were not compliant her mom would resort to physical violence and a lot of "guilting." Alexandra remembered the words her mom spoke to her in reference to having children, "God is going to pay you back for all the bad things you have done to me. Your kids are going to be so bad to you." And Alexandra recalled thinking and believing, "I am such a bad child."

Exploring her expansive painfield, Alexandra uncovered additional betrayals and their respective injuries.

"When we did move away, they [parents] lost everything. My parents lost everything in the divorce because my mom refused to sign over [property]. We had a beautiful home …like a 5,000 square foot home— custom built, five acres, with horses and things. She refused to sign anything so they lost it in foreclosure. One time when we were gone for the weekend with my dad, she sold everything…the horses [my horse], furniture. Like all these weird things that just hurt us very much. She was trying to hurt my dad, but she hurt us. She would not own her part. She would not say she was sorry."

Tapping into the life messages Alexandra previously spoke about and how they impacted her, I inquired if there were additional mixed messages.

Alexandra's flow moved swiftly, "People can't always be trustworthy. People are going to say something but their behavior is so different. My mom would be a healer and say she had all these spiritual powers… meditate and do all this stuff. And then she would do these things…" Alexandra's voice slowed, "She did have a giving heart and liked to help people that were hurting, but there was this expectation that she would get something in return."

I asked, "Did you feel that way as well? If she did something good for you, did you feel like you...." Before I could finish, Alexandra interjected.

"Yes, I owed her! I had to pay it back in some way." She thought for a moment and added, "As a kid you don't know if what you are doing is wrong. I would share too much information when we were out with friends and she wouldn't agree with it…like it might be we were strug- gling in some way. And she would pinch me really hard or kick me under the table. So I wasn't always sure what the roles were but I knew if I tried to be perfect, that was the best thing."

Alexandra and I explored the concepts of mixed messages and their inherent dangers, especially for a child. The image of the fawn re-entered my mind, imagining the difficulty of navigating its territory never knowing what was safe or what was unsafe. Whatever the discovery would be, this child—this fawn—would learn from it. Alexandra shared her next lesson.

"It was very confusing. I remember one time she [mom] was in one of her rages…and it wasn't like she was intensely violent. She did abuse us but it wasn't horrific. Ummmm, it was more verbal abuse," Alexandra's voice was serious and somber. "But I think she punched me in the face. My nose started bleeding. So I ran away to the nearest neighbor's house, about a quarter of a mile away. They knew us and everything. It was a small community. And I was like, 'My mom is trying to hurt me.' And I had never told anyone about it, and they didn't believe me. They played it out like I was overreacting and then she [neighbor] had to drive me home. And so I just had to apologize to her [mom]. And I thought she was going to go into a fit, but she just was quiet. And then she asked, 'Why did you say all those things?' I didn't know what to say...I thought, 'Maybe I'm crazy. Maybe that didn't happen!'"

I remained quiet, giving Alexandra that space to speak her truths. Her voice returned to its steady flow recalling a turning point in her life.

"But just one day I couldn't take it anymore. I had a 4.0 GPA. I was in honor classes. I was in 7th grade. I was on the math team. And, I told my science teacher what happened...that my mom was abusing us and it was really bad at home. And of course, CPS [Child Protective Services] was activated and they took pictures. I had bruises, and scars and stuff. It wasn't horrific, but it was enough. And then that was the catalyst that led to the divorce." Alexandra breathed deeply and disclosed, "And then she [mom] made these accusations that my dad was molesting my sister and I. And so that had to be investigated. She had told some of the neighbors that my dad was a bad person and was doing this. When I would walk to school, the neighbor kids would throw rocks at us and call us names. It was a really bad time.... a really bad time for me."

As Alexandra named the injuries and injustices which filled her betrayal field, I listened intently honoring their existence and her endurance. I remained quiet.

Her voice broke once again, revealing the depth of her pain, "I didn't have any friends at school. I couldn't emotionally relate to kids. They would joke around about stupid stuff...and I was like, 'That is not funny, it's stupid.'" Alexandra paused briefly; then spoke as though she was giving a declaration, "It was war...like a war but nobody else was living in it." Alexandra's softened her tone but not her resolve. "So, I would eat lunch in the library. I would escape to the library and read my books, every day. I had no friends. I felt very isolated....very worthless. The things I focused on were getting straight As, and being on the math team. I was teased for my grades. And then I developed early so I would get made fun of for that. I felt like no matter what, I couldn't be good enough."

Alexandra's words, "It was war...like a war but nobody else was living in it," captured the essence of betrayal with its insidious and ubiquitous nature. It is a force which is all-encompassing, and yet it is completely isolating. Alexandra's vast field of confusion, worthlessness, and powerlessness challenged her at every turn. I remained in wonder of her instinctual compass and her intuitive survival skills.

As we continued exploring her betrayal narrative, Alexandra described her disappointment in moving before the end of her eighth-grade school year. Not only would she be starting her thirteenth school, but not graduating with her eighth-grade class robbed her of the opportunity to be recognized for all the accomplishments she had achieved. In high school, Alexandra again worked very hard and was active in cross country track, French club, student government, and math team. Although she was having positive experiences in high school, she lived at friends' houses much of the time, sensing that her dad's house was unsafe with roommates who were dealing drugs. Alexandra believed that her dad did not know, or was not aware of the drug activity.

Although I felt as though we had covered much of her narrative, I checked in with Alexandra regarding the pattern of betrayals by her mom and how Alexandra would categorize them.

With her familiar strong flow, she explained, "It wasn't until maybe I was about eight or nine, but from that point on there would be episodes where I would feel so detached and bad. And there were other times, where I had such lovely memories [with my mother] playing in the pool with us and being silly. So, it wasn't all negative. But as I got older, especially as I entered early adolescence—those tween years... kinda eleven or twelve—I don't remember anything good really. As I got older, I just remember it getting worse."

Briefly paraphrasing the territory we had covered, I then probed further, "We have talked about the pieces from early childhood through your teen years. Are there any gaps you would like to fill in or experiences from that point forward you would like to share?"

Alexandra added, "My mom had two sisters who lived in California. They had children and I was close to them. My mom would get into fights with them and we wouldn't see them." She thought for a moment. "Another piece of the betrayal is that I lost touch with my Columbian family. I also rejected them because I associated it [Columbian family] with my mom."

As we continued to examine Alexandra's betrayal field, she described the ensuing years as being "episodic betrayals." After the divorce and moving with her dad to another town, Alexandra did not see her mom from age twelve or thirteen to about twenty-three or twenty-four, except for a handful of times. Two significant events—Alexandra's graduation from high school and her mom's remarriage—resulted in re-injury for Alexandra with her mom displaying fits of rage. During those years of separation, Alexandra described her coping mechanism, "I would pretend that she was dead. That was the only way I could deal with it. Otherwise, I would think, 'This is my fault that all this is happening.' Even though I knew it was hers too, I felt like I was deserving of this because of some of the stuff she told me."

As they had done before, Alexandra's choice of words, "I would pretend that she was dead. That was the only way I could deal with it," carried with them the ramifications of reoccurring or episodic betrayal. With her maternal source in her life sporadically endangering her sense of safety and security, the adolescent moved into a new field of protection. She purposely stepped out of her childhood emotional environment filled with betrayal and entered prematurely into her motherless role—a fawn on her own.

In the years after high school, Alexandra described her achievements in college, completing her undergrad courses and obtaining her first Master's. Because one of her best friends moved to Austin, Texas, Alexandra decided to join her there for a period of about a year. During this time, Alexandra's mom and sister were living in Houston where they started to reconnect with one another.

With a soft resignation, Alexandra described their relationship, "I would go and visit her sporadically. But inevitably, we would get in fights." Alexandra thought for a moment and continued, "I did recognize she was a lot calmer. She had done a lot of her own work—a lot of meditation and spiritual work to deal with her anger. It was causing her to be calmer." As her flow of words moved swiftly and steadily, she added, "Never once has she apologized for her part. So, I would go and visit her and handle one or two days and then she would do something or say something. 'You're not calling me enough. You're not doing enough. You're not a good daughter.'" With familiar exasperation and a hint of laughter, Alexandra declared, "'So, I'm out!' And I wouldn't see her for months. 'Okay...I'm out. Cool.' And it's gotten better as I've gotten older and had my own kids."

Sensing there was more, I waited.

"Then, about five years ago, she moved back to Columbia. She comes to the United States about once a year. I see her at family reunions. I've gone to Columbia to see her and I went to see her house. Actually, it was very pleasant and I had a good time. However, she has very poor boundaries and self-containment issues."

Alexandra explained further by contrasting a significant dynamic in the relationship with her mom to that of her dad, his remarriage, and his three children with his new wife. Where her mom would favor

Alexandra's son and her sister's son over Alexandra's adopted daughter, Alexandra's dad and his family were close, inclusive, and filled with unconditional love.

As I observed the differences in Alexandra's emotions while describing both sides of her family, I followed up with our final question, "When you think about the relationship as it is defined now with your mom, whatever the contact may be, is there ongoing betrayal?"

Alexandra's voice was serious, "So what I know with my mom, I can never be truly vulnerable with her because she will use it against me. And, she is really uncomfortable with negative emotions. If I feel sad...she always says, 'You need to be positive.' I say, 'No...we have emotions for a reason.' She kind of undermines me. I know she is proud of me because I am a psychologist, but she thinks I'm going to take in negative energy and it's going to impact my soul...all sorts of stuff. So, I cannot be honest and forthcoming about my life and what I do. So, I can't be vulnerable with her. I have to have extreme, extreme boundaries. And I have acceptance that this is the relationship I have with her. I don't call her very often and she definitely gives me a lot of grief about that. I have really good boundaries and I don't take on a lot of her stuff. But, we do not have a close mother-daughter relationship at all. And, it's never going to be that way. What I yearn for is more than she can give me and I recognize that."

As we came to the close of the betrayal narrative section, I visualized the image of a stately and statuesque young doe standing alone in her field of safety while simultaneously scanning her environs. At the same time, the betrayal fence which earlier had defined her past existence was now replaced with rows of towering protective pines. Alexandra's words explained their existence: "I can never be truly vulnerable with her because she will use it against me."

Moving into our next section, I wondered how this emerging doe found her way amidst the uncertainties and adversities surrounding her.

Brokenness From Betrayal ...

Because Alexandra had previously disclosed areas of brokenness, I asked her to share whatever came up for her as well as her life messages she received in her relationship with her mom.

Her words flowed, "I think... I didn't feel good enough. That was the core belief I grew up with. I was not good enough. I can really identify that. The messages were: adults were not trustworthy; people were inconsistent; you have to really be aware of what peoples' behavior is and what they expect of you and mold to whatever it is; and, a huge people-pleaser." She paused briefly, then elaborated, "When I was in college, I was a resident assistant. I remember I went to a training for children of alcoholics and I broke down crying. Even though my mom never drank or was an alcoholic, everything they identified in the family system I could relate to. I was sobbing. It was like, 'They are talking about my family.' It was the first time I realized all these things I didn't know and why! And what I learned from it is that my worth is in how well I did, how much I achieved, and how much people liked me. And so, the message I got was, 'Sacrifice yourself as long as everyone else is okay...then everything else is going to be okay.' So, those were the messages I got as a child."

I probed further, "What about as a female, as a daughter?"

"Those messages I got were from my dad. Those messages which later I had to do a lot of work around were, 'You should be smart. That is very important. Education is important. And it doesn't really count unless you look a certain way, unless you look good.'" Alexandra spoke firmly, adding, "Both my mom and dad were very critical on people's appearances, their looks...anything! Yes, these messages of appearance and also because we always had to appear put together. My mom spent so much time making our clothes, making sure we looked nice, making us look presentable. Appearance was really important!"

Thinking about the conditional pieces attached to Alexandra's life messages, I asked a related question. "Did you feel acceptable in *any* way?"

"I felt acceptable if I was performing, if I was achieving, and if people liked me. If people were unhappy or there was conflict, I couldn't tolerate it. I couldn't tolerate the idea of disappointing."

I dug a little deeper into the question, "Did you ever feel acceptable to your mom?"

"I never thought about that...I am guessing 'no......'" Alexandra answered thoughtfully. "I felt we could get along for short periods but no matter what we would always end up in a disagreement. I would upset her in some way."

I returned to our previous question, "Other short-term and long-term implications from the brokenness?"

Without hesitation, Alexandra explained, "Short term, looking back, definitely some symptoms of PTSD. I definitely had nightmares. I had visceral reactions. Like all the time my nervous system was activated. I had a hard time settling, distractible. I had a hard time sitting in my body. I had incredible anxiety that something bad was going to happen to my dad, my sister, and my brother, and if it did, it was going to be my fault. Safety concerns. It's not that I thought my life was in danger or that my mom was going to kill me, but I just thought she was unstable. So I thought, 'When is this going to end? How much damage is going to happen before it ends?'"

As an outlet for her emotions, Alexandra described several ways of coping with her circumstances. After the divorce and when she and her dad moved away, she recalled "crying a lot;" however, she also took up running. She became more self-reliant, learning not to ask for things because "there was no money." During her high school years, Alexandra earned her own money, supported herself, and learned how to be on her own. From the age of 17, she "didn't depend on anybody."

I gently inquired, "Other disorders besides the anxiety? Depression?"

"I think so... the crying spells. At night I just felt so lonely." Alexandra's voice diminished, almost inaudible. Then, it rose slightly, "I had an amazing cat that would snuggle with me when I was really sad." A muffled chuckle snuck though. "And I did have friends, but I felt such loneliness."

I waited. Then asked, "Anything else to add on short-term implications or long term?"

With conviction, Alexandra responded, "What I wanted to do with 'my mom out of my life,' is that *I wanted to make my life the way I wanted it.* So, I actively made a decision that I am going to do all the things my mom would not allow me to do which is to have friendships, to have people over, and I'm not going to be worried that they are going to say something wrong and she is going to blow up at them." With enthusiasm and excitement, she pronounced, "I decided to get into sports. In high school, I found out I was actually pretty decent in sports and I love it! I love it! And so, I did really well in cross country and track." She punctuated her accomplishments and stated, "I created my own sense of community."

I waited. Alexandra's voice spilled out.

"And the other thing I did was really immersed myself in service work and volunteered a lot since I was fourteen. I volunteered in a number of different soup kitchens, with school or without school. From then until now, I am still actively volunteering. Especially in my early twenties."

After sharing some of the positive aspects of her decision making, Alexandra disclosed challenges which surfaced in choices regarding her relationships.

"So, long-term ramifications, I think I definitely have some attachment issues and that played out in relationships. When I did get in a relationship, I would expect…and I've only been in a few, I'd expect too much from them. And then if they needed me, which I kinda of attracted, then I would feel suffocated."

Alexandra shared how she found herself in a physically and emotionally abusive situation with her third serious relationship. She described how she tried to save him and how she felt she was "replaying feelings from her childhood." Knowing that she had relationship issues, Alexandra chose to address them after she was married and responsible for the co-parenting of her adopted daughter. Because she had begun her doctorate program, Alexandra was mandated to be in therapy. It was during this time where she addressed her issues around codependency and self-worth, and where she had the opportunity to go deeply into self-discovery and healing.

Explaining their long-term impact on her, Alexandra shared additional life messages, "Other messages I learned later on were that 'Family does not have to be blood-related. They can be the people you chose.' So, my family, my tribe, my people—no matter where I go—I find the best humans and they are so amazing!" Her voice lowered, "All the messages I learned…keep quiet, don't tell anyone what's wrong, be a people pleaser, don't rock the boat…all these things, I had to just unlearn them." And then with a steady stream of words, she revealed her current messages, "I am vulnerable. I am not perfect. I let people know what is going on. I feel my emotions with containment."

Pondering her messages, I inquired further, "Are there any other pieces you would like to share to your brokenness?"

"I ended up, which I realized in therapy, developing an anxiety disorder, generalized anxiety disorder. I couldn't sit with myself; I couldn't be at rest. I was always worried about what other people were thinking. I was always worried about performing. Replaying conversations over again. It was pretty significant, impacting my quality of life. "

I asked, "Were you a perfectionist?"

Alexandra cheered, "Oh yeahhhh!" We both laughed. "I remember always doing…human doing. Always being. Those aren't my words, but I remember being exposed to that later. Yeahhh…."

As we came to a close in this section, I asked a related question, "Do you think the brokenness from your mom helped you to be a better mom?"

With her familiar strength, Alexandra spoke, "Absolutely. Because of the healing I had and what I was forced to do. Two things… I'm never going to repeat what she did. I wasn't going to be abusive. I wasn't going to be physical. Second thing, I knew there had to be a better way. And I would see someone else doing something different with their children, and I would take a note of it. There were times where I would fall into those old feelings and have an overreaction, but I would start identifying them when I would have an overreaction and self-correct."

As Alexandra briefly described some of the struggles, as well as parts of her recovering she experienced within her marriage, with her daughter, and with herself—I was struck by her words, *"I wanted to make my life the way I wanted it."* As I pondered them, the image of the maturing doe surfaced surrounded by a fertile field of messages supporting and strengthening her—"I am vulnerable. I am not perfect. I let people know what is going on. I feel my emotions with containment."

I was confident there was more healing to unearth in the grounds before us.

From Brokenness To Wholeness...

Because Alexandra had spoken briefly about when she first thought of addressing her brokenness in relationship to her mom, I moved into the next question with the understanding for her to share if there was more which deserved attention.

"Alexandra, when did you first consider addressing your injuries, wounds, or brokenness? What was that like for you?"

"I think, obviously, we talked about age eight or nine, that I started noticing that something was going on. In high school, I really wanted to address it and I just didn't know how. So, I think informally what I did was the connections, creating my own sense of family community with people in my school. And then I became a team leader...I wasn't the best runner in my running club but I instigated this secret kind of way where we could make these secret buddies." An excitement started to build in her voice, "We would draw names out of a hat and we would make them stuff or bake them stuff before the race so they knew somebody was cheering them on! And then we would kidnap them for their birthday and dress them up really funny and take them to breakfast. So everyone would know that was going to happen on your birthday. I became the 'birthday fairy,' and I still hold that name." Alexandra's voice softened again, "Just creating these meaningful connections in my life. And then the service work...I was doing a lot of service work."

Alexandra thought for a moment and then described how she rejected spirituality for a long time because of her mom's spirituality. Alexandra felt it was a 'façade.' In her words, "How could someone claim to be so spiritual and be so violent and mean?"

Alexandra returned to her recovering journey. "I tried to go to a therapist in my early twenties. I had a really hard time being vulnerable because, 'What if they found out how bad I was?' I couldn't get past that self-criticism and things like that. So, I ended up by accident becoming a psychology major just because I wanted to graduate and that is what I needed to do." We both chuckled, understanding the demands of college experience and its many constraints. "So I was a psychology major and I got my first Masters in Leadership and Management. I worked for a non-profit with the Girl Scouts and then at another non-profit in California where I was case manager for adults with cognitive disabilities and physical disabilities."

Alexandra described that it was working as a case manager when she met her husband who was also employed there. After they married, Alexandra decided to continue her education and entered grad school to study clinical psychology. It was during this time where Alexandra began her formal healing.

Alexandra's words came gushing out, "Through that process there was so much self-discovery. I was like, 'Oh my gosh...I have so much work to do!' So, I was twenty-six when I started the program and that's when I really actively started doing my own healing work. Because you are exposed to that material...you have to look at yourself all the time." An intensity accompanied with a strong positivity filled Alexandra's voice, "And when you start going to practicums and internships and working with clients, of course your stuff comes up! Absolutely!" Her calm strength returned, "So my stuff came up and I started working on that. And I did a lot of good work around anxiety but I couldn't really touch my mother issues that much...a little bit."

For clarification, I inquired, "Was this with a one-on-one therapist?"

"Yes, one on one. I had two I worked with. One for a time and then another one. The second one...she came from a psychodynamic place ...orientation...so we did a lot of family of origin work so that is what kinda helped me to address the issues around my mom. Because of the insurance, I had ten sessions with her...ten weeks. It was great." She thought for a few moments and added, "Informally, being like a 'Big Brother'... 'Big Sister,' and then being a mentor through my college for five years. I think that was healing in itself because that just feels healing. You get more out of it than the little mentees."

Exploring further, I asked, "Did you feel like you took on a mother role? What made it healing for you?"

Returning to her serious and somber tone, she recalled, "I think that once again that if I was such a bad person, I don't think these children or these people would connect to me. They could see me. They could accept me. I could be more vulnerable and gentle and silly. I could crack jokes..." For the first time in our interview, I noticed how Alexandra's eyes lit up and how her spirit sparkled.

She continued, "And then I had an awesome, awesome internship at a children's hospital where I was a psychology intern. So part of what I did was worked doing neuro-psychological testing—pathology and endocrinology. So, I worked with the families. One part I got to do was in consulting where a patient would be there and they would want someone from psychology to see if there were underlying psychological issues that were interacting or were there."

Alexandra enthusiastically described her successes during this internship. Once again, she found she was able to connect with the children, even when others were not able to do so. She recalled staff telling her, "If there is a patient who won't take one of us, then we will call you. We know that you have the secret." The glow in Alexandra radiated as she described her feelings during this time, "So, I felt like a 'super star!' I finished my dissertation and it got published, and I got to present it at a conference!"

Alexandra's successes were followed by a transitional period where she and her family moved to a smaller town. Alexandra struggled finding a job, especially as a pediatric psychologist. Eventually, she found work in a drug and alcohol treatment center, where she had no experience.

With exasperation accompanied with elation, Alexandra described her time there, "What I learned from that experience is that I was forced to be vulnerable and to do my own work. If I didn't, my clients would see it and call me on it. So that intensity, it was almost like another internship because I was running groups." Alexandra described how she felt ill-equipped in her new role as a psychologist in a treatment center and how she was often challenged by her clients. She added, "What I learned is that I had to be vulnerable....had to do my own work. I learned....I was exposed to Brene' Brown...I was exposed to all these things and I was like 'I have self-worth issues.' I just dove into it, informally with other therapists and colleagues because the culture of the organization was great. I learned soooo much. I got so many gifts from these clients. They had gone through sooo much adversity and they were being vulnerable. They were learning how to heal. They were recognizing their character defects." Alexandra grabbed a breath and her stream of words flowed swiftly, "I learned about the 12 steps and immersed myself in the *Big Book*. I started asking myself these questions... 'What is going on? What is my part? What is codependency?' I learned soooo much, not as a client but as a therapist. You're healing, maybe not in the same role as the client, but you are still doing your own work!"

Alexandra continued working at the treatment center until 2012 when she opened up her private practice, but remained contracted with the center. It was during this time where she almost got divorced, with "everything falling apart." She explained that there was "just so much, not anyone thing". Her family made the decision to enter therapy and committed to doing their own work for a year.

With her familiar strength and steady voice, Alexandra explained the healing which took place, "We had a couples therapist every other week. We each had our own therapist [except for their young son]. "That [therapy] changed the language we talked about. We became vulnerable. We had boundaries. We were able to discuss when we had overreactions." Alexandra took a deep breath. Then, added, "And that is when I was able to have so much more peace with my mom. I guess it was really recently where I was able to have conversations with her … and I was longing for a deeper connection and feeling that pain [but] without going into despair or asking, 'Why did this happen to me?'" After describing her more traditional forms of recovering, Alexandra described other avenues, "So, a lot of my healing has been informal through this job [working as a psychologist] which was incredibly challenging. And then I have great friends and amazing colleagues. And I just love that we can use that language [therapeutic and authentic] and be honest and share those moments like 'This is a shame core that I have.'"

I sat still, anticipating more.

Alexandra's voice was couched in layers tenderness. "And then of course, I found my own amazing therapist. I love her. And so she has helped me the last few years. I did individual and she would see my husband and me for couples therapy. Every once in a while, I would need a booster and she would bring him in." A warmth smothered her soft words, "My husband is amazing because he is so willing to do this work. He understands it is a process. He has his own journey but we use our language even with our kids."

Wanting to know more about Alexandra's healing with her therapist, I gently probed. "Is there anything from your individual therapist which really stands out for you? Is there a methodology which connected with you? Other?"

"Yes, she did a lot of attachment work repairing attachment, understanding the attachment wound. She is the one who really put together when I was having overreactions. She helped me put that together, she really did. She is the one who helped to validate..." Alexandra paused and continued, "My daughter's view right now is a little bit distorted. She blames us for having this horrible family and my therapist would say, 'So she is not really seeing it all the way....she is only seeing things from this lens.' And so it really helped me because when she [my daughter] is mad at me, that can take me back to not feeling good enough. That is the thing that takes me back."

Alexandra breathed in slowly, and then spoke, allowing her flow of words to slow slightly, "There are a lot of things where I'm not perfect, and I am sooo okay with that. But with my daughter sometimes, that is where 'I am not good enough.' And I blame myself. It is my fault that she having the problems she's having. It's pretty painful to go through. She activates my shame core. But through my own work, the attachment healing work, and having someone who sees me and see all the parts of me...and she sees me at my worst." Alexandra's gentle strength within her voice emerged and grew in intensity. Her posture shifted. The gentle doe's stately pose revealed her inner truth. Every word was deliberate and purposeful, "She accepts me. She likes me. She believes in me! She believes ... that *I am good enough*!" Alexandra's voice slowed. She spoke pensively, "She even refers clients to me." Softly but succinctly, Alexandra concluded, "She has been kinda like a mentor in a way...."

Alexandra's words—*she accepts me, she likes me, she believes in me, she believes that I am good enough*—brought forth the image of the open field. However, this time the doe was not alone. I tenderly suggested, "She has been sort of like a mother....?"

A whirlwind of warmth engulfed us both. I stared into the startled eyes of the brave doe before me, uncertain if I may have overstepped. Alexandra gasped, "Ohhhhh....." Her tears flowed and her words slowed to abrupt starts and stops, "You are absolutely right...she is old enough to be my mother." She wiped her eyes, but the stream could not be contained, "She has been there for me through really hard times." Her voice gushed forth with emotion. "I feel that unconditional love. Oh I do...I feel that unconditional regard. She sees me and she believes in me and I can go to her." I sat quietly as the doe basked in her rays of understanding. The sudden startle in her eyes was replaced with a steady serenity. "Oh my gosh, I never thought about that. I think that is probably part of that healing process...why I feel so much more okay now. It's so obvious but oh.....wow..."

We both sat quietly for several moments, honoring Alexandra's healing truths. Alexandra's insight into discovering and identifying a maternal presence in her life and its profound implications of moving her *From Brokenness To Wholeness* carried a multitude of thoughts, feelings, and emotions. Each one represented a gift—a part of the fertile field which Alexandra had purposely crafted and mindfully created throughout her healing journey alone. Alexandra's acknowledgment of a trusted beloved older doe, one who "had been there through really tough times" and given "unconditional love and unconditional regard," would change the landscape of her field significantly. The enormity of it all and of its enrichment into her place of wholeness would take additional time to process.

The slowing swirl of warmth in the room settled down, bringing with it a peaceful comfort and calm. Mirroring Alexandra's emotional depth and yet containing it, I expressed my feelings, "That is so beautiful, Alexandra. So beautiful." Giving her additional time to absorb her newly discovered truth, I reflected back Alexandra's journey, validating and affirming her voice, "Alexandra, what I am hearing is that your healing really took place in several different areas of your life. In your education and in your work with clients was learning how or giving yourself permission to *make yourself vulnerable around the most vulnerable.* There was that connection and that safety. And still, you took that risk."

I paused, then continued, "The second area would be in your clinical field internships and in your own work in therapy around self-discovery, attachment work, and addressing issues such as anxiety. The therapist-led work, if you will. And then combining that with your ongoing work as a therapist understanding that when we are serving clients, we are also attending to our own levels of healing as *we are being vulnerable with them.* And following, this last piece which was indeed huge—when your family and each individual made the decision to each embrace your own therapy. And with that, this amazing beautiful connection with your therapist who has mentored you and mothered you, and who has allowed you to be your authentic self. And, as you have said has met you with 'unconditional positive regard.'"

Alexandra nodded in agreement as I was speaking. And when I concluded, a whisper snuck through the tears, "You are absolutely right. The only piece I would add would be the connection to my community and their support system. *Because I am vulnerable with them,* I am real with them. They see me and I see them. That's huge."

Wanting to make sure all areas were covered, I asked Alexandra if there was anything else before we moved into the next section. In her own therapy, she recently had uncovered how working with kids helped her with inner-child healing. Alexandra disclosed, "I could be a kid, and be carefree. Things I couldn't experience as a child. I had to be a grown-up for so long. I wasn't allowed to be silly and free. And there was no emotional safety. And so even though I was the adult, I was craving that space."

As we were getting ready to move into our last section, the image of the field once again flooded my mind. However, this time it was filled with an assortment of flowers, and green foliage, and small furry figures playing behind the ponderosa pines. In the distance was graceful mature doe whose presence was no longer needed to guide and protect, but to serve as a reminder to the younger doe of how her vulnerability had served her well, and how it would continue to do so.

Wholeness To ...

As with the other daughters, moving into *Wholeness To ...* brought with it an ease for the daughters and me. Naming the gifts of one's healing journey is a welcoming part of each daughter's narrative and of our time together. I eagerly dove into our first question.

"Alexandra, where are you today in relationship with your mom?"

"I have a relationship with her, so that feels very nice. It's just a relationship with very strong boundaries. And what I know about that, is we can't go to any places of vulnerability." Alexandra recalled a recent example, "When my father died, she just kept trying to call me and I just couldn't take her calls. I couldn't be the strong one in that communication, which I am. She'll say whatever she says, and I usually can let it go and not take it on. But because I was so emotionally compromised over the death of my father, I could not... So, our relationship is not super deep but it is something and that is really, really nice. "

Alexandra described how her children, especially her son, have a relationship with her mom. In her own words and with a sweetness in her voice, Alexandra revealed, "I can see my mom in general being a better grandparent than she was a mother. That's kinda neat."

In a related question, I inquired, "Alexandra, where are you today with *yourself* with your mom?"

"Well, I have acceptance for what the relationship was. I forgive her. I understand that she was a very wounded human. I am not justifying her behavior. I have compassion and understanding. And I also believe she has made a lot of changes in her life: she's calmer, more centered, less reactive." Alexandra reflected and added, "And she married somebody almost fifteen years ago. And he loves her and she loves him and I see her being very happy in this relationship. And so that is also nice to see my adult parents have a much healthier relationship." And with her familiar gentle strength, Alexandra concluded, "Do I wish that she and I were close? Absolutely. But I have acceptance that is not going to happen. And every time I have tried, it has not gone well. She is just not able to be there in the way I would want her to."

Moving away from the mother-daughter experience, I asked, "How do feel about *yourself* today, and why?"

Alexandra's stream of words flowed smoothly and serenely, "I feel like the experiences I went through obviously helped shape me to be who I am. I am grateful I had the ability to face adversity and try different ways of moving through that healing, rather than being stuck in that wounded place. Because I was wounded, and I could have stayed there but I chose not to. And all these circumstances in my life kinda helped me in the path I'm in today. In general, I feel pretty content with myself. It's been years since I've struggled with anxiety disorders. Am I on the anxious spectrum? Absolutely! But, it is no longer debilitating. I use what I teach my clients—meditation and mindfulness. And, a little humor and humility! And, I like myself." Alexandra laughed lightly and I joined in. "I'm not perfect and I'm okay with that. I think I'm a good human, in general. I think I model the morals that I want for my kids, and nieces and nephews. I try to help other people, not just in my clinical work but in general, people who need help."

Her voice softened and slowed, "I love my kids… I love my husband…I love my friends… I love my community. I love where I live. I feel very content. I have all my basic needs met. I am aware things can change. Nothing is permanent. I feel today that if and when something bad happens, I am going to be okay." Her voice strengthened, "I'm going to be okay! I'm not saying I won't struggle or that it won't be easy, but I'm going to be okay. And that is the opposite from when someone experiences an anxiety disorder. All you are trying to do is grasp for control because the fear is the worst thing imaginable is going to happen. Now, I'm like 'I don't have control….and I'm okay!'"

We both basked in Alexandra's healing truths, reveling in their renewal. Tapping into the growth from her past to present, I asked, "Compared to your life messages as a child growing up, what are your life messages today? What is your internal dialogue you say about yourself?"

Alexandra popped right in, "I think for a long time I justified my pain, anger, and anxiety because of the bad things that happened to me as a child. And then at some point, I remember saying, 'Yeah, bad things happened to you—that's absolutely true, and you are choosing to stay there.' I realized that can't be an excuse for me not to heal. What I learned was trauma can occur and it can stop us from living a really full rich life. Are we going to be impacted by our history and our path? Absolutely. But we don't have to be held there, stay in that place. It can inform our future but it doesn't have to completely say what it looks like. It helped me to activate my own resiliency and believe in other humans' inner resiliency." Her voice took on an unusual intensity, "I truly believe...I truly believe we cannot do it alone. We *cannot* do it alone!" Her tone deepened again, "It doesn't have to be a therapist. It doesn't have to be formal. It can be informal like having a support system or asking for help. Being vulnerable and courageous enough is a vital part of the whole experience of being human and living." Alexandra chuckled, "Am I preaching? Are those messages?"

We both laughed, enjoying the levity of the moment. I inquired, "Are there other messages? Self to self? Woman to self?"

With her familiar strength, the statuesque doe stated, "As I am older, I realize, I am good enough. My worth is definitely not based on my appearance or how I look. I like to be healthy and work out because I feel better." She paused and pronounced, "My inner dialogue is....*I am enough!* I mean that is really it, '*I am enough!*'" The doe held her position and maintained her poise. "This is good enough! And today, I wake up and I am ready for this amazing day! I am pretty positive. I am pretty silly. I don't take myself too seriously!"

Continuing with our line of questioning, I asked, "Your self-talk as a mom?"

Alexandra punctuated her life message, "Oh, my self-talk as a mom, 'I'm good enough! And if I make a mistake, I own it. I do a re-do, a correction. I don't have to be perfect. There is no perfect in parenting." Tenderly, she added, "I am much more mindful about my parenting. I feel like I am a pretty decent parent. "

Sensing the importance of her role as a mom, I sat quietly, respecting her truths—*I am good enough...I don't have to be perfect....I feel I am a pretty decent parent.* The image of the field opened up, this time with a maturing lovely doe and a young lively buck grazing nearby but remaining under the loving gaze of a steady mother-doe. I gently segued into our next question.

"From your betrayal experiences with your mom, which life lessons have served you well and which ones continue to do so?"

"Resiliency. You know, that you don't have to live in a wounded place. Healing is possible for all humans. I am not trying to minimize other peoples' trauma histories…and say, 'Oh they can get through it.' I don't know what their journeys look like or how impacted they will be; however, I do truly believe we don't have to live in that wound. We have the ability to experience a better quality of life, whatever that looks like. My own journey has helped to believe in the work I do. I really enjoy what I do."

Alexandra described the importance of maintaining a balance in work and with her personal life. While disclosing how external motivations were not important to her, she stressed the significance of knowing her limits and of living an abundant life. In her own words, she shared a critical life message, "I don't have to save people. It is unattainable and unrealistic. I learned that, and I have good boundaries around that. "

Alexandra's inner strength continued to unfold. I explored bit further, wondering if there was more to unearth, "Other life lessons which have served you well?

A smooth, serene stream of words followed, carrying with them a message of inner depth and healing, "As I child I was told I was very emotional, over emotional. And so, what I have learned is that—and it is what I tell kids—emotions are a gift. And it is learning how to hone that gift so that it doesn't burn us out. My ability to feel deeply and to be able to feel *it*….and then….ahhhh….. I can move… and be back… and be present." Alexandra replayed her lesson, "So my ability to feel my emotions but not stay in them helps me live a full life. Emotions are there for a reason. We can tap into them but not to the point that it is all we are doing—just being an emotional being. An important life lesson is having that balance." She chuckled warmly and added, "What is the secret of life? Balance and moderation! It's what it always comes back to!"

Staying in the lightness of our conversation, I moved into our last question, "Alexandra, where do you wish to go from here? Is there something beyond wholeness?"

"Absolutely. I think just continuing on my healing journey. Sometimes I feel pretty darn good and then something will occur and I'm like, 'I'm not doing as well as I thought I was.' I will seek out some guidance or someone to bounce ideas off of. I think just having those informal mentors in my life is important. So continuing the self-discovery." Alexandra's voice lowered, but held its resolve, "I would also like to have more of acceptance about the relationship I have with my daughter and my hope is that as she enters adulthood that she can have a desire to have a relationship with me, woman to woman. I yearn for that relationship and I'm also in acceptance that it may not be the way I want. So, there is some pain because it taps into my mother's relationship which is not the way I wanted it and now my daughter's relationship is not the way I want it. What helps with that is that I have sooo many other relationships with women..."

I was still, allowing time for Alexandra's truths to settle. I knew she had touched upon an ongoing piece of brokenness, one which she continued to give herself permission to work through when possible and also to let go of when needed.

Alexandra's stream began again, flowing calmly and consistently, "Professionally, I would love to continue helping families. I love it when the child comes in but I also love working with the parents too." More intensely, she added, "Using my research and using my training...and just being a venue for change; that is so amazing! And then, above that, I'd like to do something more global, in my community area. Something with helping to destigmatizing mental illness and trying to promote awareness. Doing little things to create a path of small social change. Addressing issues such as 'What is mental health? And why is it important to talk about it?' All sorts of areas I truly believe in."

While acknowledging Alexandra's goals in moving beyond wholeness, I pressed a little more, "Alexandra, I am wondering what is at your core? What is moving within you and motivating you deep down inside?"

Alexandra smiled. Her face glowed. "I think I am really so glad we came up with that understanding...or that connection about my therapist and how she has been instrumental in my own healing, not just clinically, but in that attachment place where she really represents a mother figure. And that she is still there...oh...that is going to tear me up..." She wiped her eyes and sighed, "How lucky and fortunate I am. I am so grateful to continue to utilize that. And when self-worth issues come up, to continue to address them. And they do come up."

Knowing our time was coming to a close, I again waited, affirming Alexandra's newly discovered truth and the significance it carried with it. Mirroring her voice, I asked, "Any final or concluding thoughts?"

The gentle doe before me perked up and stared straight at me. Her voice was spirited, "Just that this has been awesome! This has been amazing! This has helped me to create a full narrative from start to where I am right now and kinda re-integrate it in a less fragmented way and see some of these connections. It helped me to touch back to some painful moments but I recognize I am not in the pain I used to be when I talked about it. And also, it helped me recognize the growth and all the aspects that helped me in my healing process. It's kinda cool! Thank you so much!"

Alexandra's words—*…it helped me recognize the growth and all the aspects that helped me in my healing process*—filled my spirit and flooded my mind. This amazing daughter—this steadfast doe—who once wandered amidst a field of adversity now stood solidly within fertile grounds of family, friends, and community. Surrounded by the elements which she chose to embrace along her path to wellness, this graceful doe courageously uncovered her truths and integrated them into her authentic being. Although her voice—her flow of self—was still for now, the doe's strong, steady, and yet soft dark eyes reflected a wholeness deep within and revealed its inner truths…

I Am Vulnerable ~ I Am Enough

Follow-up Reflection...

The past month was busy with the winter holidays, and the 2017 New Year celebrations filled our schedules with all their accompanying gatherings and goodies. And so, Alexandra and I made the decision to conclude our time together after we both had a chance to settle back into our routines. Four weeks passed since our four-hour interview, and winter's white coverings blanketed our environs.

As was true with the other daughters, I looked forward to checking in with Alexandra. With a hot cup of tea strategically placed on my desk, I once again, arranged my tape-recorders, reviewed my notes, and placed my call to her. Within a few seconds, her familiar secure soft voice greeted me on the other end.

After a mutual brief sharing of our holidays, I moved into our first question. "Alexandra, how did you feel after our interview? Any thoughts, feelings, or reflections that you would like to share?"

With a calm confidence, Alexandra disclosed, "It was really nice to have that narrative from birth until now….some of the challenges, and strengths…and the growth." She tenderly added, "And I did meet with my therapist since our interview and I let her know one of the things we discovered in my narrative—she had been like a mother figure…feeling that attachment." Almost in a whisper, Alexandra uttered, "It was really neat. I wanted to share that with you."

The warm glow from weeks earlier re-entered the space between us. I swallowed, giving myself a moment while honoring Alexandra's truth. I mirrored her soft voice, "That is so wonderful."

When the emotion lifted, I moved on, "Anything else after that day? How you felt?"

With her familiar strength and stamina, Alexandra concluded, "No, nothing that came up. It was definitely more intense than I had anticipated but also really affirming." Her voice slowed, validating each piece of her experience. "I was so honored to be there. But nothing else like, 'Oh, I shared too much.' I felt honored. I felt good. It was really nice."

Moved by her words, I thanked Alexandra for her participation and for the gift of her narrative. And as I had done with the other daughters, I reviewed a few issues with her around anonymity and confidentiality, and then I prepared to read a section aloud from her written narrative. As it was with each daughter, it was critical to me in sharing each daughter's voice that I do so with the utmost regard and respect. Taking in a deep breath and calming my spirit, I began.

As I read, I pictured the steadfast doe listening on the other end, positioned in her field and basking in her healing truths. And, as had occurred with each of the daughters, when I came to the end of the passage, I waited, wondering if I had done them and her justice.

There was a long pause. I waited, not saying a word. And then, as the doe gazed upon the vast field of truths lain before her, a humble murmur was slowly dislodged from her spirit and made its way through, "It... was..... inspirational."

Mirroring Alexandra's tone while the lump in my throat began to recede, I concurred, "Yes, inspirational..."

The doe's voice rose again, "I'm so excited...I am thinking 'Is that me?' Oh my gosh, Holli, what a wonderful thing right now when I am going through some tough times," Alexandra breathed in deeply and exhaled slowly, creating space for tears to form and spill. Alexandra wept quietly, "What an affirmation." I remained still, giving her tears time to display their meanings and speak their messages. The doe returned to her poised posture and concluded, "Thank you so much for letting me be a part of this study. It's amazing. It's wonderful. I am so thankful."

Listening to Alexandra's words brought forth images of two fields—one of little fawn struggling amidst its brokenness and one of a steadfast doe secure amidst its wholeness. By sharing her narrative and affirming its presence in her life, this gracious doe has come full circle, honoring a journey which took her from unearthing her most fractured pieces and turning them into her most treasured healing truths...

I Am Vulnerable ~ I Am Enough

7 "I Am The Phoenix That Has Risen From The Ashes" – Bettina

Reflection

January 2017 has welcomed winter in all her wonder. As I thought about winter, she is like a bridge—saluting the ending of one year and signaling the beginning of another. Over the past few days of working in my warm office and watching the pines sway in the brisk blustery winds, I too felt I was nearing the end of an eighteen-month journey—"The Daughters Project." When I started in August 2015, I gave myself two years to complete this study. However, I continued to keep a pulse on the themes and messages which were coming through the daughters' narratives, allowing them to guide me in lieu of a preset timeline. And as I prepared to begin the process with a daughter who I believed would be my last, I knew that her participation in "The Daughters Project," as was true of all the daughters, would add another layer of depth to this study. After neatly organizing my materials into a new crisp folder, I thought about how my path crossed with Bettina's.

In August of 2016, I facilitated a colloquium workshop *Breaking Through Betrayal* at a local college for Masters' level counseling students and licensed counselors and therapists. Introducing myself to the students, I described the history behind my interest in the topic of betrayal as well as my current project—a qualitative study entitled "Daughters Betrayed by Their Mothers: Moving From Brokenness To Wholeness." I did not elaborate on the study because I wanted to keep the focus on the workshop at hand. At the end of the workshop, many of the attendees waited to speak with me one on one. Some had more personal stories or comments around the topic of betrayal which they wanted to share; others had questions or were searching for guidance in their work with betrayal. I noticed one female who stood toward the end of the line, waiting patiently until the others finished and were on their way.

Approaching me, her soulful energy filled the space between us. Although the classroom was packed wall to wall with students, I remembered her thoughtful questions and reflections throughout the workshop and her strong interest in the topic of betrayal. And even though the students had introduced themselves at the beginning of the workshop, I asked for her name again.

With a smile and a melodic rhythm, she answered, "Bettina." Her name, as she would relay to me later, was important for her to use in "The Daughters Project."

Bettina graciously thanked me for the workshop and we began to connect very easily and comfortably, discussing different facets of "betrayal." As we were concluding our conversation, Bettina paused and then inquired, "If you are still seeking participants for your "Daughters' Project," I would be very interested."

Enthusiastically, I gave Bettina my contact information and briefly disclosed my timeline as well as application procedures and protocol. Over the next week, I promptly received Bettina's biographical information. As I read through it, I was moved by her breadth of experiences and by her expansive lens with which she viewed the world.

I learned Bettina was 55 years of age and was born in Germany. Although she has lived in the United States for thirty-three years, her words revealed what determined home for her, "I never felt like I belonged in Germany, but I can't say that I am American either. I am a citizen of the earth and the land has always spoken to me more loudly than the nationality to which it has been assigned."

In response to religious or spiritual identification, Bettina described how she was brought up Catholic and soon discovered it was not her "cup of tea." Her parents allowed her to leave the church when she was a teenager and both parents left the church as adults. In her own words, Bettina shared, "My relationship with the divine is very personal—[I] have never followed a faith, though Buddhism has left its mark on me. In the recent years, the 'Oneness Community' that began in India has been an important influence, as has been Matt Kahn most recently. If there is a thread that is continuous through it all—it is 'nature' and non-ordinary states of consciousness which I go into spontaneously some of the time and more predictable through the practice of Authentic Movement—(trance) dance, solo time in nature, soul craft practices and sacred sexuality."

Responding to questions regarding sexual orientation and relationship status, Bettina disclosed how she would identify as "mostly heterosexual though I had my share of explorations in my younger years that included polyamory and homosexual relationships." And although Bettina responded that she has "been considering the possibility of a relationship with a woman," she also noted that her relationship with a recent boyfriend was moving into friendship and "I am taking time in celibacy for a while until I am clear what I really want/need and what things need to be sorted out within myself before I endeavor another relationship."

After reading through the breadth of Bettina's personal background, it was evident how it was equally complimented by her educational and professional pursuits. Bettina holds a Bachelor's degree in Humanities with an emphasis in Psychology. However, she has obtained many additional hours of training in a number of body work modalities with an in-depth study in Ortho-Bionomy. Bettina has also received training in the areas of wilderness and vision quest guidance as well as visual and martial arts techniques. Other modalities of education included process-oriented psychology, authentic movement, and sand-play therapy.

Because of her wide range of experiences, I wasn't surprised how Bettina's career interests and pathways reflected that diversity. In her own words, "I work with people from pre-birth till death, quite a few couples, some children and whole families including their animal friends. I have been teaching bodywork for thirty years, and trauma resolution for ten." In addition to her somatic-based trauma work as well as bodywork and energy work, Bettina also described her incorporation of hypnosis and clearing techniques into her practices.

As I was reaching the conclusion of Bettina's biographical landscape, I noticed how similar themes of widening her experiences continued into her future interests and paths. Along with several writing projects in the works, Bettina shared how she looked forward to "...spending more time in the wilderness [and] dedicating more time to art and music." She also stated, "I have been busy for too long and not always with the things that really feed me."

Moving into her last few sentences, I was struck by the integrity and intensity of Bettina's words, "My mother's dying has been unraveling patterns I did not even know existed and I am incredibly excited to find out 'who is in there' that isn't about imprints from parents, society, and the coping mechanisms I had to develop...quite an amazing journey."

Thinking about Bettina's words, I looked out my office window. Another very cold and blustery day. Although winter is signaling the end of a year and perhaps the closing chapter to the Daughters' interviews, clearly it is saluting the beginning of a new year welcoming in the messages of another powerful voice and her truths.

Setting

It snowed almost continuously the past week leaving a fluffy white coating sprawling across the rolling grounds and blanketing the steep roof tops. The wind made her voice known by hurling clumps of snow through the pines. While the winter concerto played outside with all its harmonic crescendos, I too felt a familiar excitement start to build inside of me. The past couple of days, I, once again, organized my notes and tape recorders in preparation for the pre-interview phone conference with Bettina. As I sorted through the forms and biographical information, I re-read Bettina's explanation as to why she desired to participate in "The Daughters Project."

> My mother took leave of her body seven months ago. In the last years of her life, dementia softened many of her patterns of needing to manage and criticize others. During those years, I had a chance to complete many of the difficulties I had with her and come to peace with her.
>
> Since her death, I have had the opportunity to celebrate the ways in which my mom was an inspiration, and also examine levels of injury that our relationship had engendered that I had not been aware off before.
>
> Once my mom left her physical vehicle, a surprising number of patterns shifted inside of me and profound changes are occurring in my life. Some of these changes are gifts of grace and some have taken intense focus and dedication to my own unfolding and healing.
>
> Being able to reflect on my relationship with my mom with a witness, to celebrate what has been healed and most likely become aware of places that need more of my attention, so I can truly know the preciousness of who I am, feels like amazing gift to me.
>
> Besides all that, I so appreciate the opportunity to share my journey, so it may help others on their path.

A huge lumped lodged itself inside the back of my throat. I took a small sip of warm tea, feeling it dissolve and slide away. Another daughter. Another enormous responsibility placed upon my shoulders— to bear witness and to do justice to Bettina's journey *From Brokenness To Wholeness*. I took a larger sip of tea allowing its warmth to fill me.

As I dialed her number, a quiet enthusiasm descended upon me. I eagerly awaited her voice.

Within a few moments, Bettina's rhythmic German accent filled the space between us. We chatted briefly about the series of recent storms and the uneasy emotions they carried with them. However, as we continued to settle into our conversation, the volume of the wild winds and shooting rain outside my office window lessened and then disappeared. I moved into the first question of our check in.

"Bettina, do you have any concerns or questions about today or about the process ahead?"

As Bettina had done previously in our email exchanges, she inquired about the parameters around sharing publically or professionally regarding her participation in "The Daughters Project." She disclosed confidently, "I speak very personally about my process with my clients and my students. And I just have a feeling there will be much to learn for people from your book. I am not really sure what the question is. I just kinda feel like what you are doing is so important and I wanted it to be available to people. It's going to be a process of me letting people know I participated in this project. I think it is important to protect client privacy, but as far as I am concerned I don't think there is anything really that has to stay confidential. I do a lot of reflecting but I also know that when I am speaking or being asked questions, things come out of me that I didn't even know were in there!" A soft laughter broke through. Bettina added, "I'm not sure how I am going to feel about it by the time we are done but at the moment, I don't have any hesitation. I want to be clear, authentic, and truthful."

Listening to Bettina's willingness to remain open and authentic regarding her narrative and her natural desire to share her process around "The Daughters Project" with others, I validated her feelings as well as her intentions. Aside from maintaining the integrity of the qualitative study and any copyrighted materials, I supported Bettina in sharing her process in ways which were meaningful and purposeful to her. As with all the daughters, I reaffirmed the intensity of participating in a qualitative study such as this, and I recognized the potential need for securing healthy outlets or safe harbors as an extension of their ongoing healing. I encouraged Bettina to follow her intuitions, tethering herself to those practices which served her well.

After answering a few questions around elements of "The Daughters Project" such as number of participants, estimated length of the final product, and how each daughter's words were transcribed and integrated into written narratives, I segued into a foundational question.

"Bettina, when you think of the word "betrayal" today, what meanings or connotations come to mind?"

Bettina replied, "What you said at the colloquium....and I forgot the exact words you used....what really landed with me is it was a betrayal by assumed relationship. And my mother...." Bettina paused, and then continued, "I actually said to a friend once, 'It's kinda funny why we have this assumed relationship that parents should be taking care of their children when so few do.' It's really kinda funny. But I think we are wired biologically and psychologically that our families are a safe place to be...and mine wasn't. I had stuff with my dad. But my mother didn't protect me. She wasn't consistent. She asked me to be head of household when I was really young. All that felt like a huge betrayal as far as what my capacity or ability was to go through a normal childhood development that I didn't get to have. I mean I was the boss of the family by the time I was nine and that is what everyone called me."

Bettina's voice remained strong, "That is what betrayal was for me. She did not fulfill her role as mother in the way that we generally think about. And she also did not protect me from injury from others. So that was another big piece that I consider betrayal. And in a lot of ways she wasn't capable of being a partner to my father so I stepped into the role of surrogate wife. I felt like I needed to protect her and to make sure she was okay. So there were all these ways in which I did not get to be a child."

A heaviness descended between us carrying with it the broken pieces of betrayal. I sat quietly, honoring them.

Bettina explained, "She was bipolar and narcissistic. And she also did not take her meds."

I listened.

Bettina's voice returned to its spirited tone, "Does that cover it? The list goes on. I have a loooong list!" Her laughter lightened the moment. "I can laugh about it now. I mean there are times when I don't laugh about it. But now I can see how it all happened." Her closing words captured the essence of her being. "Does that make my life easy? Not at all. Has it helped me to become an unbelievably amazing person? Yes. Is there still stuff to heal? Yes."

After we confirmed the date of our four-hour interview and said our goodbyes, I relaxed in my chair and breathed in deeply. Reflecting upon the betrayal pieces in Bettina's life, "She did not fulfill her role as mother in the ways that we generally think about. And she also did not protect me from injury from others," I couldn't help but contrast them with her wellness tapestry of present—"Does that make my life easy? Not at all.

Has it helped me to become an unbelievably amazing person? Yes. Is there still stuff to heal? Yes."

As I had with each daughter before, I thought about her presence and her placement in "The Daughters Project." There was a reason why Bettina's narrative came last. I wondered what lessons and messages her voice would bring. I wondered what her healing truths would reveal and then gift to others. I wondered what processes enabled this extraordinary daughter to move *From Brokenness To Wholeness.*

Outside my office window, the Sun poked Her face through the foliage and the tall pines. Nature bearing witness to the journey ahead.

Beginning

One month after our pre-interview conference, I prepared for the four to five-hour interview with Bettina. Because we live in the same area, we decided to conduct our interview in my home. After laying out some gluten-free cookies and arranging an assortment of teas, I glanced out the dining room window, appreciating the bright blue skies. Although we were nearing the end of February, cloudy rainy days descended upon us and darkened our skies more than customary. A sharp briskness remained in the air; however, the cleansing rains left behind a bouquet of renewal and refreshment. I felt ready and energized thinking about the process ahead. As Bettina's car pulled up to the house, I carefully checked my recorders and my notes, making sure everything was in place. After adjusting the fireplace to a low quiet flame, I greeted Bettina at the door.

With her arms full, Bettina ascended the stairs to the main living areas following my lead. While settling into our chairs around the dining room table, Bettina laid a large collage of family photos, drawings, and illustrations against a nearby wall and explained how the display would bring significance to our interview. She also placed a striking portrait of a cat etched by her mother on the dining room table. Bettina commented on the importance of honoring the process ahead of us.

Bettina asked softly, "I wanted to check and see if you are okay with a prayer before we start?"

Matching her tone, I replied, "Yes. I am absolutely okay."

For the next few moments, Bettina graciously expressed her gratitude for the opportunity to participate in "The Daughters Project." She acknowledged the scope of betrayal and prayed that "the benefits go out to all women who have been betrayed...and to the benefit of all beings." She asked for "guidance and protection..." and what was shared was "held in the Sacred." Listening to her words, I sensed a safety and warmth enter our space. I too prayed, asking for what was of paramount importance to me with each daughter and each interview- that I would honor their truths and their voices, and I would do justice to their narratives.

At the close of prayer we paused, giving ourselves time to absorb our mutual requests. Taking in a deep breath, I began.

"Bettina, how do you refer to your mom, or how did you refer to your mom? How has that changed over time?" And I added, "I know with your narrative we are also talking about variances in language."

Bettina quickly responded, "So, when I was little, I called her *mammi* which is similar to mama. And then as I got older especially once I reached my early twenties…or maybe later, I started calling her by her first name. Ummm, it was a very significant moment when I began calling her by her first name because it became really clear that she was not *mom*. There were moments where I would address her, for example on her birthday, by *mammi*—the mom name—but it became really clear it was inappropriate to pretend because she really wasn't really capable as a mother.

My sister and I, first me and then my sister later in life as she grew older, were my mother's caretaker in a lot of ways. It was a really poignant moment. My brother continued calling my mother *mom* until the end of her life and my sister and I didn't. And I only did it when it was like a term of endearment to let her know I still thought of her as my mother, as well. But the inner conflict of calling her that when she wasn't actually able to be that was too great. It felt inappropriate."

After clarifying that *mammi* was the German word for mother or mom, I moved into the next question, "Bettina, how does it feel today to talk about your mom? And has that changed over time?"

Bettina breathed in deeply, then slowly exhaled, "A big spectrum. I feel so liberated since she died. Our relationship has been able to become what it could have been hadn't there been so much injury and incapacity in her life. Because she was this conglomerate of a total inspiration and a disaster…and everything in between. And so, I feel incredible joy to be able to relate with her now on the other side in a way that feels much more appropriate. I feel a lot of sadness that we had not a lot of that," Bettina's voice softened and broke. Her tears surfaced and flowed. "I feel sad that I didn't get to be mothered. And so it is everything. I feel immense gratitude to her….ummm…how she ended up leaving the planet. It was probably the kindest most skillful thing that she did. It allowed my sister and I to be present with the process and she didn't put anything out." Her voice strengthened, "Having been who she was …it was hard for her to be truly present for other people. She wanted to but she couldn't. And the fact she ended up dying without a big hoop-a-la at the end and that the hospice doctor had checked in and said she was good for another while, and then, she died four hours after that."

Bettina's voice slowed but held its steadiness, "I had already made the decision that to be there for her actual transition would not be good for me. As it turned out it was all pretty amazing. I got to do all the ceremony after I found out she had died." Bettina described her process of meeting with a Buddhist Lama who helped her and helped her mother "to leave," and "who [now] is fully liberated."

I gave the silent space between us time to settle us both, being mindful of how it felt for Bettina to speak of her mom, eight months after her passing.

Bettina's voice returned to its spirited tone, "She is good. She is really good. And, it is such a relief. And the relief that I have that I no longer have to worry about her. I don't have to wonder in the physical plane what kind of treatment or what kind of process...and on the emotional plane, I don't have to keep holding her anymore."

Bettina further explained her process of ceremony for her mom. Referring to her collage, Bettina pointed out a photo which illustrated "the place of refuge." Because her mom loved nature, Bettina designed and built a large bark house—a spirit house—on her property. Part of Bettina's journey in coming to terms with why her mom was hanging on was the understanding that, "A young part of her [mother] was so injured and so bewildered that until that part had healed, she couldn't leave." Bettina's words resonated with peace, "Shortly after the spirit house was completed, she went into hospice."

I paused for several moments honoring Bettina's experience. Although I knew we would be revisiting Bettina's present feelings toward her mom later in the interview, the enormity and emotionality of Bettina's ritual in healing from her mom's betrayals and the additional release and renewal which came from a very intimate and spiritual process, was one of sacred meaning.

When I felt the grieving space had been respected, I moved on to our next question.

"Bettina, we have spoken of the word *betrayal* and about its connotations. How does it feel for you today and how does it feel to use it in relating to your mom?"

Bettina's voice was light and lilted, "I have been thinking about this a lot the last few days. It is such a funny thing because on this material plane, lots of betrayal. Like this feeling of...it was all upside down... 'I had to take care of you. You were oblivious. I was the one guiding the way so much of the time.' And then in this bigger picture, now that I am on the other side of it, kinda the perfection of the insanity that I lived through. And it's not just with my mother and so... For this human girl, the betrayal was a disaster! And, for this adult being who is a much more spiritual being, I can just see how the betrayals—by my entire family but especially by my mother and father—have also created who I am. I could never be doing what I do if I had not been through the hell I've been through." Bettina's words took flight, "So it's all very relative. I don't wish this on other people, but holy cow—this has made into who I am!"

We both enjoyed the levity in her words. While I changed the tape, Bettina stretched her limbs. I noticed how she liked to move, and how it seemed to relax her and land her back into a place of clarity and calm. Sensing she was ready, I moved into the next section.

Background

"Bettina, how would you describe your family as you were growing up? How many siblings in the home, parents, or other family?"

"So, I was born and raised in Germany. Both of my parents were pulled out of high school at the very end of the war so they were both pretty traumatized; my father more than my mother. And I believe him being as sensitive of a man as he was he never recovered from the trauma of what happened during Hitler's reign and the Nazis burning books." Bettina described him further, "My father was a philosopher from the time he was very young and later spent time with people like Schopenhauer. At age seventeen when he had to go to war, he was literally one of last people out of his particular holding area that didn't end up being a prisoner of war. Everyone else after him was shipped off to Russia or wherever. My father—hurting anything was highly difficult for him—so to have to go to war was about as horrible as it gets. Thank goodness because he was so smart they ended up putting him more with technology and decoding Morse code. So, he didn't have to go out on the battle field and kill people. I don't think he would have survived. So, he took to alcohol shortly after all that he went through and struggled with alcohol all of his life. He was in and out of rehab many times. He was highly addicted to tobacco and almost burned our house down. In my early life, my father seemed to be the much bigger problem. It was so obvious. He was alcoholic. He was absent. I'm going to say although nobody looked at it that way, I'm thinking he was somewhere on the

Asperger's autistic spectrum. He was absolutely brilliant and really shut down."

I listened.

Bettina's voice lowered, "He totally loved me. And he had no way of expressing it. He was so repressed. He actually had a lot of sexual energy." Bettina reflected and added, "My father was a highly sexual man, highly sexual. He never touched me, but man... The lust that I saw in his eye as I started to become a young woman felt very, very unsafe. My mother would comment on it and not help." Bettina resituated herself and disclosed, "And later on he took his life. He took his life when I was thirty. It was very intense. So, there is betrayal on a lot of levels." She took a deep breath, "That was a long time ago. I had a long time to wrestle with that. And we're good. And I'm good too!"

Delving further into her background, Bettina described how the relationship between her parents was very strained. She added, "I don't have a lot of memory of my really early life. But when we moved to a new house when I was six, that is when the majority of my memories are pretty clear. And that's because my mother was pregnant late in life. She was thirty-nine. So, I have an older brother. I remember he was excited to have a sister and all I could think of at that time was, 'Oh shit. I'm going to be changing diapers and I'm going to be a baby-sitter.' And I was not excited. At that time, I don't think I was conscious that my mother was mentally ill, but something in me knew this was going to be trouble. At age seven, I became 'Mother.'"

As I envisioned a little girl performing the duties of an adult, I learned more about how Bettina was expected to be one.

"I was my mom and dad's favorite child. They were both happy to have a girl. My older brother was viewed as a huge threat to both my mother and my father." Bettina added, "I was super brilliant and so I became his [my father's] surrogate spouse. My mother was brilliant but she wasn't intellectual. And I was highly intellectual. The moment I could talk, my father latched on to me. I was trained in platonic discourse when I was five!" Bettina's laughter broke through, then subsided. She spoke resolutely, "I was my parents' favorite but this amount of responsibility I had to shoulder—[being] my sister's parent and my father's surrogate spouse. By the time I was nine, everyone called me 'the boss.' I was always the 'acting oldest.'"

I listened intently, capturing the image of a disordered nest, parentless and unprotected.

Bettina described her brother as being very violent and very scary. He abused her physically and he exuded tremendous power over her. In her words, Bettina explained, "I did not feel safe. My parents couldn't protect me. They had no idea how to set boundaries with this crazy person." After Bettina described some of the accidental head injuries her brother endured during childhood as well as their apparent longer-term repercussions, I moved back into Bettina's role in the family.

"Bettina, could you elaborate a bit more on your role as 'boss'?"

"I appeared to be the only person who had an overview and who had the capacities to do something about what was going on. Obviously, some of it was delusional, but I saw what was going on and I tried to set it right. My brother didn't have any interest and my sister was a lost child. My father was brilliant but couldn't change a light bulb. My mother was creative but chaotic."

Bettina described how she left Germany when she was sixteen to study in the United States as an exchange student. Years later, at age twenty-three, she would move permanently to the United States. In reflecting on her role, she added, "I remember thinking, 'I've got to get out of here.' I was the one maneuvering the strands making sure nobody was going to flip out. I was going to completely lose it or get lost."

Thinking about the fragility of both parents, I inquired how her father supported the family. Bettina explained he was head of a small TV station focused on cultural events. Her father traveled to Greece and Mexico, conducting tours and writing books. In her words, Bettina shared, "He was absent a lot. He had a lot of affairs. He worked until he killed himself. He was philosopher—a visionary."

I waited for Bettina, mindful of the difficult territory we were covering.

Her voice took on an unusual heaviness, "I felt a huge sense of responsibility of having caused him [my father] so much suffering in his life. It was one of my hugest pains growing up. I'm like this huge burden to my father. He was so unhappy in his own skin. As a teenager, it was so brutal. I was so tired of it. I remember saying to him one time, 'Why don't you just kill yourself instead of doing it in little steps over time.' His disease was bad enough that he threw up every morning–every morning. His liver was a disaster. He had these tremors. Watching him toward the end of his life was just...so painful."

Taking in Bettina's words, I connected with her sense of responsibility as she not only tended to herself but also for her intended caregivers.

She described more of her family dynamic, "One of the huge betrayals with my mother, is that she kept using me as a confident for her marriage troubles and her upset with her husband. She was highly codependent, and she made me codependent in the process." Bettina paused and continued to explain her injury from this betrayal, "Basically, the message that I got was 'men are more trouble than they are worth'....and 'you can't really make them accountable.' She just complained about him [father] but she participated in it. She would say, 'We don't want to get divorced because of you guys.' So, there was this whole feeling of being a burden. The more she talked about how unhappy my dad was and how difficult it was for her to live with him, the more I just went, 'Marriage, forget it. Having children, forget it. Having love, forget it. It's all totally impossible and why even try.'" Bettina's voice slowed but remained strong, "It gave me this false sense of importance because I was the one she confided in. I was in-between my parents and I was getting ground up. My mother using me in some ways what she couldn't fulfill with my dad."

Reflecting on her role and of the parent-child reversals, the image of a young but formidable bird came to mine. With both parents floundering, she was forced to find her way and formulate theirs. I wondered how she found the courage to leave the nest altogether.

As we moved into our concluding questions on background, Bettina shared how she finished high school in Germany and lived at home for two more years. Although she remembered her parents were in the process of separating, she remained occupied with her studies. At age nineteen, she moved out of their house.

Bettina recalled, "I was so mad at my dad. I was still helping my mom. My sister was helping but my dad had separated himself from the family altogether." Bettina described the hardships on her sister, caring for both her father and her mother into their later years.

Sensing there was more, I remained still.

Bettina paused for a few moments and then added, "I do want to share that my maternal grandmother was a huge positive influence in our lives. She would make order and bring calm. She was very unemotional but rock solid, very loving. She read books to me and baked. She was one of the few stable elements in my life. I have enormous gratitude for her, putting up with the insanity of our family."

I thought about how there are those external elements in our lives which can bring us nourishment in the most unexpected and unconditional ways. I wondered if there were additional sources which fed her soul and brought her remnants of truth.

Bettina described the strong cultural influence imparted from her paternal grandparents: classical music, philosophers, books, and nature. Her voice remained secure. She situated herself upright and erect in the chair, almost like a bird ready to take flight. "It's part of what kept me sane…having some sanity even if it isn't in the home." She paused, then punctuated her statement, "Understanding it doesn't have to be this way, I have some reference point for what it is like when somebody is actually present."

I sat quietly, at one with this remarkable resilient bird sitting across from me in her statuesque pose. I replayed her words—*I have some reference point for what it is like when somebody is actually present.* Approaching her betrayal narrative in more depth, I became acutely aware of how bearing witness was essential to Bettina's process.

Betrayal Narrative

Because we had touched upon Bettina's betrayal narrative in the previous sections, I encouraged Bettina to allow her thoughts to flow naturally, even if there was repetition. As was true for all the daughters, it was important that her narrative emanate from its authentic roots.

"Bettina, when did you first start thinking about your betrayal narrative in reference to your mom? And, what was that like for you?"

Bettina's steady spirit sprung forth, "The first betrayal was when I was age seven and I'm going to have to be mom. I just intuitively knew she didn't have it in her to take care of this child by herself. We did have help. She did have people come in from other countries who wanted to learn German. They were called au pairs. They were live-in young women who would help out with the children. So, it wasn't all on me, but there was a lot of it." Bettina thought for a moment and added, "Nobody protected me from these inappropriate responsibilities. It was probably in my teenage years where I grokked that something was really upside down. I remember the book *The Primal Scream* came out, and I had been wondering about myself because I would get feedback from my peers like, 'What is up with you? Why are you so over-bearing? Why do you have to control everything? Why can't you just trust?' On the other hand, my parents gave me so much freedom. I could be out to all hours of the night when I was a teenager. I was completely independent. I started spending the night away from the time I was twelve or thirteen. And I started to see how different that was. Other people had to be home by 10 pm."

I listened, remaining present.

"Because I got good grades, I leveraged that [freedom]. Somebody should have put their foot down. I could have been killed. I consider that a betrayal because I wasn't protected. I wasn't protected from my brother. I wasn't protected from my father. I wasn't protected from inappropriate things later in life from all that freedom I had." Bettina's voice halted briefly, "There was sexual abuse from a friend of the family that my parents didn't know about. I finally did tell my mother many years later. But they were oblivious. To me that's a betrayal." Bettina hesitated for a moment. Her voice softened, "I can see in the pictures up until age seven and what happened after that...and that's when the abuse happened in the friend of the family's house where we were invited to go on vacation. I repressed those memories until years later."

I sat quietly and observed. The elongated bird nestled herself into a soft blanket I had provided earlier that morning. She seemed to know well how to comfort herself.

Bettina elaborated more intimately on her betrayal narrative with her mom, "The fact that my mother didn't protect me became apparent. The combination of way too much responsibility and her not protecting me, not acting in a role of mother at the time. I figured that out when I was in my early teens. And then I read *The Primal Scream* book, and they say you have to be eighteen before you can do it [therapy], I thought, 'I'm not going to survive. I'm so screwed up.' I knew something was off, and mostly I thought something was wrong with me."

Wanting to clarify the nature or pattern of Bettina's betrayals, I posed a more specific question, "Bettina, it sounds like the betrayals by your mom and others were chronic or ongoing. Would that be accurate? Would you speak to that?"

Bettina sat straight up, perched with confidence and clarity. "It was very chronic in its unpredictability. So, the beautiful parts of my mother were....I didn't even know that other people didn't make their own birthday and Christmas presents. Like we would spend hours at the dining table making things until I was probably...fifteen. My mother loved creating and she was phenomenal in the crafts department. She talked to everything...to the trees, the birds, the insects...and she would have conversations with everything. She gave me this appreciation for nature and for art. It was such a spectrum of absolute beauty and art and expression, which also took me a while to figure out that wasn't normal in other families, and she was so, I mean so out of the box. She was very, very bipolar." Bettina's spirit soared. "When she was in her manic phases....oh man...it was amazing! She was the light of the party. She would instigate all these really fun things. She would do vision boards...and this was in the seventies! Not run-of-the-mill stuff!"

We both chuckled. Our laughter lingered for a moment as Bettina repositioned herself, tucking her long limbs in and around her like a bird nesting itself.

Bettina's voice slowed and softened, "What was consistent was there were very few times my father didn't drink. There were times where he did stop smoking, which I was really glad for. There were times where my mother would be stable for a while, not for very long. And the older she got, the worse it got. By the time I left Germany at twenty-three, she was pretty not stable."

Gently, I inquired, "May I ask what were the depressive episodes like?"

"She would just become really....ummm.... there were times where she was institutionalized so I don't know exactly what happened. Both my parents were institutionalized, my father for detox and depression. My mother for depression. That happened later when I was older. It wasn't like she wouldn't get out of bed when I was younger. Later in life, she wouldn't."

Bettina sat quietly for a few moments. Vividly, she recalled her past, "When she came to the States to visit, I basically had a twenty-four seven job putting her back together. My sister used this example, and later on I was really sad to realize how true it was." Her voice intensified as she revealed her sister's description, "'We were all just logs in the fire.' She [our mother] was very narcissistic. And so she would be sucking energy. She would be in this really depressed state and then somebody would come around who was vivacious and she would wake up. She would absorb from other people. And during the last ten years when she had in-home care, we would see some of these relatively vibrant people who over the course of time they were with my mother... just kind of turned grey."

As I listened, the image of a mother bird feeding off of others and depleting them instead of providing nourishment entered my mind. Bettina's words completed the picture.

"In my forties, I had all this chronic pain and I sought out a truly talented healer. She said, 'Your mother has an energetic feeding tube into you and she has been taking your energy from the time you were born.' Bettina breathed deeply, then explained, "During that time, she felt so toxic to me. There were about three or four years where I could hardly have any contact with her. I wasn't living in Germany anyway. She felt so toxic to me; I felt like I was being devoured by a vampire. It was a really rough time. I hated my mother during that time. I just went, 'How could you do this to me?'"

The images of Bettina's words flooded my mind: burning logs, toxic flames, and a ravenous vampire. Not only an "upside-down" nest filled with betrayals, but nestled within it a stoic bird suffocating amidst a bed of burning embers. I refocused on the vision before me.

The elegant bird repositioned herself in her stately stance and pronounced, "That was probably the biggest betrayal that I experienced. It's not just that you are incapable...you're feeding on your own daughter! That is not okay with me! If I am going to rate the betrayals, that was the biggest betrayal of all."

The weightiness of Bettina's words smoldered between us. And yet, the resilient creature before me continued to unearth her truths and speak them.

Bettina described how her mother had opportunities to get well, but her mother stopped her medication and dropped out of therapy. Bettina viewed it as another betrayal because "she [her mother] took it out on us." Reflecting on her past injuries, Bettina's steady voice recalled, "We are paying for your inability to stick with the process. We are all paying for it, all the time." She returned to her prior metaphor, "We were just logs in the fire ...just the sense of being used for her not taking responsibility."

Replaying the intensity of Bettina's words—*we were just logs in the fire*—the nest which once resembled a bed of charred remnants was now a ghostly relic, crafted and consumed by its creator. And still, buried beneath ashes of parental responsibility and accountability, two young birds struggled to serve their mother.

Sensing we had covered a wide spectrum of Bettina's betrayal narrative, I checked with her to see if there were any other specific pieces she wanted to add. Bettina described that within the betrayal of being given so much freedom, there was also a lack of guidance by her mom in the more intimate areas of her life: conversations about sex, rite of passage, and birth control. One of the messages Bettina received from her mother and father's lack of involvement was, "Grownups are incompetent. They are useless. They might be making some money, but they are useless." Bettina explained further, "They are clueless about relationships, with life and with love. They are just moving objects through space."

As we came to the close of this section, Bettina disclosed that her parents were "not malicious but basically wounded, unskillful, not healed people." She described how extremely painful it was to her spirit that she could not help them. She spent her entire life trying to fix her parents. As Bettina revealed more truths, her voice lowered, "I remember at workshops when asked what we would wish for if we could have the perfect parents, and all I ever wanted to see was my parents in love."

The gentle bird wept softly, "I just wanted them to hold hands and be happy. And for us not to have to be responsible for their happiness. I would have been fine with all the other challenges. But, the fact that they didn't [have love] and we just tried to patch that all up...and we felt responsible for their unhappiness, that was really, really hard."

While Bettina cozied herself in the chair, I observed as she soothed her inner being with movement and deep breaths. I thought not only the expansive nature of betrayals Bettina had experienced but of the betrayal environment which had taken so much from her. And although we had touched upon pieces of her brokenness in her betrayal narrative, I knew there was more to uncover.

I took a deep breath with her as we prepared to unearth additional painful embers.

Brokenness From Betrayal

"Bettina, we have spoken about some of the brokenness you experienced from your mom's betrayals. Can you speak to other ways in which the betrayals impacted or affected you?"

Without hesitation, Bettina spoke, "I'm going to say what stands out the most is my physical body. I started having serious illnesses and was hospitalized when I was really young. They couldn't figure out why my immune system wasn't working. They did endless tests and I was always sick: tonsillitis, strep throat, and sinus infections. And then as I got a little older it became urinary tract infections, yeast infections, and a malfunctioning digestive system probably when I was seven. Very serious, serious, serious digestive issues. Probably celiac but nobody knew. I also had periods from hell. I was down for the count. I was anemic for many, many years."

Bettina reflected for a moment and added, "But this has really just occurred to me because I have been dealing with this forever. I think it is a combination...I think I inherited microorganisms from my parents which were really destructive. I really believe it is the level of stress I lived under. I didn't even know how stressed I was and it never gave my immune system a chance. I was basically in over-sympathetic stimulation my entire life. I didn't have self-regulation around my nervous system. I just didn't know what it would be like to relax."

Recalling the level of stress imposed upon her and its impact on her health, Bettina described how her body reacted counterintuitively to relaxation therapy. She also disclosed her emotional responses as she worked through sexual abuse in psychotherapy. When her therapist asked her to recall a memory when she was safe, Bettina responded, "I am not safe anywhere. I am not safe in the office. I am not safe in my house. I am not safe in my bed. I am not safe ANYWHERE!" Bettina took in a deep breath and exhaled slowly. "I did not grok this until recently—how severe my overactive sympathetic basically kept me at the edge of my seat my entire life. And I didn't know it. I really didn't know until recently how really high strung I was. It was almost impossible for me to relax unless I am out in nature for extended periods of time, preferably with someone who protects me."

Connecting the impact of her unsafe feelings to her choices in relationships, Bettina explained, "It is also what has gotten me into relationships that I knew were not good for me because somebody would protect me for a while. Because I experienced no protection at home to speak of, I am highly vulnerable to somebody offering protection."

Focusing on Bettina's messages—*I am not safe. I am not safe anywhere*—I explored further, "Bettina, in an earlier section describing your betrayal narrative, you referenced your life messages on how you viewed men. In your *Brokeness From Betrayal,* will you speak to other life messages—the internal dialogue you said to yourself—from your relationship with your mom or from your environment?"

Bettina's voice sprung forth, "Bodies don't work. Bodies are not reliable. Nothing really is reliable. My take away from all this drama in a bad way—from the brokenness is *that nothing works.* God doesn't help because if there was a God, none of this would have happened. Adults are for the most part pretty useless and self-involved. Marriages don't work. Having children is a really bad idea. And…we make really bad choices as humans. That was the biggest thing—you can't really trust humans and their choices. My father was an alcoholic and killed himself and my mother was a mess. I had this sense that nothing was working. It took me a long time… to learn from nature that there is some basic resiliency that has nothing to do with logic. The fact that I have kept coming back, it was a little bit like a tree. If you cut me down and you don't give me enough water, I am going to still stick out my little sprout. I am like that. I didn't give up."

Sensing the strength of her inner spirit, I probed further, "Are there messages you said to yourself about *yourself*?"

The lone bewildered bird spoke her truths from years past, "There is something seriously wrong with me. I can't digest my food. I am sick. I can't have relationships." Bettina breathed in slowly. Exhaling, she punctuated each word, "What is wrong with me, and I gotta fix it. I gotta fix it. Part of my life I felt it was wrong for me to be here. It was wrong for me to be here…but I worked that out. Thank God." The bird sat erectly. Her posture revealed her strength. "I felt this determination that I had to fix it. There was a piece of me that knew that I was resilient but it wasn't a conscious thing." Her voice lowered, "What is still lingering is that self-worth is often times still related to what I am producing for others. Having had a narcissistic mother there wasn't really a whole lot of unconditional love. It would peak through every so often. But mostly it was, 'What are you going to do for me?' One of my messages is that I absolutely did not believe there would be any love if I wasn't producing, or bringing them inspiration, or if I wasn't coming up with solutions for their lives. And that is how a lot of my relationships ended up. I was just providing."

Thinking about Bettina's life message—*I was just providing*—and of its importance and impact upon her, I asked, "Would you like to speak further as to how your brokenness affected your choices or roles in relationships?"

Bettina replied with gentle authority, "Human design has helped me so much to help me make sense of my life. The way my human design is that it is not so easy for me to receive, and then combining that with having to be producing and being competent, really receiving and getting support has been difficult. Some people have wanted to give to me and I wasn't very available to it because I didn't think I deserved it. Some of the time, I was really finicky. I am just so used to fending for myself. This is part of my practicing going toward wholeness, to say when somebody offers me something that I don't go into my knee-jerk, 'Well, first of all you can't do it anyway because it isn't going to work and secondly it is a lot easier to do it for me myself!'" We both laughed in unison, recognizing the roots of codependency in her statement. Bettina's voice settled back down, "My expectation that my needs were going to be met were so low. And anytime anyone ever gave anything to me, I never anticipated that there weren't strings attached. I wondered, 'What is the price tag going to be?'" She paused briefly, then continued, "Another message was there is no expectation for things to last. And some of that is good because it gives me realism; it prepared me for grief. It is no stranger in our lives. And simultaneously, I have no confidence whatsoever in the solidity of relationships and love and care for each other. That's not good. That's created a huge amount of struggle." She reflected and added, "In the last year, I've learned why I was attracted to people—what worked and what didn't."

Bettina stretched out her limbs and then pulled them in close to her long slender frame. The image of an extraordinary bird entered my mind, one which flies far ahead scanning the landscape for safety and protection. One which searches for the solutions and provides for those following behind. One which anticipates and plans but expects little. One which sacrifices her own wellbeing so that others may claim a semblance of their own. One which turns to Nature to find her source and rebirths herself in the process.

Although we had sifted through the ashes of brokenness and identified their respective injuries, I sensed their healing properties were in close proximity. And thus, I remained open and present as Bettina shared her journey *From Brokenness To Wholeness*.

From Brokenness To Wholeness

Bettina and I took a short break. While I warmed our teas, Bettina walked outside, basking in the warming of the day and briefly immersing herself in nature. Having removed her shoes and socks, she buried her toes in the small patch of grass which typically was where our adopted family of deer took their afternoon naps. I thought it only natural that Bettina would be drawn to the same area of beauty and comfort.

After returning to the dining room table, we settled smoothly back into our process. Given the territory we had already covered with respect to brokenness in relationship to her mom, I moved to the second question, "Bettina, when did you first consider addressing your injuries, wounds, or brokenness? What was that like for you?"

Bettina responded, "In my very younger years, I was working with horses, and that was my solace. I basically earned some of my lessons by taking care of horses. There was a horse that I had been working with and loved—a stallion—but he was taken away. The woman [owner] had promised me that she would take me with...and she didn't. That was absolute devastation for me. That is when I really immersed myself in school and going more toward the arts." Bettina described in more detail her understanding of herself and her situation, "Even younger, I was clear I needed help. And then, as a teenager my mother started going to these Zen retreats. I wanted to go and they wouldn't let me because I wasn't sixteen yet. And then, one of the things that really helped me was that a friend of my mother's opened up a pottery studio and I had the key to it. I soon became kind of the manager of that studio. And I was self-taught at throwing pottery. It's kinda what kept me sane because German high school is academics...academics!"

I listened closely as Bettina explained the rigorous course work and expectations of German high school. Connecting with how Bettina was more drawn to the creative, artistic fields of study, I sensed how her frustrations were often in conflict with her need to persevere and in contrast with the academic expectations imposed upon her.

Bettina's voice remained strong and steady, "After I got done with high school, and I was so glad that was over, I started traveling. I went to Findhorn, the community in Scotland where they were working with all the nature spirits. They started showing the world we are out of balance in our relationship with nature. I spent some time there and then I came back to the States and traveled all over."

For the next several minutes, Bettina described a multitude of experiences and how each became a fertile ash in her mound of brokenness. In her words, "I hitchhiked all over the country. I was raped at gunpoint. Nobody knew where I was or when I was coming home. I hooked up with Native Americans, did fire dancing, went to the Grand Canyon with cowboys, and participated in women's circles. The adventures I had were off the charts! I was a total, total wild girl. I did endless amounts of adventure... and I did it my own way."

Bettina reflected for a moment and concluded, "In part, living all that freedom even though it was very dangerous and I did a lot of counter-productive things, and I hurt myself and I got hurt, there was something really liberating for me to feel this incredible sense of 'I can do it. I can do anything.'"

Thinking about Bettina's journey *From Brokenness To Wholeness*, I thought about how often times it is more of a journey *out of Brokenness To Wholeness*. Sometimes, it requires that we bury ourselves deeper in our pain in order to get to the core of it before we can surface from it. I remained fully present as Bettina continued to share how she lifted herself out of accumulated layers of brokenness.

After leaving Germany at the age of twenty-three, Bettina returned to the States permanently. She explained, "I started doing my recovery work because I realized I had sexual abuse in my history. It was all happening at once. I went to school, and I worked full time, and I did my recovery work. It was insane. But, it was very empowering because I felt like 'I'm starting to get a handle on all of this.' I did workshop after workshop. I was in therapy pretty much all the time...all the time."

I gently inquired, "Was this with one therapist or were there others?"

Bettina's voice held its authority, "Different people. I never did very well with just talk therapy alone. So it would be hypnosis or body work and talking, or authentic movement. I was always doing some kind of therapy. A few years as of late, I mostly did co-counseling with somebody...more like supporting each other. Really, really deep work definitely resolving some developmental trauma." She took in a deep breath and repositioned herself. She continued, relating her healing work to her professional work, "In the process of what I was offering my clients, I was doing a tremendous amount of work. How I figured out I had sexual abuse is that I had gobs of women who had sexual abuse. It took me a long time to figure out it was okay to have boundaries and that my value wasn't based on what I could provide sexually or otherwise. And so, in the early years my sexual experiences were bordering on date rape or other experiences which were not good for me. I realized I didn't have a voice. I would be highly sexual and then go into shut down. So, I took all these workshops around sexuality. I did the Human Awareness Institute. I did a lot, a lot of work."

Even after much recovery, unearthing tender ashes of sexual abuse and its recovery can evoke sparks of injury or vulnerability. I remained still for a few moments respecting Bettina's position and her process.

When the space between us felt secure, I moved ahead. "Bettina, will you elaborate more on how your work or different facets of it has been a part of the healing process?"

With Bettina's familiar strength, she offered, "Oh sure. I almost had to see my clients heal to trust that I could heal. Often times, people say, 'You have to have been there before you can guide people.' For me, it was the other way around. There were lots of things I had to see....like my clients healed. Then, 'Oh, if they can do it. I can.' I never thought I could be whole enough to have a real life. It took a looong time for me to realize, 'Other people are getting better. I can get better.' I listened closely to what I said to people. I said to myself, 'I think I'll try that'!"

As we both chuckled softly, Bettina expressed the need to maintain her integrity with her clients and with herself. She stressed the importance of not being hypocritical and thus embracing her own self-care with the same intention she gave healing to others.

Bettina shifted and moved again. When I observed that her legs were neatly tucked beneath her and her arms in close, I began, "Can you speak to anything in particular in your experiences which helped you to address your brokenness with your mom?"

Bettina lingered for a moment. Calmly, she revealed, "Everything did it in its own way. Each was a piece to the puzzle. I can't say that there is any *one* thing. All that work around sexuality was hugely helpful and it repaired the insanity of my relationship with my mother and my mother's non-relationship with her femininity. It was really interesting how my parents collaborated in not having me be a woman. Like my dad said, 'You don't ever want to be dependent on a man. Get a really good education so you will never be dependent on a man.' And my mother did not live her femininity, so I had no role model. So doing all that work around my own sexuality about relationships and all of that was huge because I had no idea. I had no role model in her what a healthy relationship is...what sexuality is. So, that work was totally necessary in the process of recovering."

Bettina sat quietly, sifting through the layers and reflecting on them.

Her voice regained its volume, "Art therapy actually was huge for me. I took art therapy training. I hosted it so that it made it possible without spending a ton of money. I did a whole big piece on my mom. I did a whole series on what I experienced my mom to be at the time. That was when I realized she had this feeding tube into my system and was taking from me. It was an incredible process of realizing how I had been rearranged by her narcissistic tendencies. And my art therapist walked me through to create what it was. I wrote a whole story about it. A huge piece of healing happened in that process. In the end, she encouraged me to create safety for myself in this process of dismantling the false self that I had developed in order to deal with my mother. I really felt like that was a turning point." Bettina shifted, soothing herself. "I still needed to stay away from her for a while which wasn't hard because I was here and I was really busy with work. The art therapy was so helpful...and part of why it came to me was because of nature. And, in part, *my* connection to nature was given to me by my mother. She was so connected to nature." Bettina took in a deep breath. Then, exhaled her healing truths, "On one hand, she was a monster. On the other hand, she was this angel."

The energy in Bettina's voice filled the space between us. Wholeness seemed to be spilling out from the mound of ashes and could not be contained.

The statuesque bird sat up erectly. Her wholeness revealed its source, "I want to acknowledge this. It is almost like the remedy is right next to the poison. And, it is like that in nature." She explained further, "I fell into a prickly pear cactus once and I had stickers all over my body that I couldn't get out. I looked like a porcupine! But what happened, I asked everybody, 'How do I get these spines out?' They said, 'You have to cut the pear...you have to shave the spines off the prickly pear and then you cut it in half. And then you do a poultice. You actually bind the prickly pear to your body and it will draw the spines out.'" Wholeness continued to pour out as she spoke, "Well that worked! That is how I feel about my mother! There were pieces of my mother which were so toxic and right next to them was the remedy—my love of nature and art and expression—they were my remedies to the toxins!"

Although the lovely bird sat still, her voice took flight.

"I am not a victim anymore. I am so not a victim anymore. That was a big piece of my brokenness. People around me reflected that. They would say, 'We're tired of you complaining about what's not working in your life. We are tired of you complaining about what these men or these people have done to you. If you don't want it, do something else.'" Her truths soared. "I don't see things that way anymore. I am not a victim anymore."

Bettina's words—*I am not a victim anymore. I am so not a victim anymore*—remained suspended between us. The vision of the unsafe, unprotected nest consumed in ashes was replaced by beautiful branches and sacred spices forming a pyre nest. And the fragile bird who was once starved by the very elements which were to nourish her was now in the process of re-emerging.

Bettina's words affirmed her current reality.

"Holli, if my story had ended maybe two years ago, I'm sure I would not have felt qualified to be part of your study. Even though I had done all this work, there was still this serious self-doubt about my lovability, about my worthiness, about whether anybody would show up. But, it is not true anymore."

As we moved into the final section of *Wholeness To ...*, I thought about each daughter's journey *From Brokenness To Wholeness*, understanding it is not a destination but a process. I wondered what significant changes had taken place in the past two years to propel Bettina into a stronger place of wellness. While changing the tape, I noticed how Bettina wrapped her long arms tightly around her body. The lovely bird closed her eyes and gently caressed herself. After a few moments, she stretched her limbs, folded them inward, and moved into her perched position.

Her newly-formed truths awaited witnessing.

Wholeness To

I moved into the first question, "Bettina, where are you today in your relationship with your mom?"

Her voice was peaceful, "I am the only one of the children who made peace with her long before she died. Years ago...and more so as I went along. I didn't need her to be anything different. When I was there [Germany] almost four years ago to clean up the mess my brother had created, I told her, 'This may be the last time I see you. It is very challenging for me to be here.' That was an intense thing to say...very intense. It's true." She explained more fully, "We talked on the phone.

But then, we developed more and more of a relationship as her mind got more and more confused. The dementia was a blessing. I actually had not thought about it until just now. Some people say when you get dementia, you get mean. My mother stopped manipulating. I think that the energies which were orchestrating her life that had taken hold of her left because she wasn't useful anymore. She finally at the very, very end came back to God. It was one of her biggest pains." Bettina breathed in and added, "And then, there is more of a relationship in the non-physical. And that is good."

Bettina reflected back to her time spent with the Tibetan Lama while her mother was still in hospice and affirmed the peace she experienced in knowing her mother was able to leave the physical plane. She recalled her thoughts, "I am totally fine with the fact that I am holding her hand from afar. I don't want her attaching herself to me. She has had enough of my life juice. I love you but I am not going to subject myself to you anymore. I am going to celebrate your beauty. I'm not going to hate you."

Elaborating more on her relationship in the end time with her mom, Bettina referenced once again the building of the spirit house and its significance. In her words, "It was a big, big process. I knew it was a sacrifice, but it wasn't a self-betrayal. If I had gone to Germany to take care of her, that would have been self-betrayal. I was able to offer my skills to her and offer healing. It didn't eat up my life energy. This activity showed me that I stopped being anxious. Now that I had a clear place to focus...and not just...when is the next shoe going to drop? When is the next disaster? When is the next crisis? When is the next decision?" With a confident steadiness to her voice, Bettina claimed her truths, "When building the spirit house, I would have really clear times to tend to her and the rest of the time was mine. So, it was a really clear differentiation between codependency, self-betrayal, and actually informed mature loving action."

As I thought about the informed, mature, loving action Bettina had performed, I moved into a more intimate area in Bettina's recent past with her mom, "Bettina, could you speak about your mom's funeral and how that played a part in your healing? I believe you gave the eulogy?"

"Yes. For me, the eulogy was a huge healing peace. And it was scary as hell! Here was my brother who had not spoken to me. There were relatives I had not seen or spoken to in years. Friends of my mother's I had not seen or spoken to in years. I had been gone. I had lived in the States longer than I lived in Germany. And my German is rusty. I had to write it out. I had to practice. And basically, I rehearsed how to speak this eulogy in German. And I only had about five or seven minutes to speak."

Bettina took in a deep breath, exhaled slowly, and recalled more details, "In Germany people don't speak at the mortuary. It is supposed to be a priest or someone singing something. One of my mother's long-term friends for spiritual guidance spoke, but I spoke too. And it was so important to speak the truth. Speak the truth about how sketchy my mother was without being disrespectful. Speak the truth about the beauty she had brought to us when we were kids. To speak about the suffering she went through. I cried. I was up there saying, 'I feel embarrassed, and shy, and emotional.' I cried. And it totally changed everything …how this funeral went. For me, I knew there was not going to be a memorial. I knew I wasn't going to be back in Germany any time soon. It kinda brought me closer to some of these relatives I really hadn't had any contact with." Bettina spoke with intention, "But most importantly, it was this feeling that I honored myself, and I honored my mother, and I honored all of us with truth—with beautiful truth. That was so healing….so healing."

Basking in the light of her truths and how their glow reflected in her wholeness, I moved into a related question. "Bettina, what are your life messages today? How do you feel about yourself today?"

"Some of what we have talked about…really that change. I am not going to say I have fully arrived in self-care and self-love. But the amount of progress I've made has *everything* to do with it. To be able to say, 'You're worth it. I love you'. In the past, some of my self-care was done grudgingly. Now, the self-care comes from a true self-love. Being single and celibate is a total act of self-love. No more giving myself up. No more getting tangled up. I know how dopamine-addicted I am. I am always learning. I am always looking for new experiences. I'm like, 'Where is the next thing?' And now, just to go, 'No.'"

Bettina spoke of recent losses in her past: her precious companion cats, lovers, and friends. She stressed how "something shifted" in her. In her words, "I came to a place of acknowledging I deserved my own attention. I deserved my own love. Until I gave that to myself, why should anyone else? It was really that clarity of this old spiritual saying, 'You attracting what you are putting out.' When I looked at what I was attracting, it definitely had gotten better. Before, I had people in my life who were not empathic or who were narcissistic. And I'm not going to pretzel myself anymore to see if somebody on the outside is going to give me what I want. I am going to give it to myself. That came from a deep place of recognition." Bettina spoke firmly and with finality, "And I believe because I don't have to worry about my parents anymore, my nervous system is settling down."

"Bettina, from your betrayal experiences with your mom, what life lessons have served you well and which ones continue to do so?"

"Kinda what I said before. The other side of betrayal is how incredibly strong this had made me. For example, although I felt deep injury not having spiritual guidance, I did have the space to find my own way and didn't get indoctrinated by anything! There are lots of traditions I take pieces from but there is none that work for me in their entirety. And had I been brought up in one, I probably would have gotten pretty hooked because of the imprint. I don't have that. I get to choose! Again, on one hand huge injury. On the other hand, huge opportunity!"

Bettina's truths continued to surface and spill out, "My mother's love of nature has been the most restoring aspect of how I can heal myself. Knowing how resilient I am. It's probably hypothetical, but if I had had a normal life, I would never have discovered all that I have discovered." Her voice strengthened and moved at a rapid pace, "I would never have been driven to investigate all that I have investigated! I would never have uncovered all that I have uncovered! I have this immense gratitude for all the skills and resources I have developed—for all that I had to find in order to make it...to heal."

Bettina's spirit was set free and her voice soared.

"And now that I can say, '*I am the phoenix that has risen from the ashes,*' it is extraordinary! The wisdom I can bring to people. The compassion and the knowledge I can bring to people. The inspiration!"

Across from me, the statuesque, stunning bird sat perched on a nest of wooded beauty. Her words ignited, took flight, and carried with them flames of renewal and of rebirth—*I am the phoenix that has risen from the ashes.* Their messages would gift others across nature's endless horizon and then return to her as she continued traveling her path from *Wholeness To*...and beyond.

Tapping into the mindful intention of her healing, I gently inquired, "Bettina, understanding that wholeness is not the end of the journey, where do you wish go from here?"

Her voice lowered again, "It depends how we define wholeness. I don't think humans can be whole. Knowing how limited our perspective is, I don't pretend to get to the end of it. One thing that is really clear to me is that I am coming back. I came to the States to be an artist. I didn't have enough time to become an artist that would likely be able to make a living just doing art. I want to make more space for my creativity and for nature, art, self-generated ceremony, sacred theatre, and more time for prayer."

The pensive bird shifted. Then settled. "I am in the process of restricting my business so I don't have to spend so much time one-on-one. I am not willing to sit in the energy of suffering. It is not good for my nervous system and it is not good for my digestion. I'm getting more and more selective about who I am accepting into private practice. I also want to create more content online. I write pieces as I feel inspired, but I don't want to feel any pressure to write books at this time. I'm moving more into a coaching and advising position. And for work I'm coming back to teaching seminars, but on a bigger scale so I don't have to do so many of them. I just want more time to sit and pray."

Bettina reflected for a moment, "I also think it is important to continue recognizing ourselves. Until we recognize our own beauty, our own worthiness, our own preciousness…it is going to be very hard for anybody else to do it. So, I am going to continue to work on that." Bettina thought for a moment and recalled a pivotal experience, "I actually had a woman in my life briefly who said she wanted to adopt me and she saw my beauty. The first time she gave me a session, she cried as she led me out the door. She said, 'I just want to thank you because you have no idea I get how hard it is for you to be here. And for you to be such an angel on the earth at this time is really extraordinary.'" Bettina's voice quivered slightly, "It was one of the first times I could barely let it in. Her recognizing me helped me to recognize me, and… me recognizing me. And since then, more people have said similar things appreciating what I bring to the world." She paused and then gently pronounced, "I'm proud of myself. The fact that I can say this without feeling self-conscious, it is really true."

The healing in Bettina's words sparkled, lighting the space between us. Its glow spread a halo of wellness around her. I sat quietly admiring this brave bird whose flight was not over but whose inner strength lay secure in a nest of truth.

Coming to the close of our time together, I thanked Bettina for her compassion and courage. I thanked her for the privilege of bearing witness to her narrative and of trusting me with her truths. Bringing our interview full circle, we closed in prayer. As Bettina gave thanks for our time together and for the process we shared, the image of *the phoenix rising out of the ashes and rebirthing itself* took hold. As she rose, her wholeness emerged from the flames, attached itself to her elegant wings, and displayed its truth across the exquisite skies -

"I stand behind what this is and what this evolution has required. It's good for me that people know."

Follow-up Reflection

Although winter was officially still on the March calendar, spring made an early entrance over the last few days in the western part of the United States. Her sudden emergence brought much welcomed warmth along with a multitude of scented blossoms. The buzzing in the air signaled the arrival of bees, reminding human inhabitants of nature's cycle of regrowth.

In preparation for Bettina's post-interview conference, I thought about her narrative, and the other daughters', and how each of their words brought empowering messages of human resilience and renewal. I reflected on the cyclical nature of human healing, with each season gifting us with ample opportunities to recover and regrow. I was excited to check in with Bettina, wondering where her wellness wings had taken her since our interview several weeks ago.

After arranging my notes and clarifying questions, I re-read the last section *Wholeness To* , wanting to do justice to Bettina's words. As was true with all the daughters, hearing their narratives read back to them proved to be quite emotional. And thus, for me the weightiness of the task was surpassed only by the immense gratitude I felt for each daughter. After sipping my tea, I glanced at the clock. Almost noon. I placed the call.

Bettina's voice was spirited. We briefly chatted about the warm weather and the fresh bouquet of beauty surrounding our environs. Sensing a lightness in her voice, I eagerly asked my first question, "How have you been feeling since our time together? How are you feeling today?"

Without pause, she replied, "So, I was really tired after we got done. It was a lot. It was good that I didn't try to do anything else that day. But there were no big upheavals. I was a little stirred up. I don't think I've ever rolled out that whole story—all at once." Bettina paused and added, "I had a therapy session set up for afterwards and all that went fine."

Bettina described how she was able to move through our process, feeling settled and yet keeping up with life's business and dynamic nature. We were both in agreement that the extraordinary degree of self-care Bettina implemented prior to our interview as well as the emotional, psychological, and spiritual preparation she had embraced materialized in her feelings of being "settled."

I gently inquired, "Bettina, is there anything else which has come to your mind since our interview or anything you have thought about which you would like to change or amend?"

Bettina chuckled, "I don't think so....and that is almost like 'that's a long time ago!'" I joined in the laughter. Bettina continued, "To be honest, I haven't had much time to think about it. There has been so much dynamic movement the last few days. So, there is nothing off the top of my head. There might be something when you ask me questions, so maybe would could do that?"

"Of course," I replied. And as I had done with all the daughters, I spent the next several minutes checking a few issues of clarification within Bettina's narrative. Before moving into the reading of the *Wholeness To ...* passage, I paused and explained the significance of Bettina's tagline and of its integration into the narrative, "Bettina, the tagline I chose for you is, *I Am The Phoenix That Has Risen From The Ashes.*"

Before I could continue, Bettina tenderly responded, "I love that. Thank you."

Over the next twenty minutes, I read. I was mindful of the meaning each word carried with it and sensitive to its potential impact upon Bettina. There were moments, as there had been with the other daughters, where I too felt the waves of emotion flowing through the messages and spilling out into the space between us. As I spoke the last few words, "I stand behind what this is and what this evolution has required", my voice broke for a moment. I composed myself and delivered her courageous words, "It's good for me that people know."

I sat quietly and waited. I could hear Bettina's soft sniffles and slow sighs in the background. I gave her time to sit with her nest of truths, giving witness to their rightful position and place.

Bettina's voice was low and intentional, "In an odd way, you have had insight into my life that nobody else has had. I feel very seen, and heard, and represented through the way you are doing this. So I feel grateful you took the time to share this with me because it is really powerful, especially to hear the spoken word and to hear the emotion that comes with it as you are reading about it." I listened. Bettina added, "What I so appreciate is your receptivity and your crafting with the words. Hearing you talk about it..." Bettina's voice quivered slightly, "your level of care and the capacity to see beyond the words."

I swallowed and took in a deep breath. "Bettina, thank you for trusting me with your voice. Thank you for your courageous being and compassionate spirit. Thank you for all that you bring and give to the universe."

Bettina's voice was fueled and took flight. I visualized the elongated bird sitting in her statuesque and stately posture. "We could all be drug addicts or in a mental institution or been really bitter, but instead we have taken this and done something else. This is also one of the reasons I wanted to be part of it ["The Daughters Project"] because there is a bigger message about it all. One of the things I've been wanting is to reach more people and through your book, I get to do that. So, it feels like this incredible win–win situation."

As I listened, her wings carried timeless truths. "That is how I want life to be. I want a world where there is reciprocity, generosity, sustainable peace and movement away from scarcity, fear, overwhelm and stress." As her voice intensified, her messages soared, "I want a place of being held where we can bring forward our best potential. It is my biggest desire to inspire others with new possibilities to wholeness."

The image of the beautiful bird re-entered my mind. From her unsafe upside-down nest, to its scattered embers and charred skeletal remains, to the rebuilt pyre set ablaze, Bettina's path *From Brokenness To Wholeness* was a sacred testament to Nature's cycle of rebirth. Its legacy has been and will continue to be clearly marked by those bearing witness to her truth...

I Am The Phoenix That Has Risen From The Ashes

Part Two: An Analysis

An Analysis
A Strand of Pearls

The purpose of "The Daughters Project" was to explore, discover, and examine experiential recovery themes within the narratives of a given population of females. The guiding questions for the study were as follows: (1) What are the life experiences and life messages of daughters betrayed by their mothers? (2) How can daughters betrayed by their mothers move from brokenness to wholeness? And, (3) How can presenting the voices of daughters through personal narratives create new meanings for the interviewer and readers regarding the healing of daughters betrayed by their mothers?

Utilizing twenty-five pre-established questions to guide the interview process, each daughter shared her narrative in response to them. In addition to exploring and examining the recovery themes within the daughters' narratives, I have also discovered other themes which contribute to the overall essence and extended meanings within the study. Thus, their inclusion is important.

Several weeks after the final daughter's narrative, I scanned the multitude of words filling the pages before me. With the daughters' shells wide open and their pearls polished and poised, it was time to string their truths together with trustful precision, timeless respect, and tender regard. Just as the interviewing process along with the transcription of the daughters' narratives proved to be a profoundly transformative experience, revisiting and analyzing the themes within each one and in relationship to one another also gifted me with a deep personal source of growth as well as a gratifying professional challenge. Although my heart was heavy with responsibility, my spirit was light, lifted by the healing and the hope each pearl represented.

Guiding Question #1:
**What are the life experiences and life messages
of daughters betrayed by their mothers?**

Beginning Strand – Names and Feelings

Given the subject matter, daughters betrayed by their mothers, it was important to explore how and why daughters chose to refer to their mothers this way and to explain their present-day feelings as they spoke about their mothers as women who betrayed them.

Although almost all daughters used the word "mom" or "mother" during their upbringing, each qualified its usage. One daughter disclosed using "mother" because it was "less intimate" while another daughter explained how she called her "mom," "but I don't think of her as mom." She further explained how the word "mom" equated with feelings of emptiness, disappointment, and negativity. One daughter described using the word "mammi," German for mama, when she was younger but as she got older called her mother by her first name because "It became really clear that she was not my mom." Another daughter, who currently refers to her mother as "mom," disclosed, "There was a time when I didn't call her by her name and for years I didn't talk about her." Two daughters adopted other names one when referring to their mothers. In times of deep pain, one daughter referenced her mother as "The Betrayer," explaining it was "a form of protection." With agreement among her family members, including her mother, one daughter has utilized the word "the womb" for the past twenty years because "she gave birth and sort of gestated me...a sort of storage facility for nine months."

In reviewing the daughters' narratives around their current feelings in discussing their mothers as betrayers, I found agreement in their descriptions of acceptance with several comparing it to the last stage of grief. Each daughter also described other qualifying emotions.

- I do not feel any guilt or shame in talking about my mom. If talking about my mom is going to contribute to my healing journey, I carefully evaluate it and decide.

- I am in a really good place because I don't have all that negative energy. I am totally open.

- It has definitely changed. I don't feel the same emotional pain I did before.

- It feels fine. Not particularly charged. It is what it is. It is sad.

- Talking about her is still a little uncomfortable for me. But it doesn't illicit the same pain it used to.

- A big spectrum. I feel so liberated since she died. I feel incredible joy to be able to relate with her now on the other side. I feel sad that I didn't get to be mothered.

Summary

Because the words "mom" and "mother" carry with them various connotations of nurturance, safety, and unconditional love, betrayal mother-wounding is not only experienced internally but it is compounded externally by cultural interpretations and social perceptions of mothering. Furthermore, talking about or referencing mothers in ways which are contrary to familial or societal traditions can be viewed as unacceptable and inhibit the voices of those experiencing betrayals by their mothers.

Therefore, in seeking participants for "The Daughters Project", I hypothesized that daughters who chose to participate would feel secure in talking about their mothers and in telling their truths. And although there appeared to be an underlying sadness within the daughters' voices when disclosing "the loss of not having a mother," their readiness to be a part of the study was clearly revealed in their levels of peace and acceptance.

Reflecting on the weightiness of mother-norms placed upon these daughters, I thought of real pearls and how their authenticity and strength were formed out of adversity.

Background Strand – Family, Role, and Early Life Messages

Throughout all the narratives, it was evident there were levels of dysfunction within each family system. The "betrayals" of/by the mothers served as the underlying foundation from which ensuing unhealthiness took hold and formed within the family and/or exacerbated an already fragmented system. Although several mothers were referenced with regards to specific diagnoses such as Alcoholic, Bipolar, Borderline Personality Disorder, and Narcissistic Personality Disorder, in general mothers were described as the following: angry, aggressive, anxious, depressed, detached, self-absorbed, violent and volatile. To varying degrees, all mothers were verbally, emotionally and physically abusive.

In describing their families, daughters consistently used the word "chaotic," whether or not alcoholism was a part of the dynamic. With slight variances in the degree of pathology within the family system, the role of fathers was strikingly consistent in that they were under-functioning, unable, or unwilling to be present as a parent. Three sets of parents divorced and one separated; however, mothers remained the primary betrayers.

In this background strand, each daughter was asked about her role in the family. Although the daughters varied in birth order, most identified as the parentified child describing their roles as "the acting oldest," "the adult in the house," "the mom in the home," "the caregiver of the mother," "the first line of defense for younger siblings," and "the one to make sure everyone was okay." Although not all mothers were alcoholics or addicts, the family systems mimicked a diseased dynamic casting daughters into the roles of the lost child, rescuer, peacemaker, and pleaser.

In my Master's program studying lifespan development, I was drawn to Albert Bandura's Social Cognitive Learning Theory. Bandura suggests that as children grow and develop, they learn about themselves and their environments from their life experiences. Within my theoretical orientation, I have adopted the belief that each of those life experiences, whether positive or negative, then translates into life messages—the internal dialogue we say to ourselves about who we are and how we feel about the world we are in. Because of the importance of life messages to this study and to their respective journeys, I asked daughters to share their early life messages. There was remarkable consistency in how each daughter viewed and thought of herself in reference to betrayals from her mother. In their words:

- I didn't feel important. I didn't feel valuable. Mostly, I felt invisible.

- I did not feel as smart. My mom loves my sisters more than she loves me.

- I felt I wasn't good enough. There was something wrong with me. I was on my own.

- I did not have a mother. I protected my sister.

- I thought I was stupid. Adults lie. They do not tell the truth. We always had a façade. I felt like a bad person constantly trying to prove to everyone that I wasn't.

- I did not feel safe. At age seven, I became mother. I've got to get out of here. I had a feeling of being a burden [to mom].

Summary

In reflecting upon these young pearls whose formative years were marred by violations of innate trust in the mother-child relationship, their early life messages are clearly and understandably reflective of those betrayals. During these trust-building years, the confusion around the lack of nurturance and unconditional love was internalized as a lack of self or defect of self. Feelings of worthlessness such as shame, doubt, guilt, and inferiority accompanied these maladaptive life messages. As vulnerable as these young pearls were, it was also extraordinary how each one stepped into or took on roles which far exceeded their ages and stages of development. This has led me to conclude that although each daughter's early life messages were extremely contrary to healthy psycho-social development, these same experiences formed a layer of nacre around the grain of sand, protectively coating her injuries with a translucent film of resiliency.

Betrayal Narrative Strand – Connections and Patterns

From my years of previous study and work around betrayal, I expanded its meaning to include three explanations:

- An investment into someone or something met with rejection and or abandonment.
- A profound trust which is profoundly violated.
- A truth which becomes a lie. A belief which is shattered.

In designing the study "Daughters Betrayed By Their Mothers: Moving From Brokenness To Wholeness," I purposely defined the word "betrayal" in accordance with a broadened perspective. Thus, in the Letter of Invitation and the Informed Consent, "a mother who betrayed" covered a wide range of connotations and applications.

The word "betrayed" should be interpreted in its broadest sense including mothers who were absent, abusive, alcoholic, or unavailable. It may include mothers who were bipolar, borderline, narcissistic, or who suffered from other mental and/or physical disorders. It implies any violation of trust between participant and her mother; it encompasses a mother's inability or unwillingness to provide unconditional love, nurturance, protection, and support for participant. The betrayal occurrence(s) may be either short term, episodic, or ongoing.

The purpose of daughters sharing their betrayal narratives was two-fold. First, I wondered when daughters initially thought about their betrayals in connection with their mothers and how they felt. Secondly, I was interested in uncovering any patterns of betrayal among the daughters' experiences and how those occurrences or sequences impacted each daughter.

With regard to connecting their betrayals to their mothers, all daughters were in agreement that the word betrayal was not part of their young vocabulary; however, all had *a knowing or an awareness* around their betrayals from age five to about age seven. Although two daughters recalled never remembering a healthy mom, they noted an escalation of symptoms during the same age span.

During these formative years of *knowing*, daughters expressed strong feelings of *confusion* over what a mother was supposed to be and what they were experiencing. This was evident in their descriptions:

- There was a shift in mothering. She was present physically but abandoned us emotionally. I felt like I was holding a secret. I felt like something was wrong with our family.

- Others (girls) said she was mean. She was angry all the time. I couldn't talk to her. There were discrepancies in her mothering. I was discounted.

- There was physical abuse. Never a sane person. There was emotional abuse. I was left to figure it out for myself.

- I knew she was crazy. This is not how it is supposed to be.

- There was fighting and chaos. I did not know how to deal with it.

- By age seven, I was going to have to be mom. There is something really upside down.

Although there were variances in their descriptive phrases regarding the lack of mothering, daughters repeatedly referenced their mothers as being *mean*. This *meanness* unleashed a sense of worthlessness among the daughters who expressed feelings of guilt, inadequacy, and self-hatred.

Within the narrative strand, daughters disclosed how feelings of confusion were amplified when comparing their families and their mothers to friends' households. Daughters reported "other mothers were not like her" and shared their feelings of embarrassment and shame. During these early years, daughters also described growing feelings of distrust and disgust toward their mothers who continued to choose destructive behaviors/relationships such as unhealthy partners, substance addiction, and conflict with family members and others. A sense of powerlessness over their mothers' behaviors also contributed to daughters' feelings of over-responsibility for self, siblings, and family in general, contrasted with fears regarding lack of protection and safety.

In the investigation of patterns of betrayal among the daughters' narratives and their ensuing impact, several themes emerged.

It was very evident that all daughters experienced chronicity in their patterns of betrayal. Several daughters described periods of less disturbance or episodic bouts of self-regulation; however, all daughters concurred that these periods of relative calm were typically short-lived followed by intense relapse or further regression into unhealthiness. While one daughter referenced her pattern of betrayals as "layers added onto layers," two daughters described their betrayal occurrences as "living in a war zone" with consistencies in its "unpredictability" and "living on high alert."

Within the chronic nature of the betrayals, daughters also described the worsening or escalation of their mothers' injurious behaviors over time. Throughout their adolescent, teen, and young adult years, daughters "lack of having a mother" was internalized as deeply embedded self-deprecating life messages.

- I am a bad person. I am a bad child.
- I am not good enough.
- Something is wrong with me.
- I am not wanted.
- This is my fault. I am not going to survive.

In addition to these feelings of worthlessness, another theme which emerged from the betrayal narratives was the degree of impact on the daughters' sense of powerlessness, not just over their circumstances and worth but with their voices. One daughter described her mother as "the silencer of my voice" while another was told "to keep my mouth shut." Two daughters disclosed they "could not speak out or speak to her" or "could not express emotions, be honest, or forthcoming." One daughter described, "[When] I got into my mom's face...I risked further retaliation."

Throughout the betrayal narratives and embedded within the chronicity and intensity of their injuries and injustices, each daughter expressed another *knowing*—an acute awareness of her current reality. Before they had reached adolescence, all daughters acknowledged and understood "being on their own," and "not having a mother to show the way." As they grew and matured, daughters also developed a *knowing*

of their inner voices and their messaging which cultivated an innate sense
of self-direction and survival:

- I want to get out of here.

- I wanted to get away.

- I had no desire to go back home.

- I had to get away.

Summary

In my analysis of betrayal and developing a working theory around
degree of injury from betrayal, I believe that the principle of degree of
occurrence is a reliable predictor to the degree of impact. In referencing
the degree of occurrence, there are two applications to consider: first, the
number of times individuals were betrayed; secondly, the frequency of
exposure to the betrayer and/or the betrayal environments. In my work
with victims of ongoing or chronic betrayals and/or with individuals
who continued to have frequent contact with the betrayer and/or
betrayal environment, they most likely endured devastating and debilitating consequences, especially when victimized throughout childhood.
Thus, the chronic nature of betrayals experienced by all the daughters
and their ensuing emotional, psychological and physical ramifications
were to be expected. The severity of the betrayals , with their extremely
abusive components, further augmented their degree of damaging effects
on the daughters.

Within *Breaking Through Betrayal: And Recovering The Peace
Within 2nd Edition* (2016)," I uncovered and identified three States of
Being—*Confusion, Worthlessness, and Powerlessness.* These three States
of Being are the key clinical components to accessing and assessing
injury from betrayal. The hallmarks of each State of Being are
identifiable by the following presentations and characteristics:

- **State of Confusion:** An individual desperately tries to make sense
  out of someone/something which does not make sense. An
  individual feels lost.

- **State of Worthlessness:** An individual recognizes she is 1) not as
  important or valuable as she believed; 2) not as important or
  valuable as another or other person, place, thing, opportunity,
  need or desire; 3) not important or valuable at all. An individual
  feels robbed and redefined.

- **State of Powerlessness:** An individual vacillates between two
  debilitating extremes: 1) feeling controlled and changed by her

betrayer and betrayal environment; 2) trying to control or change her betrayer and her betrayal environment. An individual feels desperate and frightened.

My investigation into and analysis of betrayal led me to conclude that an individual who has been betrayed, will navigate through these three debilitating States of Being, typically presenting in the order identified and bringing with them a host of physical, psychological, and behavioral manifestations.

Thus, I found it remarkable how each young daughter was able to formulate her *knowing* about "not having a real mother," while navigating the first State of Being, the chaos of confusion. This *knowing* was not only psychologically incredibly painful but it fueled each daughter's destructive life messages of worthlessness, intensifying feelings of shame and self-doubt. At the same time with all maternal sources of trust non-existent, I believe this initial *knowing* provided the basis from which each daughter learned to trust in herself and in her truths.

Although I am well-aware that "loss of voice" is a common manifestation which accompanies betrayal trauma, as the interviewer I found this to be one of the most difficult discoveries regarding all the daughters. I believe the emotional development of a child requires safety and space to express herself. When the need to speak, or to be heard, or to express emotion is silenced or suffocated, it damages the core being— the ego—of an individual. However, as I examined the betrayal journeys of the young pearls into their adult years, I was moved by the *knowing* of their inner voice and its instinctual messages of direction. Just as the particle of sand provided the necessary chronic irritant in order for the nacre to continue it secretion, the evisceration of each daughter's voice by her mother created a safe space for its subtle and sustainable self-emergence.

Brokenness form Betrayal Strand – Life-long Messages and Their Impact

Early into my studies of psychology, I was also drawn to Erik Erikson, a well-known theorist of psychosocial development across the life span. Although there are limitations to Erikson's *Eight Stages of Psychosocial Development* with regards to its factual analysis, I have found it a reliable tool for assessment of impact on an individual's development when used in conjunction with life messages. Therefore, as I analyzed the themes within the *Brokenness from Betrayal Strand*, I examined the daughters' life-long messages (those which they continued to carry with them from childhood) along with newly adopted life messages and explored their connections to short term and long term impact. At the same time, I was mindful of how their navigation through betrayal's States of Being, continued to influence or impact their brokenness.

Because all the daughters, to varying degrees shared pieces of their brokenness within the *Betrayal Narrative* itself, I encouraged them to honor their voices and their truths by freely disclosing what came up for them, even if there was repetition. I found that messages which were repeated or rephrased served to highlight their importance to daughters and to this study.

As I began stringing together the daughters' life-long and current messages from their brokenness, I discovered how their early violations of mother-child trust continued throughout their lives. Keeping in mind the importance of the successful meeting of basic needs in Erikson's first stage of psychosocial development, Trust vs. Mistrust (ages 0-18 months), it was not surprising to me that all daughters expressed a complete inability to trust and clearly identified a fear for their safety. Given the chronic nature of their betrayals, daughters continued to carry these pieces of brokenness with them throughout their developmental stages. However, what struck me was the depth to which the harsh, inconsistent, unpredictable, and unreliable "mothering" not only shattered any hope of security but also completely destroyed any sense of belonging or acceptance. This was evident in their messages:

- I must not have been wanted. I was not wanted.

- I am not good enough. I cannot do good enough. I call it the not-enough syndrome.

- I don't fit in this world. I shouldn't be here.

- There are good people and then there are people like me. There are worthy people and then there are people like me.

- I don't feel good enough. I was not good enough.

- There is something seriously wrong with me. Part of my life, I felt it was wrong for me to be here.

According to Erikson's theory, when a child is not able to move through a psychosocial stage with positive ego development, the child will carry those deficiencies into her ongoing developmental stages, hindering to varying degrees their successful navigation as well. At the same time, I believe it was the ongoing nature of extreme criticism, control, and chaos exhibited by the mothers as well as their respective degree of severity which negatively impacted the daughters' ability to move through the stages of Shame and Doubt vs. Autonomy (ages 18 months—3 years); and Guilt vs. Initiative (ages 3-6); and to achieve positive ego development. This was evidenced in the early life messages of each daughter and their impact upon them.

- I had to be vigilant and assess my circumstances. I had to implement protective measures.

- Nothing I do is right. I can't speak good enough. I can't dress good enough. I'm always striving to do better.

- You are not right. You are a tramp...a disgrace.

- I carried around shame. On the emotional caste system, I was at the bottom—the untouchable.

- I couldn't tolerate people being unhappy.

- I didn't know how to relax. It was impossible to relax.

During these early stages of development, daughters also reported experiencing high levels of stress not only from their betrayal trauma but also from additional psychosocial stressors within the family. Their impact was felt at young ages as daughters presented with a myriad of physical manifestations such as anxiety, anxiousness, hyper-sensitivity, nightmares, over-sympathetic stimulation, and an overall sense of "not being able to relax" or "settle oneself." At a very early age, one daughter disclosed how her body reacted with serious digestive illnesses while "living under a level of stress" which never gave her immune system a chance. As daughters matured into adulthood, the long-term impact of their brokenness manifested in clinical/medical disorders such as anemia, bulimia, depression (with a few reporting suicidal ideation and/or attempts), Generalized Anxiety Disorder, social anxiety, and Post Traumatic Stress Disorder. Several daughters noted their codependent personalities with compulsive needs to "control their environments" and others struggled with managing obsessive or repetitive thoughts, all in an effort to "calm worries about what others would think."

Stringing the life messages of brokenness together with my observations of the daughters' disadvantaged journeys through Erikson's Stages of Development, I clearly identified how these maturing pearls suffered greatly, especially as they moved through the stage of Industry vs Inferiority (ages 5- 12). Because daughters were not encouraged and reinforced for their *own* competencies, but instead learned early on to "sacrifice myself as long as everyone else is okay" or "self-worth is related to what I am producing for others," daughters internalized profound feelings of insecurity, inferiority, and inadequacy which they carried with them into the next stage—Identity vs Role Confusion (ages 12-18).

Within Identify vs. Role Confusion, Erik Erikson describes the importance of individuals discovering who they are, what they are all about, and where they are going in life. Within the freedom of exploring differing roles (vocationally and romantically), young people establish a positive identity. One of the most difficult discoveries within this strand was uncovering the depth of "loss of identity" for the all the daughters. Two daughters described a "fractured sense of self," while another disclosed how "betrayal ate away at who I was and am." Several daughters explained their "inability to give, receive, or feel love," as well as finding it difficult "to be vulnerable and ask for what I need".

As daughters moved into young adulthood and beyond– Intimacy vs. Isolation (ages 18-40), their profound sense of inferiority and their fractured sense of identify combined with the compounded deficiencies from previous psychosocial stages impacted their relationships on several levels. However, it is my observation that the degree of trust violation between mother and daughter during the very earliest stages of development and its chronic nature set the groundwork for the difficulties daughters encountered in entering into, committing to, and securing safe caring relationships. Several daughters had relationships with highly abusive, alcoholic or addicted, and emotionally absent men. One daughter reported a pattern of "being split from my own needs in order to avoid conflict." Another discovered how her attachments issues led her to "expect too much" from a relationship while simultaneously feeling "suffocated" if someone was too needy or too dependent upon her. Several daughters viewed themselves as individuals who were "not able to receive love" or "not available because I didn't think I deserved it." One daughter expressed, "no expectations for things to last and no confidence in the solidity of relationships" with regards to love and care.

Not just in the strand of *Brokenness From Betrayal* but in other sections as well, daughters shared how the betrayals from their mothers impacted their decisions regarding other potential relationships, in particular in becoming mothers themselves. Two daughters, who later become mothers, made promises to themselves at very young ages regarding their role as mothers. One daughter pledged that, "If and when I am a mom someday, I will never, ever be like my mom. I will do it differently." Another promised, "I'm never going to do what she did...I wasn't going to be abusive. I knew there had to be a better way." A different daughter disclosed how her decision not to become a mother was based on her *knowing* of "never feeling comfortable around children, not wanting anyone dependent on me, and not knowing how to give love," while another shared, "I wouldn't be able to give to that child what it needed...so it is not right for me." Another daughter disclosed how her life messages about "adults being useless and self-involved" and that "marriages don't work," led her to *knowing* that "having children is a really bad idea." And one daughter's anger-filled environment fueled her *knowing* that, "Families are something you get out of, not into," along with, "there is no positive association of the mother-child relationship." It was very evident that all daughters were well-aware of their capacity to be mothers and based their decisions not only on what would be best for a child, but also for themselves.

All throughout the stages of development from birth to adulthood, daughters shared the profound impact of betrayal by their mothers in describing their feelings of worthlessness. However, one of the most difficult pieces which surfaced consistently within their brokenness was daughters being shamed by their mothers. Being shamed was experienced directly through the physical and emotional abuse daughters suffered and from the demeaning name labeling such as "Horrible Holli," "The Boss," and "cry baby." In addition to being shamed, daughters often carried feelings of shame over their appearances and reported "never feeling pretty." Another daughter who was not properly dressed or cared for felt like "Pig Pen." Daughters also felt shame over their broken families and their inability to "fix them," and "blaming [themselves] for not being able to make their mothers happy." The shame daughters internalized also contributed to feeling socially awkward, isolated, alone, and "not like anyone else."

Summary

Given the degree of betrayal injury experienced by daughters along with their degree of occurrence resulting in compounded deficiencies incurred throughout the daughters' formative psychosocial stages of development, it is to be expected that their impact would be far-reaching and long lasting. This was evident in the daughters' life messages about themselves and their environments. In stringing these messages together, I have identified three over-arching themes of brokenness which provided a context from which to understand their short term and long term impact.

- A lack of trust in their mothers and in the concept of motherhood
- A lack of belonging or acceptance

- A lack of self-worth

Thus, without any sense of security, attachment, or importance combined with extremely adverse experiences and psychosocial stressors, daughters' health was impacted physically, psychologically, and emotionally on many levels. Their relational health was impacted by destructive patterns, in particular with investing into unhealthy partners and/or in their diminished capacity to invest intimately and safely. And, their inner-personal wellbeing was impacted by the weightiness of shame combined with a duty to take care of their mothers.

As I finished stringing together the strands of *Brokenness From Betrayal*, there was one underlying theme which had emerged previously, but which presented itself more fully. Its glow was remarkable. One pearl reported, "I could not depend on anyone so I became very self-reliant. I learned I could invest into other areas which gave back to me." Two other pearls shared turning to sports where they experienced feelings of accomplishment and community. One pearl disclosed how she earned her own money in high school, supported herself, and "learned to be on my own." Two pearls disclosed how their gifts and talents—academically, artistically, and athletically—significantly altered their self-deprecating life messages, "When I'm doing something good, I get something good," and "By ninth grade, school was my savior."

Reflecting on the gestation of the daughters' wounds, I was reminded of how the oyster continues its secretion, slowly and steadily adding layer upon layer of nacre over the irritant to form its coatings of strength, sustainability, and beauty. I thought of the daughters and of their *knowing* and how it had first surfaced to tether them to their formative truths. And then over time, their *knowing* secured them more firmly to their sense of direction and survival. I found it remarkable how amidst years of mother-wounding, their *knowing* took hold, transforming itself into timeless, translucent layers of resiliency.

Guiding Question #2:
**How can daughters betrayed by their mothers
move from brokenness to wholeness?**

Brokenness to Wholeness Strand –
Protecting the Injured Self and Producing a New Self

Stringing together the themes within the *Brokenness to Wholeness Strand*, I found a consistent pattern of healing among the daughters. Although their journeys and paths were diverse, all daughters moved through a process of *protecting the injured self and producing a new self*.

Protecting the Injured Self

One of the insidious aspects of betrayal injury is the degree of emotional, psychological, and physical energy which is expended navigating through the three States of Being. Additionally, a tremendous amount of energy is consumed in taking on various roles of responsibility for the betrayer and within the betrayal environment. Consequently, individuals who have been betrayed in a chronic nature learn to navigate from an external locus of control. In particular for children, their sense of survival comes from what their betrayer and/or betrayal environment is dictating. Thus, their focus is constantly turned outward.

However, as was discovered in their *Background, Betrayal Narrative,* and B*rokenness from Betrayal Strands,* daughters began formulating a *knowing or an awareness* around their betrayals from their mothers at young ages. I found it remarkable how the daughters' needs to self-protect were voiced within their early life messages of "I want to get away" and "I had to get away." Although their locus of control remained predominantly external throughout their teens, daughters demonstrated an innate ability to self-protect by turning their focus inward and tending to their needs. With slight variations in age, daughters chose to move away from their mothers after finishing high school. One daughter, whose mother lost custody when she was young, chose to live with her dad but declined having visitation with her mom. In moving away, one daughter expressed how this was, "My opportunity to make a decision for myself...not really caring about what anybody else thought," while another described her need for independence from her mother and her desire to create "environmental conditions to start healing."

In working with victims of all kinds of betrayal, I have found that it is not impossible but it is very challenging to remain in the environment of the betrayer and to focus on the wounds of self. Even under the best circumstances, victims are continually triggered and/or reinjured and thus recycle through the states of confusion, worthlessness, and powerlessness. By moving away from their mothers and staying away, the daughters chose the first critical step in moving *From Brokenness to Wholeness*—clearing the needed space both for the cultivation of an internal locus of control and for the creation of conditions necessary to continue protecting themselves.

Producing a New Self

Another piece to the insidious nature of betrayal injury is the thinking on the part of the betrayed that *someone or something else needs to make it right*. With most betrayals, this person or source is typically the betrayer. Although this mindset is understandable, I believe this invites further injury to victims as they tether their healing to the actions or non-actions of the betrayer. More importantly, this thinking does not afford victims the opportunity to do their recovering work.

Throughout the examination of the daughters' journeys *From Brokenness to Wholeness*, I found daughters' ages ranged from early 20's to early 40's when each first began her recovering path. However, there was a common thread in each daughter's thinking—a commitment to *righting herself*. I found this to be extraordinary given there wasn't a single trigger or factor which precipitated this thinking but rather a maturing trust in her *knowing* of what her betrayal experiences taught her and what her life messages from her mom spoke to her. Several daughters noted how the presence of other healthy maternal figures in their lives such as grandmothers, family friends, teachers or mentors within their community, served as "surrogate moms" or "role models for what it is like to be a woman." These connections strengthened their desire and their commitment to move forward taking responsibility for their wellness.

I believe that distancing themselves physically from their mothers along with adopting the mindset of *righting themselves* laid the foundation for each daughter's journey *From Brokenness to Wholeness*. As I continued exploring their narratives searching for themes in their healing, I found it intriguing how the daughters embraced a wide range of therapeutic methodologies, teachings—both formal and informal—as well as professional and personal growth experiences. However, once again as I strung the pearls together, there was remarkable consistency in their shared experiences of *Producing a New Self*—a healing process of awareness, insight, and understanding.

Awareness

Holding a *knowing* about one's brokenness from her mother is a beginning. Being able, ready, and willing to expand upon that awareness exploring its degree of impact and injury on the self is much more difficult. For the daughters, this was a slow, tender process which began in quite a unique way for each one. One daughter described her awareness as "coming in through the back door," as she worked through her painful relationship with her father first, not yet able to address her mother wounds. Another daughter revealed how she entered counseling to work on her marriage, but "was in total denial for some time." Then, she described how, "I knew and felt my mom did not love me…but I had no idea of the pain around it." Another daughter described her awareness around "starting to repeat some of the same patterns as my parents," and "wanting a different life…a safe place to come home to." A different daughter entered therapy at age fifteen because "my father was dying" but didn't address her mother issues until her twenties. And yet, another daughter who started therapy in her early twenties "had a really hard time," wondering what would happen if they "found out how bad I was." And, one daughter began taping into her awareness as she traveled the world, "living all that freedom" and liberating herself from her mother.

During this period of opening the shell to their brokenness, most daughters were confronting challenges in their physical and emotional wellness and in their intimate or significant relationships. However, each daughter stayed the course, never wavering from her commitment to *righting herself.*

Insight and Understanding

As I examined the process of *Producing a New Self,* I found the daughters' levels of investment into their recovering work extraordinary. Each daughter placed her trust into the hands of professionals, bravely embracing insights into the genesis and gestation of her mother wounds. This work was extremely difficult and demanding of self. The daughters remained determined.

Daughters sought out different therapeutic settings and approaches which suited their personalities and preferences. While all daughters worked with licensed counselors and therapists, several incorporated the healing teachings of spiritual leaders and of Nature. Four daughters worked exclusively with female therapists while two preferred male therapists. With either gender, all daughters reported on their insights into the importance of a maternal or paternal transference with their therapists. Daughters described feeling "loved, seen, accepted, liked, and believed in." Others disclosed the importance of "learning about trust and healthy boundaries," "being reparented," and experiencing "uncon-ditional love and recognition."

There was clearly no "one approach" in *Moving From Brokenness To Wholeness.* Daughters described comfort and safety in embracing a variety of therapeutic tools and strategies. Through approaches such as attachment work, art therapy, cognitive-behavioral, psychoanalytic and talk therapy, daughters were able to further their insights into their betrayal trauma while tending to the healing of the fractured self. Daughters described the value of other therapeutic methods such as authentic movement, dance, body work, human design and hypnosis. Several daughters drew from healing lessons within Nature. All daughters not only attended therapy over periods of several years, but they also re-entered therapy as needs and issues surfaced.

Several daughters expanded their insights into themselves, their mothers, and their families through numerous opportunities such as pursuing educational degrees, advanced trainings, and professional internships. Most attended adjunct venues of healing such as self-growth classes or institutes, support/12 Step groups, and many furthered *Producing a New Self* through recovery readings. Regardless of the source, all daughters reported that as their insights deepened around how and why their betrayal trauma from their moms injured the self, their healing deepened as well.

In Erik Erikson's *Eight Stages of Psychosocial Development*, he suggests that an individual's unresolved navigation through any prior developmental stage will hinder her ability to complete further stages successfully. This may result in a more unhealthy sense of self and fragmented ego. However, Erikson also purports that individuals have the capacity to resolve prior stages at a later time. In my work with betrayal injury or trauma of any kind, I utilize a life messages thera-peutic approach to assessment, intervention, and treatment and in working through unresolved stages of development. I have found this approach to be very successful in eliciting and expanding individual's understanding in making connections between sources of brokenness and their impact on the self. Furthermore, when there has been healing work in resolving prior developmental trauma, life messages are a reliable indication of levels of wellness or wholeness and/or stages needing further attention. Thus, in designing the interview questions, the inclusion of daughters' life messages was an integral piece throughout the study.

As I methodically examined the daughters' narratives, I focused on how their recovery work or other growth experiences deepened their understanding of their mother wounds and how it impacted their life messages. The daughters' messages clearly reflected their restorative properties.

One daughter described the depth and breadth of understanding which took hold as she interned in a women's shelter and connected with their narratives of abuse and trauma, "I identified my self-deprecating life messages of self-blame and self-hatred from my mom," and "was able to release layers of shame." While working with her therapist, another daughter disclosed being able to "face the loss of sense of self." With more understanding of her mother wounds, she further uncovered, "I learned I was not good enough. If I learned it, it was worth trying to relearn who I am." When another daughter's understanding took hold, she described how she was able to reframe prior life messages of "over-responsibility for her betrayers". She then released their hold over her and replaced them with new life messages: "Who these people [betrayers] were…understanding who they were before I was even thought of. Understanding I wasn't their problem…never their problem!"

A different daughter disclosed how her understanding of her "need to have my life look a certain way to compensate for what I didn't feel or what I had inside" helped her to identify and work on "my idealization of other people" and "my devaluation of self." And still, one daughter described how her work in a drug and alcohol center increased her understanding into "issues of vulnerability," and motivated her to address "my self-worth issues." And, another daughter disclosed how her work of "dismantling the false self that I had developed in order to deal with my mother" was a turning point in her understanding of how she dealt with her mother.

In synthesizing the life messages within the daughters' process of *Producing a New Self,* I found remarkable consistency in their successful revisitation of and navigation through prior early developmental stages of trust, initiative, and autonomy. This manifested in numerous ways: 1) in the daughters' capacities to trust in themselves, in relationships with their therapists and healers, and in those worthy of their trust; 2) to individuate from their mothers and establish their autonomy; and 3) to demonstrate initiative and commitment as they invested into their recovering work. Further evidence of positive ego development is reflected during the psychosocial developmental stages of competence, identity, intimacy, and generativity: 4) Without exception, every daughter excelled in her respective professional field exhibiting extraordinary levels of competence; 5) Each reintegrated life messages of positive worth and image in the healing of her identity and of self; 6) and lastly, every daughter established and invested into intimate relationships, friendships, and communities creating safe spaces of acceptance and attachment.

Thinking about the daughters and their extraordinary journeys *From Brokenness To Wholeness*, I pictured a beach beautifully showcasing a small display of shells. Upon closer examination, their openness revealed their translucent truths. Each one hosted the cultivation of a unique pearl comprised of layers upon layers of awareness, insight, and understanding. And each one had been transformed by the years of nacre carefully and steadily restoring her trust, belonging, and worth.

Summary

Betrayal injury, as with most presenting issues, does not usually stand alone. Therefore, it is important to note that as daughters confronted and addressed their mother wounds, at times many were also healing co-occurring disorders and/or other forms of childhood trauma or relational challenges. I found it remarkable how each daughter consistently remained open and aware to unearthing additional layers of injury and tended to them in timely ways. In addition, because of the work each daughter invested into her recovering and because of her degree of awareness, insight, and understanding of what wholeness felt like (and feels like), it was not surprising that each pearl was (and is) protective of her wholeness and proactive in maintaining it.

In learning about the formation of pearls, I discovered that today most pearls are farmed because of the rarity of real pearls. I learned that whether a grain of sand finds its way into an oyster's shell or if it is implanted, it may take anywhere from four to six years for the layers of nacre to from a perfect pearl. The process cannot be rushed or it will sabotage its growth. Reviewing the daughters' narratives, I was reminded that the process of *Protecting an Injured Self and Producing a New Self* occurred over a span of fifteen to thirty-five years. And although the daughters' journeys to wholeness are never finished, the longevity of each pearl's mindful, purposeful, and steadfast investment into *righting herself* is an indication of its polished authenticity and its powerful legitimacy.

> *Guiding Question #3:*
> **How can presenting the voices of daughters through personal narrative create new meanings for the interviewer and readers regarding the healing of daughters betrayed by their mothers?**

Wholeness To Strand –
Lessons of Acceptance, Resiliency, and Giving Back

Throughout the entire process of planning "The Daughters Project," carrying out the interviews, transcribing the daughters' narratives, and conducting their ensuing analysis, I challenged myself to remain open and receptive to whatever lessons would come my way. Given my lengthy interest in and study of betrayal, I drew from my prior knowledge allowing it to guide me through the process. However, as I navigated through every stage of preparation, interviewing, listening, reflecting, and writing, I was professionally informed and personally transformed by the voices of the daughters and their respective messages. Moving into *Wholeness To*, the *Lessons of Acceptance, Resiliency, and Giving Back* proved to be no different.

Within the *Wholeness Strand,* one of the areas of examination was each daughter's current status in her relationship with her mother. There were several important variances to consider within the context of their relationships: two daughters' mothers were no longer living, three daughters have limited or no contact, and one daughter has frequent contact. However, there was remarkable consistency in the daughters' descriptions regarding their feelings of acceptance around their mothers.

- I have no relationship with my mom. This was her choosing. I understand my mom more. It does not excuse her behavior. It explains it. I have a peace and an acceptance about it.

- She died at age 87. My beliefs about the relationship are more positive. I've made progress over the years. I'm accepting her for who she was.

- I have my life and my mom is not in it. I am protective of my family and my life. I no longer look at the things in my childhood that happened to me. They are things that were given to me.

- I don't have a mother. I have this mental patient that I have some custodial responsibility for. It's hilarious and it's heart-breaking. It is on my terms. I feel completely at peace. I don't want any more. I don't need to have any less.

- I have a relationship with her so that feels very nice. It's just a relationship with very strong boundaries. I have acceptance for what the relationship was. I forgive her. I have compassion and understanding.

- I am the only one who made peace with her before she died. Years ago, and more so as I went along. I didn't need her to be any different.

Accompanying feelings of acceptance, several daughters disclosed other emotions such as sadness. One daughter explained, "When I think about my mom, I feel sad. I allow that feeling, I honor it, and I let it pass. If it lingers, I say a prayer sending positive thoughts her way." Another daughter described her feelings of gratitude as she was writing a list of positives about her mom. In her words, "I am grateful that I can see the good." One daughter disclosed her feelings around loss and the similarities with grieving a death. "I don't think it's something we talk about. I have a mother, but I don't." And, whether their mothers were still living or had passed and regardless of the degree of contact, all daughters were in agreement regarding feelings of self-care and that honoring themselves and their healing truths took precedence over the relationship with their mothers.

Searching for the themes within the *Wholeness To Strand*, I revisited the daughters' current life messages and life lessons. Reading through them, I was incredibly moved by the depth of inner-personal growth and breadth of awareness, insight, and understanding. Pulling this strand together, I was struck by the glow from the pearls radiant layers of resiliency.

- I live in accordance with my healing truths. I have a choice about how I feel about myself. It is my responsibility to choose and act on it. If I stumble and fall, I can always begin again. I have choices on how I want to live my life. I choose wellness.

- Becoming a better human being is a life project. Being grateful and having faith that good is coming out of the challenge. I know what I am doing every day is the right thing, or being able to accept right here, right now is perfect. It is okay.

- I've worked really hard and continue to work hard to create the life I want to live which is different from what I had. I don't have to be perfect. It's okay for me to do my absolute best. It's okay to have to start over again.

- It's okay to be independent, self-reliant, resourceful and self-directed and I have to compliment that with my vulnerability and soft side. Contentment, happiness, and joy cannot be given and they cannot be taken away. You cannot allow your childhood to determine your fate.

- You don't have to live in a wounded place. We don't have to be held there. This helped me to activate my own resiliency and believe in the other human's inner resiliency. Healing is possible for all humans.

- The other side of betrayal is how incredibly strong this has made me. My mother's love of nature has been the most restoring aspect of how I heal myself and knowing how resilient I am.

Within the daughters' lessons on resiliency, were strong references to their ongoing work toward wholeness. One daughter disclosed how she will continue "to work on being still" giving herself time to reflect and sit with emotions before making decisions. Another daughter disclosed the importance of her boundary work, "letting go of friends who are not healthy" and "putting myself around people who are." A different daughter described her desire to "see my brokenness as actually a part of my wholeness—a part to be celebrated and brought forth," while another looks forward to "continuing the process of self-discovery." And one daughter described her longing to "create more space for my creativity, nature, art, self-generated ceremony and more time for prayer."

Approaching the final section of analysis on the *Wholeness To Strand*, I reminded myself that all daughters were in "giving" wellness professions, both in individual as well as in organizational capacities. Therefore, I anticipated their journeys beyond wholeness would reflect their giving nature. However, as I began stringing the pearls together, their polished essence illuminated the strand with powerful voices of *Giving Back*.

- I will keep a pulse on my passions and what is purposeful. Giving back is my platform for ongoing recovering. Giving back is my greatest reward.

- I want to give back to people and to the universe. There is more I can give.

- I hope my experiences will help somebody else. This is what I really want to do—give people the help I didn't have. I'd like to do more of that.

- The biggest life message I live by is 'the gift of giving,' whether it is in a friendship or kindness to a stranger. I lead with kindness. Let that be the first way I am experienced by another person.

- I will continue helping families and being a venue for change. Professionally, I will do something more global in my community to destigmatize mental illness.

- I want a world where there is reciprocity, generosity, sustainable peace and movement away from scarcity, fear, overwhelm, and stress.

Summary

In the *Wholeness To Strand*, I have purposely contained my analysis of the daughter's *Lessons of Acceptance, Resiliency, and Giving Back*. I believe their wellness speaks for itself. In my work with betrayal as with other issues, the measurement of one's wholeness is in how one chooses to live her life. It was clearly evident that throughout each daughter's journey she was able to release the pain of her past and reframe her experience in a lens of acceptance and peace. Every daughter courageously committed to moving out of the victim and survivor mode, righting and redefining herself and in the process embracing a place of renewal and resilience. And lastly but as importantly, as each daughter moved toward wholeness securing her recovering tenets and solidifying her healing truths, she utilized her personal growth for gifting others and her professional resources for giving back.

As I thought about these extraordinary daughters and their journeys *Moving From Brokenness To Wholeness*, I was drawn back to the shells on the beach. My mind returned to the grain of sand, the betrayal mother wound, making its way into the shell. Quietly it suffered. Slowly it healed. Studying the shells one last time, I honored each daughter and her journey. I whispered to each of them, "A pearl is a beautiful thing produced by an injured life." Sensing their presence, I waited. The pearls slid from their shells and joined together. Forming a perfect single strand of wholeness, their timeless truths illuminated the sea, the sky, and the sand.

Flying Solo
A Hero Lies In You
I Made Me Who I Am
The Power Rests Completely Within Me
I Am Vulnerable ~ I Am Enough
I Am The Phoenix That Has Risen From The Ashes

Epilogue – Pearls Lighting The Way

In my years in the recovering field, I have come to believe, know, and trust that addressing what is uncomfortable is necessary in order to create change. Opening up the conversation about betrayal, mothers, and daughters is no different. Therefore, I want to acknowledge each of the daughters. I want to thank you for bravely coming forward, opening up your shells, and sharing your journeys *From Brokenness To Wholeness*. By doing so, you not only have honored your voices and your truths, but you have become creators of change. You are *Pearls Lighting The Way*.

Pearls of insight and understanding

For those individuals who have been blessed to have a mother or a mother-figure who has nurtured, protected, and provided for them in the ways we associate with a mother's love, I hope the daughters' stories have cultivated an understanding and a compassionate response within you for those who have not been so fortunate. And for the daughters and sons who *know you have a mother, but you don't,* I hope the daughters' narratives have crafted new insights around your mother-wounding and have comforted you with a warm blanket of knowledge that you are not alone.

Pearls of inspiration and empowerment

For individuals who have courageously opened up their shells of wounds and who have embraced a recovering process or wellness path, I hope you have been further empowered by the daughters' journeys of commitment to the process and their ongoing work toward wholeness. And for individuals who are struggling with betrayal wounding or other areas of brokenness, it is my hope that the daughters' living examples of the power of choice, perseverance, and resiliency will stimulate a shift in your thinking and inspire you to choose wellness.

Pearls of affirmation and validation

For individuals who are in health care professions or for those who are in positions of helping others, I hope the daughters' narratives remind us of the power of listening, *really* listening. And that often times, it is not our methodologies or our strategies which create change, but simply our availability, attention, and unconditional positive regard which provide a safe space for acceptance and belonging to take hold. For any one of us who might be quick to dismiss the pain of another person or too busy to sit still with someone who is hurting , it is my deepest hope that from the daughters' stories, we are awakened to the healing properties which come from affirmation and validation of one's experience. All it requires is our empathic presence.

Pearls of Light

As I come to the close of a two year journey with "The Daughters Project", an ocean of feelings and emotions swells within me. I am over-whelmed with gratitude for the daughters and I am honored to have been entrusted with their voices. And because of the restorative ways in which the universe works, bearing witness to their narratives deepened layers of wholeness within my being. It is testament to the power of healing light one pearl reflects upon another. It is the promise of shared truth.

When I think of "my daughters", my mind returns to the shells on the beach. They are wide open, showcasing each unique pearl and her beauty. I am reminded that real pearls are not perfectly round or smoothly textured; however, they are much heavier and stronger than fake pearls. Real pearls vary in shape and size, but their overtone colors are more pure and lustrous than imitations. And although real pearls are cool to the touch, they turn warm when resting against the body's temperature. Most importantly, when held up to light, real pearls reflect a translucent depth, revealing their organic genesis and their years of authentic growth.

Every day, each of us has a choice. We can choose to remain in our injured places or we can open our shells to healing processes. It takes time and it requires much of us. However, as we embrace our journeys of recovering, layer by layer we will move out of brokenness and into wholeness. The painful pieces of our past will become our sources of rebirth and renewal. And just as it is true with real pearls, over time our truths will rest secure within us warming our souls, and they will shine through us *lighting the way* for others.

A pearl is a beautiful thing.... produced by an injured life.

Appendix A – Letter of Invitation

Holli Kenley, M.A.
California Licensed Marriage and Family Therapist
MFC 39156

Letter of Invitation

Daughters Betrayed By Their Mothers
Moving From Brokenness To Wholeness (Wellness)

Dear Prospective Participants:

The purpose of this letter is to invite you to participate in an independent project—Daughters Betrayed By Their Mothers: *Moving From Brokenness To Wholeness*—through an interview process conducted by Holli Kenley. Ms. Kenley holds a Master's Degree in Psychology, is a California State Licensed Marriage and Family Therapist, and is in good standing with the California Board of Behavioral Sciences as well as the California Association of Marriage & Family Therapists.

The purpose of this project is to explore, discover, and examine experiential recovery themes within the narratives of a given population of females. The guiding questions are as follows: (a) *What are the life experiences and life messages of daughters betrayed by their mothers? (b) How can daughters betrayed by their mothers move from brokenness to wholeness? And, (c) How can presenting the voices of daughters through personal narratives create new meanings for the interviewer and readers regarding the healing of daughters betrayed by their mothers?*

You are eligible to participate in this project if you are a female between the ages of 35 – 75, if you were raised by **a mother who betrayed*** you, if you experienced **brokenness*** from your mother's betrayal/s, and if you are now living **a life of wholeness (wellness) ***- personally, professionally, and relationally. You will be asked to participate in a 4 hour interview—either in person, via Skype, or by phone. The interview will contain questions about your family background; your mother and her role in your formative and adult years; the betrayal/s you experienced from your mother and their impact on you;

and your healing journey from brokenness to wholeness. You will be given the questions in advance for consideration and preparation. Two 30 minute conferences (pre and post) will accompany the 4 hour interview. Your responses will be anonymous.

For purposes of clarification, the following terms have been more specifically defined.

*A mother who betrayed: *The word "betrayed" should be interpreted in its broadest sense including mothers who were absent, abusive, alcoholic, or unavailable. It may include mothers who were bipolar, borderline, narcissistic, or who suffered from other mental and/or physical disorders. It implies any violation of trust between participant and her mother; and it encompasses a mother's inability or unwillingness to provide unconditional love, nurturance, protection, and support for participant. The betrayal occurrence/s may be either short term, episodic, or ongoing.*

*Brokenness: *Participant can clearly identify injuries sustained (physical, emotional, psychological, relational, etc.) and directly correlate or connect them to her mother's betrayal/s.*

*Life of wholeness (wellness): *Participant can clearly articulate and describe her healing path, recovery process, treatment program, or restorative journey which has brought her into a place of wellness and wholeness—personally, professionally, and relationally. Participant's current state of wholeness (wellness) does not imply that she is in a "perfect place", but rather she is mindful of living in accordance with her healing truths, and she is purposeful in embracing and cultivating healthy ways of being—personally, professionally, and relationally.*

Your participation in this project is completely voluntary. If you choose to participate, you are free to withdraw your consent and discontinue participation at any time without prejudice.

It is my intention upon completion of the interviewing process and my ensuing analysis and interpretation of the experiential themes within the participants' narratives to publish my findings. Names of all identities of participants will be changed to protect anonymity.

Upon request, you will be sent a copy of the *Interview Questions* along with the *Consent to Participate in Daughters Betrayed by their Mothers Project.*

Please feel free to contact Holli Kenley at holli@hollikenley.com if you have any questions. Subject line: **Daughters Project.**

Sincerely,
Holli Kenley, M.A., MFT

Appendix B – Consent Forms

California Licensed Marriage and Family Therapist
MFC 39156

CONSENT TO PARTICIPATE IN AN INDEPENDENT PROJECT:

Daughters Betrayed By Their Mothers
Moving From Brokenness To Wholeness (Wellness)

I, Holli Kenley, M.A., MFT, invite you to participate in an independent project conducted by Holli Kenley through an interview process. Your participation in this project is voluntary. Please read the information below and ask questions about anything you do not understand before deciding whether or not to participate.

PURPOSE OF PROJECT

The purpose of this independent project is designed to explore, discover, and examine experiential recovering themes within the narratives of a given population of females. The guiding questions are as follows: (a) *What are the life experiences and life messages of daughters betrayed by their mothers? (b) How can daughters betrayed by their mothers move from brokenness to wholeness? And, (c) How can presenting the voices of daughters through personal narratives create new meanings for the researcher and reader regarding the healing of daughters betrayed by their mothers?*

You are eligible to participate in this project if you are a female between the ages of 35-75, if you were raised by **a mother who betrayed*** you, if you experienced **brokenness*** from your mother's betrayal/s, and if you are now living **a life of wholeness***- personally, professionally, and relationally. You will be asked to participate in a 4 hour interview—either in person, via Skype, or by phone. The interview will contain questions about your family background; your mother and her role in your formative and adult years; the betrayal/s you experienced from your mother and their impact on you; and your healing journey from brokenness to wholeness. You will be given the questions in advance for consideration and preparation. Two 30 minute conferences (pre and post) will accompany the 4 hour interview. Your responses will be anonymous.

For purposes of clarification, the following terms have been more specifically defined.

*A mother who betrayed: *The word "betrayed" should be interpreted in its broadest sense including mothers who were absent, abusive, alcoholic, or unavailable. It may include mothers who were bipolar, borderline, narcissistic, or who suffered from other mental and/or physical disorders. It implies any violation of trust between participant and her mother; and it encompasses a mother's inability or unwillingness to provide love, nurturance, protection, and support for participant. The betrayal occurrence/s may be either short term, episodic, or ongoing.*

*Brokenness: *Participant can clearly identify and describe injuries sustained (physical, emotional, psychological, relational, etc.) and directly correlate or connect them to her mother's betrayal/s.*

*Life of wholeness (wellness): *Participant can clearly articulate and detail her healing path, recovery process, treatment program, or restorative journey which has brought her into a place of wholeness and wellness—personally, professionally, and relationally. Participant's current state of wholeness (wellness) does not imply that she is in a "perfect place", but rather she mindful of living in accordance with her healing truths and is purposeful in embracing healthy ways of being— personally, professionally, and relationally.*

DURATION AND LOCATION

Your participation in this project will consist of a live interview that will last for approximately 4 hours, with one additional 30 minute pre-interview phone conference and one additional 30 minute post-interview phone conference. If more time is needed for the 4 hour interview, both parties will agree on a designated period of time, not to exceed 1 additional hour. The interviews will be conducted in person (at a designated space), via Skype, or by phone. It is my fist preference to conduct the interview in person.

PROCEDURES

If you volunteer to participate in this project, I would ask you to do the following things:

1. **For screening processes, please submit the following:**

    a. A short biography (maximum 500 words).

    b. A short statement as to why you would like to participate in this project (maximum 250 words).

    c. Current contact information: email address and phone number/s

        ➢ **Failure to submit all above information, falsifying information, or misrepresentation of any kind will disqualify participant for this project.**

        ➢ **Please submit all above information in one word document or PDF File and send as an attachment to holli@hollikenley.com.**

    d. Notification of acceptance or non-acceptance into this project will be sent to prospective participants within two weeks from submission of screening information. Participants are not obligated to participate upon acceptance into this project.

2. **Review of Interview Questions**

    a. Participants will receive a copy of Interview Questions along with the Consent Form.

    b. Participants are required to review the questions, reflect upon their responses, and spend time in preparation for their interview.

3. **Pre- Interview Phone Conference**

    a. Before our scheduled 4 hour interview, we will schedule a 30 minute pre-interview phone conference. I will call you. This is a time for us to become acquainted and for you to ask any questions. At this time, if there are any reservations on either part, those will be discussed. Also, if either party feels uncomfortable with the process and needs to withdraw, that decision will be honored by both parties.

    b. At the conclusion of the pre-interview conference, a date and time will be set for the 4 hour interview.

4. **4 hour Interview**

   a. Prepare for your interview. Be authentic and honest. This is a time to honor yourself and your truths.

   b. Get a good night's sleep before our interview. On the day of our interview, give yourself plenty of time to relax and get centered. Make sure that all distractions are taken care of and that you have a quiet, confidential, and safe place to talk (if by phone or Skype). If we are meeting in person, a confidential place will be designated.

   c. We will utilize the questions as a guide for our interview. Although I will move through the topic areas in order, it is important for our process to be fluid and natural. I would like you to do most of the talking; however, if something needs clarification or explanation, I will step in and ask. Also, if I feel we are getting off topic, I will gently redirect our interview.

   d. At the end of our time, I will ask you if you feel that you covered everything you wanted to. If either you or I feel we need additional time to finish, we will schedule a date and time for a one hour interview.

5. **Post- Interview Phone Conference**

   a. Within two weeks after our 4 hour interview, we will schedule a 30 minute post-interview phone conference. At this time, please feel free to ask any questions, make any changes, or add any other information you feel is relevant or important. I, too, may have some follow-up questions or comments.

   b. We will conclude our time together.

POTENTIAL RISKS AND DISCOMFORTS

1. Discussing our *mothers* and their roles in our lives is a very tender and difficult topic, especially if our mothers were betrayers. For many females, even those individuals who have done extensive recovery work regarding their injuries and injustices imposed upon them by their mothers, there is often a feeling that they are betraying their mothers when speaking honestly about their experiences and relationships. It is really important to ask yourself these questions:

   - Am I am in a healed place where I can speak openly and honestly about my mother and honor my truths and myself in the process?

   - Although I may get re-injured by a memory, a flashback, or a current situation, am I grounded in my healing, in my way of being, and in my current support system?

   - What do I hope to gain by participating in this project?

2. Please think very carefully about your participation in this project. If you proceed, please know that there are risks for re-injury and for discomfort for *everyone*. As a licensed therapist, I will do all that I can to make the interview process safe and comfortable. **However, it is not my role during this process to function as your therapist.** I am here to listen as you share your narrative and to glean thematic lessons from your life experiences. If you are currently working with a therapist or clinician, you may want to consider reconnecting during the process for support.

3. Maintaining anonymity is extremely important. I will do all that I can to minimize any risk or breach of information. When exchanging information electronically, there is always some level of concern. Please be aware of this.

4. It is my intention upon my completion of this project and my ensuing analysis and interpretation of the experiential themes within the participants' narratives to publish my findings. Names of all identities will be changed to protect anonymity.

5. During any time of this project, if a participant threatens to harm herself, or another individual, or discloses any kind of abuse of a minor or elder, as a mandated reporter, I have a duty to report such offenses to law enforcement. This is a lawful breach of confidentiality.

6. There also may be 'risks and discomforts which are yet unknown or unforeseen.'

ANTICIPATED BENEFITS TO PARTICIPANTS

1. In projects such as this one, we cannot say that there will be any direct or implied benefits to the participants. If you do benefit in some manner and you feel like disclosing that information, please feel free to share that in your post-conference. Your participation may help health care providers as well as the lay audience better understand how and why a given number of females emerged from a state of brokenness due to their mothers' betrayal/s and were able to grow into a state of wholeness.

2. Although there is extensive literature on disorders or pathology of mothers and their respective impact and injury upon child-hood/adult development as well as sound clinical techniques and tools for recovery, the intention of this project and your participation in it is to benefit potential readers by providing experiential themes, lessons, and insights into healing from maternal betrayal/s based on personal stories and truths.

ALTERNATIVES TO PARTICIPATION

Choosing not to participate in this project is the only alternative to participating in the project.

PAYMENT FOR PARTICIPATION

Participants will not be paid or offered other benefits.

FINANCIAL COSTS TO THE SUBJECT

Participants will not be reimbursed for any expenses incurred by participating in this project.

POSSIBLE COMMERCIAL PRODUCTS

1. It is my intention to publish my findings from the project—
   Daughters Betrayed By Their Mothers: *Moving From
   Brokenness to Wholeness.* With your participation, you consent
   to the following:

   > *By my consent to participate in this project, I give up any
   > property rights to all information obtained through the interview
   > process, its publication, and sales of said publication.*

MEDICAL CARE FOR RESEARCH RELATED INJURY

In the event of an injury from the research procedures, no form of
compensation is available from Holli Kenley. Medical treatment
(physical or mental) may be provided at your own expense; or at the
expense of your health care insurer, which may or may not provide
coverage. If you have questions, you should contact your insurer.

ANNONYMITY

1. When the results of the research are published or discussed in
   conferences, your identity and all other identities disclosed in the
   project will be protected by name substitution or name
   replacement with numbers/letters.
2. Screening information of participants and interview notes will be
   stored in locked file cabinets. Upon completion of published
   work, such information will be shredded.

AUDIO RECORDINGS AND TRANSCRIPTIONS

1. The 30 minute pre-interview conference, 4 hour interview (and 1
   hour additional interview if applicable), and 30 minute post-
   interview conference will be audio recorded and transcribed. I
   will tell the participant when the recording is on and when it is
   off.
2. The recordings will provide accurate investigation into four
   major areas of exploration:
   - Participant's family background.
   - Participant's mother and her role in participant's form-
     ative and adult years with a focus on maternal betrayal/s
     of participant.

- Participant's life messages from betrayals including but not limited to their short and long term impact.
- Participant's healing journey from brokenness to wholeness.

3. The recordings will be the basis of my analysis and interpretation of experiential themes within participants' narratives. The recordings will also provide proof of the qualitative nature on which I am basing my findings.

4. The recordings will allow for the investigator to remain present with the participant.

5. The recordings and their transcriptions will be stored in locked file cabinets. They will be deleted upon completion of research and publication thereof.

6. First names only will be used for the recordings, transcriptions, and labels. Names will be changed to protect anonymity when transcribing recordings for presentation or publication.

Statement from Subject:

I _____ freely consent to the use of audio recordings of my words and/or actions as described above in the project—**Daughters Betrayed By Their Mothers:** *Moving From Brokenness to Wholeness*. I understand that the recordings will be used as described in the **AUDIO RECORDING AND TRANSCRIPTION** section, and that names will be changed to protect anonymity when transcribing recordings for presentation or publication. I waive the right to inspect or approve use of this material as incorporated in the work. I acknowledge that the investigator is under no obligation to use the recordings in the work described is she so elects.

I release the investigator from any claims that may arise regarding the use of recordings and their transcriptions, including any claims of defamation, invasion of privacy, or infringement of moral rights, rights of publicity or copyright. I acknowledge that I have no ownership rights in the recordings or the research.

PARTICPATION AND WITHDRAWAL

Your participation is this research is voluntary. If you decide to participate, you are free to withdraw your consent and discontinue participation at any time without prejudice.

WITHDRAWAL OF PARTICIPATION BY THE INVESTIGATOR

The investigator may withdraw you from participating in this research if circumstances arise which warrant doing so. If you experience any of the following side effects* or if you become ill during the process, you may have to drop out, even if you would like to continue. The investigator will make the decision and let you know if it is not possible for you to continue. The decision may be made either to protect your health and safety, or because it is part of the project plan that people who develop certain conditions may not continue to participate.

* Side-effects may include but not be limited to the following:

- Increase in or exacerbation of previous mental disorders or physical ailments.

- Manifestations of depression, anxiety, and other mood/psychotic disorders.

- Resurfacing of unpleasant triggers, flashbacks, or memories.

- Unmanageable levels of inner personal emotions such as stress, shame, guilt.

- Relapse or regression into unhealthy behaviors, thoughts or feelings: i.e. addiction, anger, abuse.

- Danger to self or to others (reportable by law).

- Any and all unforeseen psychosis that prohibits participation in this project.

IDENTIFICATION OF INVESTIGATOR and OFFER TO ANSWER QUESTIONS

1. In the event of project related injury or if you experience an adverse reaction, please immediately contact 911 or go to your nearest emergency room facility.

2. If you have any questions about this project, please feel to contact Holli Kenley via email—holli@hollikenley.com. You will receive a response within 24 hours.

RIGHTS OF PARTICIPANTS

You may withdraw at any time and discontinue participation without penalty.

You are waiving any legal claims, rights or remedies because of your participation in this project—**Daughters Betrayed By Their Mothers:** *Moving From Brokenness To Wholeness.*

SIGNATURE OF PROJECT PARTICIPANT

I have read the information provided above. I have been given an opportunity to ask questions and all of my questions have been answered to my satisfaction. I have been given a copy of this form.

_____

Name of Participant – please print

_____

Signature of Participant Date

_____

Address

SIGNATURE OF INVESTIGATOR

_____

Signature of Investigator Date

Appendix C – Interview Questions

Daughters Betrayed By Their Mothers. © 2015 Holli Kenley
Moving from Brokenness to Wholeness (Wellness)

Beginning....

1. How do you refer to your "mom"? Do you use that noun, or do you use a different one? Other? Can you talk about that?
2. How does it feel to talk about your mom?
3. Has that changed over time? Is it different today than a year ago? 5 years ago? Other?
4. We've talked about the connotations of the word "betrayal". How does word feel for you? How does it feel to use it in relating to your mom?

Background....

5. How would you describe your family as you were growing up?
6. How many siblings, parents in the home, other family?
7. How would you describe your role?

Betrayal Narrative ....

8. When did you first start thinking about your betrayal narrative with your mom? What was that like for you?
9. How would you like to share your betrayal narrative now?
   - Is there a chronology to your betrayal/s with your mom?
   - Was there a pattern of betrayal? Episodes? Re-occurring?
   - Other?
10. When you feel ready, please share your narrative.

Brokenness from Betrayal...

11. How did your mom's betrayal /s affect you? What do you remember thinking, feeling, and doing?

12. What life messages came to you from your mom and/or in your relationship with her?

13. What were their short term and long term implications or impact on you?

14. Are there other pieces to your brokenness which are important to share?

From Brokenness to Wholeness...

15. When did you first start thinking about your brokenness in relationship to your mom?

16. When did you first consider addressing your injuries, wounds, or brokenness? What was that like for you?

17. How would you like to share your journey from brokenness to wholeness?

    - Are there different stages?
    - Has there been ongoing work?
    - Other?

18. When you are ready, please share your journey from brokenness to wholeness.

Wholeness to........

19. Where are you today in your relationship with your mom (whether living or not)?

20. Today, where are you with yourself?

21. How do you feel about yourself today? Why?

22. What life messages do you say to yourself now?

23. As you continue to work on your wholeness, what areas are important to you?

24. From your betrayal experience with your mom, what life lessons have served you well and which ones continue to do so?

25. Where do you wish to go from here? Is there something beyond wholeness?

About The Author

Holli Kenley is a California Licensed Marriage and Family Therapist and a California State Licensed Teacher. She holds a Master's Degree in Psychology with an emphasis in Marriage, Family, and Child Counseling. She has worked in a variety of settings: a women's shelter, a counseling center, and in private practice. Counseling with adolescents, teens, and adults, Holli's areas of specialized training and experience include sexual trauma, abuse, addiction, codependency, domestic violence, betrayal and cyber bullying.

Holli is the author of seven recovery books including *Breaking Through Betrayal: And Recovering the Peace Within* (2010); *cyber bullying no more: Parenting a High Tech Generation* (2011); and her powerful memoir *Mountain Air: Relapsing and Finding The Way Back...One Breath at a Time* (2013). Her first novel *Another Way* (2015) offers tweens to teens (and their parents/ guardians) an empowering message of *discovering, defining, and determining* self-worth. In her Second Edition of *Breaking Through Betrayal* (January 2016), Holli addresses relapse as an issue of *self-betrayal* with a healing process for *self-discovery*. In her recently released book *Power Down & Parent Up: Cyber Bullying, Screen Dependence, &Raising Tech-Healthy Children* (2017), Holli provides parents and guardians with a roadmap for navigating our tech-driven world. She is also Contributing Wellness Editor for *Clear Life Magazine*.

Holli Kenley, M.A., MFT, currently works in the field of psychology as an author, speaker, and workshop presenter. Through her gentle but powerful *informative and restorative approach,* Holli engages clinical and lay audiences, empowering them with strategies to embrace well and whole ways of being. She has been a five time peer presenter at the California Association of Marriage and Family Therapists' Annual State Conferences and a featured or keynote speaker at college level clinical programs, state and national advocacy organizations, and educational institutions speaking on the topics of cyber bullying, the power of self-worth, betrayal, relapse, and sexual abuse recovery. Holli has been a guest on over 100 podcasts and numerous TV shows speaking on issues of wellness.

Prior to and during her career as a therapist, Holli taught for thirty years in public education. As an advocate of all forms of abuse and trauma, Holli supports and participates in community activism with numerous organizations: Stand for the Silent; RAINN (Rape, Abuse & Incest National Network); the "It's On Us Movement"; and the Family Online Safety Institute (FOSI), an international organization working to make the online world safer for kids and their families.

Although Holli enjoys living in the mountains and breathing in the peace and beauty around her, her mission is an integral part of her being:

> "Wellness awaits each of us. We choose the time. And yet I know from my own recovering journey that although choosing wellness is the first critical step, it is only the beginning. Through my writing, speaking, and clinical trainings or workshops, it is my ongoing purpose and passion to provide others with healing tools to create and sustain healthy change in their lives."

For more information about Holli or to contact her for your next conference, workshop, or speaking opportunity, please visit www.hollikenley.com.

Bibliography

Ackerman, R. (2002). *Perfect daughters: Adult daughters of alcoholics.* Deerfield Beach, FL: Health Communications, Inc.

Bandura, A. (2015). *Moral disengagement: How people do harm and live with themselves.* New York, NY: Worth Publishers.

Beattie, M. (1986). *Codependent no more: How to stop controlling others and start caring for yourself.* Center City, Minn.: Hazelden.

Briere, J. & Scott, C. (2015). *Principles of trauma therapy: A guide to symptoms, evaluation, and treatment (DSM -5 update) 2nd edition.* Los Angeles, CA: Sage Publications

Coplin, A. (2012). *The orchardist – a novel.* New York, NY: Harper Perennial.

David, L. "Erikson's Stages of Development," in *Learning Theories,* July 23, 2014, https://www.learning-theories.com/eriksons-stages-of-development.html

Films Media Group. (2010). *TED Talks: Brene Brown--The Power of Vulnerability.* TED.

Gurman, A. S., Lebow, J., & Snyder, D. K. (2015). *Clinical handbook of couple therapy.* New York: Guilford Press.

Hedva, B. (2013). *Betrayal, trust, and forgiveness: A guide to emotional healing and self-renewal.* Bonners Ferry, ID: Wynward Press.

Hafner, K. (2014). *Mother daughter me: A memoir.* New York, NY: Random House Trade Paperback.

Herman, J. (2015).*Trauma and recovery: the aftermath of violence – from domestic abuse to political terror.* New York, NY: Basic Books.

Janov, A. (1970). *The primal scream: Primal therapy: the cure for neurosis.* New York.

Kenley, H. (2015). *Another way – a novel.* Ann Arbor: Loving Healing Press, Inc.

Kenley, H. (2015). The power of worth. Part one –becoming aware. *ClearLife Magazine*. No.1. pp. 66-71.

Kenley, H. (2016). The power of worth. Part two – you have the power to discover, define, and determine your worth. *ClearLife Magazine*. No. 2. pp.88-97.

Kenley, H. (2016). Self-worth vs cyber-worth. 3 tips for reconnecting with your real self. *ClearLife Magazine*. No.3. pp 82-85.

Kenley, H. (2016). Unlocking cyber bullying: 3 keys for protection and intervention. *ClearLife Magazine*. No. 4. pp 66-71.

Kenley, H. (2016). Clean out digital clutter. Make room for authentic connection. *ClearLife Magazine*. No. 5. Pp 107-113.

Kenley, H. (2017). How do we become empowered? *ClearLife Magazine*. https://clearlifemagazine.com/read/wellness/ 2017.

Kenley, H. (2017) 13 reasons why: shaming no more. *ClearLife Magazine*. https://clearlifemagazine.com/read/wellness/ 2017.

Kenley, H. (2015). Tug of war wellness: three recovery lifelines. *In Recovery Magazine*. Volume 13, 2015. Retrieved from: https://inrecovery.com/tug-of-war-wellness/

Kenley, H. (2013). *Mountain air: Relapsing and finding the way back... one breath at a time.* Ann Arbor: Loving Healing Press, Inc.

Kenley, H. (2016). *Breaking through betrayal: And recovering the peace within 2nd edition.* Ann Arbor: Loving Healing Press, Inc.

Kobrin, S. (2012). *The satisfied soul. Transforming your food and weight worries.* Bloomington, IN: Author House.

Levine, P. & Phillips, M. (2012). *Freedom from pain; discover your body's pain to overcome physical pain.* Boulder, CO: Sounds True, Inc.

Levine, P. & Frederick, A. (2016). *Walking the tiger: healing trauma.* Audio CD.

Lindberg, A.M. (2005). *Gift from the sea: 50th anniversary edition.* New York: Pantheon Books.

Maltz, W. (2012). *The sexual healing journey: A guide for survivors of sexual abuse.* New York: William Morrow.

McGoldrick, M. (2016). *A clinical companion to genograms: Assessment and intervention.* New York, NY: WW Norton & Company, Inc.

Nerburn, K. (2013). *The girl who sang to the buffalo, a child, an elder, and the light from an ancient sky.* Novato, CA: New World

Library.

Netter. G. (Producer) & Cretton, D.D. (Director). (2017). *The glass castle* [Motion Picture] USA: Gil Netter Productions.

Nichols, M. P. (2014). *Family therapy: Concepts and methods.* Harlow: Pearson.

Pretzer, J. (2013). *Clinical applications of cognitive therapy.* New York: Plenum Press.

Safer, Jeanne. (2003). *The normal one: Life with a difficult or damaged sibling.* New York, New York. Random House, Inc.

Salvador, M., & Vetere, A. (2012). *Families and family therapy.* London: Routledge.

Santrock, J. W. (2014). *A topical approach to life-span development.* Boston: McGraw-Hill

Scheck, Stephanie. (2014) *The stages of psychosocial development according to erik erikson.* Norderstedt, Germany: GRIN Publishing

Smith, R. H., W, B., & Alcoholics Anonymous. (2013). *The big book of Alcoholics Anonymous: The story of how many thousands of men and women have recovered from alcoholism.* New York: Lark Publishing.

Taughinbaugh, C. (2014). *Parents to PhDs: 28 interview with parents who share heartache, wisdom, and healing through first-hand experiences.* (Kindle ed.). Amazon Digital Services.

Watson, D. L., & Tharp, R. G. (2014). *Self-directed behavior: Self-modification for personal adjustment.* Monterey: Brooks/Cole.

Wincze, J. P., & Weisberg, R. B. (2015). *Sexual dysfunction: A guide for assessment and treatment.* New York: Guilford Press.

Witchel, A. (2013). How jeannette walls spins good stories out of bad memories. *The New York Times Magazine,* Retrieved September 12, 2017. (https://nyti.ms/12CMgO)

Index

1

12 Steps, 24, 29, 41, 54–58, 61, 167, 228

A

AA, 52
abandonment, 14, 25, 29, 46, 56, 74, 78, 82, 215
abuse. *See also* sexual abuse
abuse recovery, 30
acceptance
as grief, 5
Ackerman, R., 24
addiction, 42
Al-Anon, 9, 24, 25, 40, 52, 55, 56, 89, 90
alcohol, 8, 10
alcoholism, 11, 20–26, 40, 46, 50, 56, 60, 61, 73–82, 85–89, 92, 162, 188, 197, 211–15, 222, 238, 240
anger, 6, 23, 82, 109, 115
and alcohol, 8
anorexia, 125
anxiety, 85, 115, 162, 166, 170, 221
and BPD, 110
anxiety disorder, 164, 172
art therapy, 202, 228
attachment, 145, 163, 168, 170, 175, 176, 224, 229, 241
attachment work, 228
awareness, 226

B

Bandura, A., 214
Beattie, M., 24, 89
betrayal
definition, 42
betrayal narrative, 11–17, 44–48, 52, 78, 98, 108, 113–17, 155–61, 192–97, 249
Big Book, 167
bipolar, 74, 75, 184, 193, 215, 238, 240
body image, 125
Borderline Personality Disorder, 110, 213
boundaries, 28, 35, 55–57, 60, 62, 94, 97, 104, 109, 125, 134, 160, 161, 168, 171, 174, 190, 201, 227
strong, 231
Breaking Through Betrayal, 29, 136, 143, 179, 218, 251
bulimia, 51, 125, 221

C

Catholic, 70, 180
CBT, 228
chaos, 7, 43, 110, 190, 213
chronicity, *217–18*
CODA, 52, 54, 55, 56
codependent, 24, 33, 35, 89, 164, 168, 190, 198, 204, 221, 251
competence, 229
conflict avoidant, 120
Consent Form, vii, 67, 241

Are you ready to heal?

Breaking Through Betrayal: And Recovering the Peace Within is for any individual who has experienced betrayal and is struggling to break through its bonds. Through a proven process tailored for recovery from betrayal injury, readers are invited to:

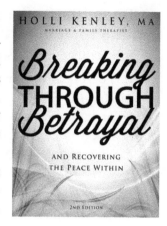

- Explore and connect with the different kinds of betrayal: rejection or abandonment; a violation of trust; a shattered truth or belief.

- Identify and move through betrayal's three States of Being—confusion, worthlessness, and powerlessness—while uncovering contributors of symptom intensity and duration.

- Revive and restore mind, body, and spirit with a 5-part recovering process for "righting oneself" and attend to re-occurrence or re-injury.

New in this Second Edition of Breaking Through Betrayal, readers are offered a unique perspective on a timeless topic—relapse. By reframing relapse as a familiar experience and redefining it as an issue of self-betrayal, readers are:

- Drawn into a safe conversation while breaking through the stigma, secrecy, and shame of returning to any kind of unhealthy pattern of thinking, behaving, or feeling.

- Invited to partake in an empowering 6-part recovering process in moving from self-betrayal to self-discovery.

"Holli Kenley shares her comprehensive approach to a situation most of us experience at least once in our lifetimes – betrayal. As a former therapist, I appreciate the author's ability to take a complex topic and turn it into an uncomplicated and well-organized read, including easy-to-follow exercises at the end of each chapter. This book is an important resource for anyone experiencing grief and loss as the result of betrayal. Read it and 'recover the peace within.'"

--Janet A. Hopkins, Editor-in-Chief, *In Recovery Magazine*

ISBN 978-1-61599-285-0
Loving Healing Press

Deep down inside, each of us knows what our truths are.

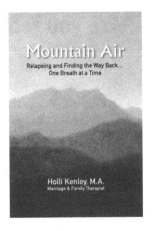

It is forgivable to lose them...

It is unforgivable not to reclaim them...

Mountain Air: Relapsing And Finding The Way Back One Breath At A Time is a brutally honest personal narrative detailing a painful decent into relapse and a powerful journey back to recovering.

Without condemnation but with passion and purpose, *Mountain Air* ...

- Embraces individuals who have abandoned their authentic ways of being for a life of personal neglect, indulgence, or self-destruction.

- Speaks to individuals who have betrayed their healing tenets— the addict who has lost his sobriety, the abused who has returned to her abuser, or the codependent who continues to rescue the uncontrollable.

- Reaches out to individuals who have maintained a life of stability and wellness, but who are eroding over time – and losing their sense of self and of spirit.

Mountain Air is for any individual who has experienced relapse and who is fighting to find his way back...

- By inviting readers to take a journey with the author as she shares time-tested lessons in the recovering process.

- By providing thoughtful and accountable exercises with each chapter that guide the reader in the reclaiming and sustaining of their truths.

"...a personal memoir out of which she extracts principles that can be generalized to all who are in recovery, inspiring them to take courage. This poetic and nature-infused account should become a standard for all therapists and all in the process of recovery."

--David Van Nuys, Ph.D., Emeritus Professor of Psychology, Host of Shrink Rap Radio

ISBN 978-1-61599-188-4
Loving Healing Press

CPSIA information can be obtained
at www.ICGtesting.com
Printed in the USA
BVHW091807121118
532890BV00003B/179/P